The Song Cycle

The song cycle was one of the most important musical genres of the nineteenth century. Famous examples by Schubert, Schumann and Mahler have received a great deal of attention. Yet many other cycles – by equally famous composers, from the nineteenth and twentieth centuries – have not. *The Song Cycle* introduces key concepts and a broad repertoire by tracing a history of the genre from Beethoven through to the present day. It explores how song cycles reflect the world around them and how national traditions and social relationships are reflected in composers' choices of texts and musical styles. Tunbridge investigates how other types of music have influenced the scope of the song cycle, from operas and symphonies to popular song. A lively and engaging guide to this important topic, the book outlines how performance practices, from concert customs to new recording technologies, have changed the way we listen.

Laura Tunbridge is Senior Lecturer in Music at the University of Manchester.

Cambridge Introductions to Music

The Song Cycle

LAURA TUNBRIDGE

CAMBRIDGE
UNIVERSITY PRESS

CAMBRIDGE
UNIVERSITY PRESS

University Printing House, Cambridge CB2 8BS, United Kingdom

Cambridge University Press is part of the University of Cambridge.

It furthers the University's mission by disseminating knowledge in the pursuit of education, learning and research at the highest international levels of excellence.

www.cambridge.org
Information on this title: www.cambridge.org/9780521721073

© Cambridge University Press 2010

First published 2010

A catalogue record for this publication is available from the British Library

ISBN 978-0-521-89644-3 Hardback
ISBN 978-0-521-72107-3 Paperback

For Alec

Contents

List of music examples   *page* ix
List of tables   xiv
Preface and acknowledgements   xv
Selected chronology   xvii

Chapter 1 Concepts   1

Chapter 2 Wanderers and balladeers   23

Chapter 3 Performance: the long nineteenth century   40

Chapter 4 Gendered voices   50

Chapter 5 Between opera and symphony: the orchestral song cycle   64

Chapter 6 Travels abroad   81

Chapter 7 Modern subjects   112

Chapter 8 The death of the song cycle   123

Chapter 9 Performance: the twentieth century   144

Chapter 10 Afterlife: the late twentieth century   153

Chapter 11 Rebirth: pop song cycles   169

Notes   187
Guide to further reading   213
Index   218

Music examples

1.1 Robert Schumann, *Dichterliebe*, no. 11, 'Ein Jüngling liebt ein Mädchen' ('A Boy Loves a Girl') to 12, 'Am leuchtenden Sommermorgen' ('One Bright Summer Morning'). 'It's an old story, / Yet remains ever new; / And he to whom it happens, / It breaks his heart in half... One bright summer morning, / I walk around the garden.' Trans. Richard Stokes, *The Book of Lieder*, p. 471. *page* 12

1.2 Robert Schumann, *Dichterliebe*, no. 1, 'Im wunderschönen Monat Mai' ('In the Wondrous Month of May') to 2, 'Aus meinen Thränen spriessen' ('From my Tears will Spring'). Trans. Stokes, *The Book of Lieder*, p. 469. 16

2.1 Johannes Brahms, *Romanzen aus Ludwig Tiecks 'Magelone'*, no. 15, 'Treue Liebe dauert lange' ('True Love Abides'). 'And whatever held the spirit captive / Then recedes like mist, / And the wide world opens its doors / To the cheerful gaze of spring.' Trans. Stokes, *The Book of Lieder*, p. 86. 30

2.2 Franz Schubert, *Winterreise*, no. 1, 'Gute Nacht' ('Good Night'). 'A stranger came, / A stranger I depart. / The month of May favoured me / With many bouquets of flowers... I cannot choose the time / For my journey: I must find my own way / In this darkness.' Trans. Stokes, *The Book of Lieder*, p. 363. 35

2.3 Franz Schubert, *Winterreise*, no. 24, 'Der Leiermann' ('The Organ Grinder'). 'There beyond the village, / An organ-grinder stands, / And with numb fingers / Plays as best he can... No one cares to listen, / No one looks at him; / And the dogs snarl / Around the old man.' Trans. Stokes, *The Book of Lieder*, p. 373. 36

2.4 Franz Schubert, *Winterreise*, no. 14, 'Der greise Kopf' ('The Hoary Head'). 'The frost has sprinkled a white sheen / On my hair.' Trans. Stokes, *The Book of Lieder*, p. 369. 37

4.1 Robert Schumann, *Frauenliebe und -leben*, no. 8, 'Nun hast' du mir den ersten Schmerz getan' ('Now you Have Caused me my

First Pain'). 'There I have you and my lost happiness, / You, my
world!' Trans. Stokes, *The Book of Lieder*, p. 443.   52

4.2 György Kurtág, *Messages of the Late R. V. Troussova*, no. 4,
'A Little Erotic'.
With permission of Editio Musica Budapest.   57

5.1 a) Richard Wagner, *Tristan und Isolde* Act II, 'Descend night of
love, grant oblivion that I may live'.
b) *Wesendonck Lieder*, no. 5, 'Traüme' ('Dreams'). 'Say, what
wondrous dreams are these / Embracing all my senses'. Trans.
Stokes, *The Book of Lieder*, p. 568.   67

5.2 Gustav Mahler, *Kindertotenlieder*, no. 1, 'Nun will die Sonn' so
hell aufgehn' ('Now the Sun Will Rise as Bright'). Trans. Stokes,
The Book of Lieder, p. 209.   73

5.3 Gustav Mahler, *Kindertotenlieder*, no. 5, 'In diesem Wetter'. 'In
this weather, this howling gale, this raging storm'. Trans. Stokes,
The Book of Lieder, p. 211.   74

5.4 Gustav Mahler, *Das Lied von der Erde*, no. 4, 'Von der Schönheit'
('Of Beauty').   79

6.1 Modest Musorgsky, *Sunless*, no. 1, 'Komnatka tesnaya, tikhaya,
milaya' ('A Little Room, Cosy, Quiet, Dear').   83

6.2 Alexander Dargomïzhsky, 'Vostochniy romans' ('Oriental Romance').   84

6.3 Modest Musorgsky, *The Nursery*, no. 1, 'S nyaney' ('With
Nanny'). 'And how those children cried out, wept. Nanny dear!
Why did the wolf eat those children?' Trans. David Fanning.   87

6.4 Modest Musorgsky, *Songs and Dances of Death*, no. 2, 'Serenada'
('Serenade') 'Magical bliss blue-shaded night, trembling spring
twilight . . . "In the darkness of stern and narrow captivity"'.
Trans. David Fanning.   89

6.5 Tchaikovsky, *Shest' Romansov* (*Six Romances*) op. 73, no. 6,
'Snova, kak prezhde, odin'. 'Again, as before, I am alone, / Once
again I am wrapped in grief . . . The poplar is seen at the
window, / All lit by the moon.' Trans. David Fanning.   90

6.6 Jules Massenet, *Poème d'avril*, no. 1, 'Prelude'. 'A chilly rose, its
heart drenched with rain, / Has just blossomed on a trembling
bough. / And I feel the sweetest folly assail me once more / To
create songs and recall the past! // All the dead loves asleep in my
soul, / Gentle Lazarus, on whom I shed so many tears, /
Laughingly raise their shroud of flowers, / And ask me the name
of my new love. // O my blue-eyed darling, dress and let us flee /
Through woods filled with melancholy and shade, / To seek a

sweet cure for our sweet folly. / The sun has wounded me with its first rays!' Trans. Richard Stokes, *A French Song Companion* (Oxford University Press, 2000), p. 306.   95

6.7 Gabriel Fauré, *La Bonne Chanson*, no. 5, 'J'ai presque peur, en verité'. (Transposed to C♯ minor.) 'In truth, I am almost afraid, / So much do I feel my life bound up / With the radiant thoughts / That captured my soul last summer.' Trans. Richard Stokes in Graham Johnson, *Gabriel Fauré: The Songs and Their Poets* (Aldershot: Ashgate, 2009), p. 233.   98

6.8 Claude Debussy, *Fêtes galantes (I)*, no. 1, 'En sourdine' ('Muted'). 'Calm in the twilight / Cast by lofty boughs.' Trans. Stokes, *A French Song Companion*, p. 111.   100

6.9 Claude Debussy, *Fêtes galantes (II)*, no. 3, 'Colloque sentimentale' ('Lovers' Dialogue'). 'Do you remember our past rapture?' Trans. Stokes, *A French Song Companion*, p. 120.   102

6.10 Maurice Ravel, *Chansons madécasses*, no. 2, 'Aoua!' 'Aoua! Aoua! Beware of white men, dwellers of the shore. In our fathers' time, white men landed on this island; they were told; here is land, let your women work it; be just, be kind, and become our brothers.' Trans. Stokes, *A French Song Companion*, p. 42.   105

6.11 Karol Szymanowski, *Słopiewnie*, no. 3, 'Sw. Franciszek' ('St Francis'). 'Little birds, little flowers . . . cheerful alleluia, holy gospels.'
© 1923 by Universal Edition A.G., Wien/UE 6968. Text: Julian Tuwim. Reproduced by permission. All rights reserved.   109

7.1 Arnold Schoenberg, *Das Buch der hängenden Gärten*, no. 15, 'Wir bevölkerten die abenddüstern Lauben' ('We Peopled the Evening-Dusky Arbours'). 'Now it is true, she will leave forever.' Trans. Stokes, *The Book of Lieder*, p. 286.
Copyright 1914 by Universal Edition. Renewed copyright 1941 by Arnold Schoenberg. Text by Stefan George.
Reproduced by permission. All rights reserved.   116

7.2 Arnold Schoenberg, *Pierrot lunaire*, no. 7, 'Der kranke Mond' ('The Sick Moon'). 'O sombre deathly-stricken moon lying on heaven's dusky pillow, your stare, so wide-eyed, feverish, charms me, like far-off melody.' Trans. Jonathan Dunsby, *Schoenberg: 'Pierrot lunaire'* (Cambridge University Press, 1992), p. 44.
Copyright 1914 by Universal Edition. Copyright renewed 1941 by Arnold Schoenberg.
Reproduced by permission. All rights reserved.   119

8.1 Paul Hindemith, *Das Marienleben* (1923), no. 3, 'Mariä
Verkündigung' ('The Annunciation'). 'It wasn't an angel
entering (understand), that frightened her.' Trans. Stokes, *The
Book of Lieder*, p. 133.
ED 2025 Marienleben Urfassung: © 1924 SCHOTT MUSIC,
Mainz – Germany. Renewed 1951.
Reproduced by permission. All rights reserved.   128

8.2 Othmar Schoeck, *Gaselen* (*Ghazals*), no. 1, 'Unser ist das Los der
Epigonen'. 'Ours is the fate of the Epigones, who live in the vast
halfway world; look, how you squeeze one more drop from old
lemon rinds.' Trans. Chris Walton, *Othmar Schoeck: Life and
Works* (University of Rochester Press, 2009), p. 124.
© 1923 by Breitkopf & Härtel, Wiesbaden.   130

8.3 George Butterworth, *Six Songs from 'A Shropshire Lad'*, no. 6, 'Is
My Team Ploughing?'   133

8.4 Ralph Vaughan Williams, *On Wenlock Edge*, no. 3, 'Is My Team
Ploughing?'
© Copyright 1911 by Ralph Vaughan Williams
Revised edition: © Copyright 1946 by Boosey & Co. Ltd.
Reproduced by permission of Boosey & Hawkes Music Publishers Ltd.   134

8.5 Paul Hindemith, *Das Marienleben* (1948), no. 3, 'Mariä
Verkündigung' ('The Annunciation'). 'It wasn't an angel
entering (understand), that frightened her.' Trans. Stokes, *The
Book of Lieder*, p. 133.
ED 2026 Marienleben Neufassung: © 1948 SCHOTT MUSIC,
Mainz – Germany
Reproduced by permission. All rights reserved.   138

8.6 Richard Strauss, *Vier letzte Lieder*, no. 4, 'Im Abendrot' ('At
Sunset'). 'Could this perhaps be death?' Trans. Stokes, *The Book
of Lieder*, p. 563.
© Copyright 1950 by Boosey & Co. Ltd.
Reproduced by permission of Boosey & Hawkes Music Publishers Ltd.   140

10.1 Sylvano Bussotti, *Pièces de chair II*, no. 7, 'Voix de femme'
('Woman's Voice').
Reproduced by kind permission of Universal Music MGB
Publications srl.   158

10.2 Luciano Berio, *Circles*, no. 3, 'n(o)w'.
© Copyright 1961 by Universal Edition (London), Ltd.,
London/UE 33022. Text: ee cummings.
Reproduced by permission. All rights reserved.   160

10.3 Brian Ferneyhough, *Études transcendentales.*
© Copyright 1984 by Hinrichsen Edition, Peters Edition
Limited, London, EP 7310.
Excerpt reproduced by kind permission of Peters Edition Ltd, London.   165

Tables

6.1 Fauré, *La Bonne Chanson*   *page* 97
7.1 Structure of Boulez, *Le Marteau sans maître*   121

Preface

The song cycles of Beethoven, Schubert, Schumann and Mahler are considered some of the finest musical works of the nineteenth century and have had countless studies devoted to them. However, the history of the song cycle as a genre had not been written before this Introduction. The purpose of this book is to investigate broader contexts for the song cycle across a range of composers and centuries, to provide starting points for discussion in the classroom and suggestions for further music to explore.

The chapters are presented roughly in chronological order, but sometimes depart from that to consider themes and ideas pursued by multiple generations. A book such as this has to be selective, and there are many interesting examples that could not be included (an overview is given in the Chronology). Focusing on cycles rather than individual songs means that there have been further losses: most notably Hugo Wolf, who published his works as collections rather than cycles, even if we tend to hear them as such today. But there is much to be gained from concentrating on song cycles, particularly a sense of how they interacted with other genres, such as symphonic and operatic music and, in the second half of the twentieth century, with popular music.

The song cycle owes its established position in part to its adaptability. For example, this evening I could hear Mahler's first song cycle, *Lieder eines fahrenden Gesellen* (*Songs of a Wayfarer*) sung by student Alex Knox with the University of Manchester Symphony Orchestra, or in a recital by Ian Bostridge and Julius Drake. I could also attend the premiere of a song cycle about characters living in a block of flats in modern Britain: according to the publicity for Alan Williams's *Twelve Storeys High* the music has a 'part-cabaret, part-jazzy, part-contemporary music feel to it, and draws on ideas from popular song as well as traditional notions of the song cycle'. The song cycle, in other words, can be many things: old, new, small-scale, symphonic, classical, popular, native, exotic, amateur, professional. Its scope is perhaps one reason why its history has not been attempted before. Getting to grips with that history, though, can help explain not only why song cycles came into fashion but also what is more surprising for a genre that began as salon entertainment in early nineteenth-century Austria: their continued appeal for a variety of performers, composers and audiences.

Most of the song cycles discussed here have dedications to poets, musicians, friends and family to whom the composer was indebted; every page of this book deserves something similar, but a brief and inevitably incomplete list of acknowledgements will have to suffice. I am grateful to Victoria Cooper and Rebecca Jones for their enthusiasm for this project throughout, and to the production team at Cambridge University Press. I have benefited greatly from the input of a number of readers: as well as those for the Press there have been Andy Fry, Wayne Heisler Jr, Zoë Kirkham, Gavin Osborn, Roger Parker, Robert Pascall, Scott Paulin, Hannah Sander, Jennifer Sheppard, Emma Shires, Sean Walsh and Susan Youens. Other friends and colleagues have improved translations, suggested and located further examples, or simply been prepared to chat about this book's progress. They include Benjamin Binder, Mark Campbell, Carl Chastenay, Ian Cull, Julian Davis, Deniz Ertan, Rufus Hallmark, Emily Howard, Martin Iddon, Roe-Min Kok, Gundula Kreuzer, Kristina Muxfeldt, Eva Schultze-Berndt, Benjamin Walton and Ron Woodley. Thanks, with love, to my parents and brother for their gentle encouragement and support throughout.

My colleagues at Manchester have made various contributions to this project: special thanks are due to Caroline Bithell, David Fanning, Philip Grange, Camden Reeves and Susan Rutherford, and to Nina Whiteman for preparing the music examples. Finally, thanks to the students at Manchester who have helped me shape some of this material through lectures and seminars.

Selected chronology

Key: date, composer, *cycle title* op. number (poet)

1815   Carl Maria von Weber, *Leyer und Schwert* op. 41 (Körner)

1816   Weber, *Die Temperamente beim Verluste der Geliebten* op. 46 (Gubitz)
       Ludwig van Beethoven, *An die ferne Geliebte* op. 98 (Jeitteles)

1817   Ludwig Berger, *Gesänge aus einem gesellschaftlichen Liederspiele 'Die schöne Müllerin'* op. 11 (Müller and others)

1818   Conradin Kreutzer, *Wanderlieder* (Müller); *Frühlingslieder* (Müller)

1823   Franz Schubert, *Abendröte* (Schlegel)

1824   Schubert, *Die schöne Müllerin* D795 (Müller)

1825   Heinrich August Marschner, *Sechs Wanderlieder* op. 35 (Marsano)

1828   Schubert, *Winterreise* D911 (Müller); *Schwanengesang* D957 (Heine, Rellstab, Seidl)

1833   Otto Claudius, *Neun Lieder von W. Müller* (Müller)

1834   Carl Loewe, *Gregor auf dem Stein* op. 38 (Giesebrecht); *Der Bergmann* op. 39 (Giesebrecht)

1835   Loewe, *Esther* op. 52 (Giesebrecht)

1836   Loewe, *Frauenliebe* (Chamisso)
       Gottlieb Reissiger, *Frauenliebe* (Chamisso)

1838   Marschner, *Bilder des Orients* op. 90 (Stieglitz)
       Franz Lachner, *Frauenliebe* (Chamisso)

1839   Carl Banck, *Des Leiermanns Liederbuch* op. 21 (Müller)

1840   Robert Schumann, *Liederkreis* op. 24 (Heine); *Zwölf Gedichte* op. 35 (Kerner); *Liederkreis* op. 39 (Eichendorff); *Frauenliebe und -leben* op. 42 (Chamisso); *Dichterliebe* op. 48 (Heine)

1841   Hector Berlioz, *Les Nuits d'été* op. 7 (Gautier)

1849   Schumann, *Lieder und Gesänge aus Wilhelm Meister* op. 98a (Goethe)

1850   Schumann, *Sechs Gedichte von N. Lenau und Requiem* op. 90 (Lenau)

1851   Schumann, *Sieben Lieder* op. 104 (Kulmann)

1852   Schumann, *Gedichte der Königin Maria Stuart* op. 135 (trans. Vincke)

1854   Peter Cornelius, *Vater unser* op. 2 (Cornelius); *Trauer und Trost* op. 3 (Cornelius)

1856   Cornelius, *Weihnachtslieder* op. 8 (Cornelius)

1859   Cornelius, *Brautlieder* (Cornelius)

1866   Jules Massenet, *Poème d'avril* op. 14 (Silvestre)
        Cornelius, *An Bertha* op. 15 (Cornelius)
        Antonin Dvořák, *Cyprise* op. 2 (Pfleger)

1868   Massenet, *Poème du souvenir* (Silvestre)

1869   Johannes Brahms, *Romanzen aus Ludwig Tiecks 'Magelone'* op. 33 (Tieck)

1871   Arthur Sullivan, *The Window or The Loves of the Wrens* (Tennyson)

1872   Modest Musorgsky, *The Nursery* (Musorgsky)

1873   Adolf Ander, *Frauenliebe und -leben* (Chamisso)

1874   Musorgsky, *Sunless* (Golenischschev-Kutuzov)

1876   Massenet, *Poème d'octobre* (Collin)

1882   Musorgsky, *Songs and Dances of Death* (Golenischschev-Kutuzov)
        Massenet, *Poème d'hiver* (Silvestre)

1885   Gustav Mahler, *Lieder eines fahrenden Gesellen* (Mahler)

1891   Gabriel Fauré, *Cinq Mélodies 'de Venise'* op. 58 (Verlaine)

1893   Ernest Chausson, *Poème de l'amour et de la mer* op. 19 (Bouchor)
        Pyotr Tchaikovsky, *Six Romances* op. 73 (Rathaus)

1894   Fauré, *La Bonne Chanson* op. 61 (Verlaine)

1895   Edvard Grieg, *Haugtussa* op. 67 (Garborg)

1896   Brahms, *Vier ernste Gesänge* op. 121 (Luther)
        Chausson, *Serres chaudes* op. 24 (Maeterlinck)

1898   Arthur Somervell, *Maud* (Tennyson)

1899   Edward Elgar, *Sea Pictures* op. 37 (Noel, Elgar, Browning, Garnett, Gordon)

1900   Roger Quilter, *Four Songs of the Sea* op. 1 (Quilter)

1901   Somervell, *Love in Springtime* (Tennyson, Rossetti, Kingsley)

1903   Maurice Ravel, *Shéhérazade* (Klingsor)

1904   Mahler, *Kindertotenlieder* (Rückert)
        Ralph Vaughan Williams, *Songs of Travel* (Stevenson)
        Somervell, *The Shropshire Lad* (Housman)
        Conrad Ansorge, *Waller im Schnee* (George)

1905   Quilter, *To Julia* (Herrick)

1906   Ravel, *Histoires naturelles* (Renard)
        Sir Granville Bantock, *Sappho* (Bantock)

1907   Somervell, *James Lee's Wife* (Browning)

1909   Arnold Schoenberg, *Das Buch der hängenden Gärten* (George)
        Mahler, *Das Lied von der Erde* (Bethge)

Vaughan Williams, *On Wenlock Edge* (Housman)

Fauré, *La Chanson d'Eve* op. 95 (Van Lerberghe)

1910 Elgar, *Cycle* op. 59 (Parker)

1911 Karol Szymanowski, *The Love Songs of Hafiz* op. 24 (trans. Bethge)

1912 Schoenberg, *Pierrot lunaire* op. 21 (Giraud)

George Butterworth, *A Shropshire Lad* (Housman)

1913 Ravel, *Trois Poèmes de Stéphane Mallarmé* (Mallarmé)

Igor Stravinsky, *Trois Poésies de la lyrique japonais* (trans. Brandt)

Ethel Smyth, *Three Moods of the Sea* (Smyth and Hamilton)

1914 Lili Boulanger, *Clairières dans le ciel* (Jammes)

1915 Szymanowski, *Songs of the Fairy Princess* (Szymanowksa)

1918 Szymanowski, *Songs of the Infatuated Muezzin* op. 42 (Iwaszkiewicz)

Richard Strauss, *Krämerspiegel* op. 66 (Kerr)

1919 Ivor Gurney, *Ludlow and Teme* (Housman); *The Western Playland* (Housman)

Fauré, *Mirages* op. 113 (Brimont)

1921 Fauré, *L'Horizon chimérique* op. 118 (Mirmont)

Szymanowski, *Word Songs* op. 46b (Tuwim)

1923 Paul Hindemith, *Das Marienleben* op. 27 (Rilke)

Joseph Canteloube, *Chants d'Auvergne* (also 1927, 1930, 1954)

Hans Pfitzner, *Alte Weisen* op. 33 (Keller)

Othmar Schoeck, *Elegie* op. 36 (Lenau and Eichendorff)

Schoeck, *Gaselen* op. 38 (Keller)

Somervell, *A Broken Arc* (Browning)

1924 Anton Webern, *Sechs Lieder* (Trakl)

1925 Gurney, *Lights Out* (Thomas)

1926 Ravel, *Chansons madécasses* (Parny)

1926 Schoeck, *Lebendig begraben* op. 40 (Keller)

1929 Ernst Krenek, *Reisebuch aus den österreichischen Alpen* op. 62 (Krenek)

1930 Schoeck, *Wanderung im Gebirge* op. 45 (Lenau)

1931 Krenek, *Durch die Nacht* (Kraus)

Schoeck, *Zehn Lieder nach Gedichten von Hermann Hesse* op. 44 (Hesse)

1933 Ravel, *Don Quichotte à Dulcinée* (Morand)

Schoeck, *Notturno* op. 47 (Lenau)

1934 Webern, *Drei Gesänge aus 'Viae inviae'* (Jone)

1935 Francis Poulenc, *Cinq Poèmes de Paul Éluard* op. 77 (Éluard)

1936 Olivier Messiaen, *Poèmes pour Mi* 1/17a (Messiaen)

Benjamin Britten, *Our Hunting Fathers* op. 8 (Auden, Ravenscroft)

1937 Poulenc, *Tel jour, telle nuit* (Éluard)

Schoeck, *Wandsbecker Liederbuch* op. 52 (Claudius)

1938   Messiaen, *Chants de terre et de ciel* 1/19 (Messiaen)

1939   Arthur Honegger, *Poèmes de Claudel* H. 138 (Claudel)

1940   Britten, *Les Illuminations* op. 18 (Rimbaud)

1942   Hanns Eisler, *Die Hollywood-Elegien* (Brecht, Eisler)

       Britten, *Seven Sonnets of Michelangelo* op. 22 (Michelangelo)

1943   Schoeck, *Unter Sternen* op. 55 (Keller)

       Britten, *Serenade* op. 31 (Cotton, Tennyson, Blake, Jonson, Keats)

1944   Krenek, *The Ballad of the Railroads* op. 98 (Krenek)

1945   Messiaen, *Harawi* 1/28 (Messiaen)

       Britten, *The Holy Sonnets of John Donne* op. 45 (Donne)

1946   Schoeck, *Spielmannsweisen* op. 56 (Leuthold)

1948   Poulenc, *Calligrammes* op. 140 (Apollinaire)

       Strauss, *Vier letzte Lieder* TrV 296 (Hesse and Eichendorff)

       Ned Rorem, *Three Incantations from a Marionette Tale* (Boultenhouse)

1949   Britten, *Winter Words* op. 52 (Hardy)

       Schoeck, *Das still Leuchten* op. 60 (Meyer)

       William Grant Still, *Songs of Separation* (Bontemps, Marcelin, Dunbar, Cullen, Hughes)

1950   Poulenc, *La Fraîcheur et le feu* op. 147 (Éluard)

       Aaron Copland, *Twelve Poems of Emily Dickinson* (Dickinson)

       Rorem, *Flight for Heaven* (Herrick)

1951   Rorem, *Cycle of Holy Songs* (Psalms)

1952   Michael Tippett, *The Heart's Assurance* (Keyes, Lewis)

1953   Samuel Barber, *Hermit Songs* op. 29 (Irish monks' marginalia)

       Rorem, *Poèmes pour la paix* (Regnier, Ronsard, Magny, Daurat, Baïf)

1954   Rorem, *Four Dialogues* (O'Hara)

       Priaulx Rainier, *Cycle for Declamation* (Donne)

1955   Pierre Boulez, *Le Marteau sans maître* (Char)

1956   Poulenc, *Le Travail du peintre* op. 161 (Éluard)

       Schoeck, *Das holde Bescheiden* op. 62 (Mörike)

       Schoeck, *Nachhall* op. 70 (Lenau, Claudius)

       Sofia Gubaidulina, *Fatseliya* (Prishvin)

1958   Sylvano Bussotti, *Pièces de chair II* (various)

       Britten, *Songs from the Chinese* op. 58 (trans. Waley); *Nocturne* op. 60 (Shelley, Tennyson, Coleridge, Middleton, Wordsworth, Owen, Keats, Shakespeare); *Sechs Hölderlin-Fragmente* op. 61 (Hölderlin)

       Hans Werner Henze, *Kammermusik 1958* (Hölderlin)

1960   Luciano Berio, *Circles* (cummings)

1961   Rorem, *King Midas* (Moss)

1962   Tippett, *Songs for Ariel* (Shakespeare)
        Milton Babbitt, *Du* (Stramm)
1963   Rorem, *Poems of Love and Rain* (various)
        George Crumb, *Night Music I* (Lorca)
1965   Franz Waxman, *Das Lied von Terezin* (poetry by concentration camp
        children)
        Boulez, *Pli selon pli* (Mallarmé)
        Britten, *Songs and Proverbs of William Blake* op. 74 (Blake); *The Poet's Echo*
        op. 76 (Pushkin)
1966   Rorem, *Hearing* (Koch)
1967   Dmitri Shostakovich, *Seven Verses of Alexander Blok* op. 127 (Blok)
1968   Rorem, *Some Trees* (Ashbery)
        Crumb, *Songs, Drones and Dances of Death* (Lorca)
1969   Britten, *Who Are these Children?* op. 84 (Soutar)
        Tippett, *Songs for Dov* (Tippett)
        György Kurtág, *Memory of a Winter Sunset* op. 8 (Gulyás)
        Barber, *Despite and Still* op. 41 (Graves, Rilke, Joyce)
        Rorem, *War Scenes* (Whitman)
        Peter Maxwell Davies, *Eight Songs for a Mad King* (Stow)
1970   Crumb, *Ancient Voices of Children* (Lorca)
1971   Rorem, *Ariel* (Plath)
1972   Rorem, *Last Poems of Wallace Stevens* (Stevens)
1973   Shostakovich, *Six Verses of Marina Tsvetayeva* op. 143 (Tsvetayeva)
        Henze, *Voices* (various)
1974   Shostakovich, *Suite on Texts by Michelangelo Buonarroti* op. 145; *Four Verses
        by Captain Lebyadkin* op. 146 (Dostoevsky)
1975   Elliott Carter, *A Mirror on which to Dwell* (Bishop)
1976   Rorem, *Women's Voices* (Boleyn, Rossetti, Dickinson, Wylie)
        Britten, *A Birthday Hansel* (Burns)
1977   Kaija Saariaho, *Bruden* (*The Bride*) (Södergran)
1978   Carter, *Syringa* (Ashbery, Ancient Greek)
1979   Rorem, *The Nantucket Songs* (Williams, Ashbery, Rossetti)
1980   Rorem, *The Santa Fe Songs* (Bynner)
1981   Carter, *In Sleep, in Thunder* (Lowell)
        Kurtág, *Messages of the late R. V. Troussova* op. 17 (Dalos)
        Gordon Getty, *The White Election* (Dickinson)
        Elizabeth Maconchy, *My Dark Heart* (Petrarch, trans. Synge)
        George Benjamin, *A Mind of Winter* (Stevens)
        Wolfgang Rihm, *Wölfi-Liederbuch* (Wölfi)

1982   Rorem, *Three Calumus Poems* (Whitman)
1983   Henze, *Three Auden Songs* (Auden)
1984   Harrison Birtwistle, *Songs by Myself* (Birtwistle)
1985   Brian Ferneyhough, *Études transcendentales* (Meister, Moll)
       Birtwistle, *Words Overheard* (Birtwistle)
1986   Gubaidulina, *Perception* (Tanzer)
       Simon Holt, *Canciones* (Lorca)
1989   Henze, *Drei Lieder über den Schnee* (Treichel)
1990   Rorem, *The Auden Poems* (Auden)
       Witold Lutosławski, *Chantefleurs et chantefables* (Desnos)
       Rihm, *Das Rot* (Günderrode)
1992   John Casken, *Still Mine* (Turnbull, Silkin, Pybus)
1993   Alfred Schnittke, *Mutter* (Lasker-Schülen)
1994   Rorem, *Songs of Sadness* (Strand, Merrill, Hopkins, Burns)
       Carter, *Of Challenge and of Love* (Hollander)
       Schnittke, *Fünf Fragmenten zu Bildern von Hieronymous Bosch* (Aeschylus,
       Pevsner)
1995   Saariaho, *Château de l'âme* (Jaufre trans. Renou and Lexa)
1996   Hans Zender, *Schubert's Winterreise: A Composed Interpretation* (Müller)
       Birtwistle, *Pulse Shadows* (Celan)
       Gubaidulina, *Galgenlieder à 3, à 5* (Morgenstern)
1998   Gérard Grisey, *Quatre Chants pour franchir le seuil* (Guez-Ricordi, Erinna of
       Telos, Epic of Gilgamesh etc.)
       Birtwistle, *Nine Settings of Lorine Niedecker* (Niedecker)
       Henze, *Sechs Gesänge aus dem Arabischen* (Henze)
       Rihm, *Nebendraussen* (Lenz)
1999   Birtwistle, *The Woman and the Hare* (Harsent)
2000   John Corigliano, *Mr Tambourine Man: Seven Poems of Bob Dylan* (Dylan)
       Rorem, *Another Sleep* (fourteen authors)
       Birtwistle, *There is Something Between Us* (Brendel)
       Judith Weir, *woman.life.song* (Morrison, Angelou, Pinkola Estés)
2002   Rorem, *Aftermath* (thirteen authors)
       Saariaho, *Quatre Instants* (Amin Maalouf)
       Camden Reeves, *Night Descending* (Tennyson, Blake, Poe)
2004   Phil Kline, *Zippo Songs* (Zappa)
       Osvaldo Golijov, *Ayre* (Maalouf)
2005   Richard Causton, *La terra impareggiabile* (Quasimodo)
2006   Carter, *In the Distances of Sleep* (Stevens)
       Jonathan Dove, *Hojoki, An Account of My Hut* (Kamo-no-Chomei)

2007   Sally Beamish, *Songs of Hafez* (trans. Peacock)
       Simon Holt, *Sueños* (Machado)
       Philip Glass, *The Book of Longing* (Cohen)
       Henri Dutilleux, *Le Temps l'horloge* (Tardieu, Desnos)
       Michael Finnissy, *Whitman* (Whitman)
2008   Mark Glanville and Alexander Knapp, *A Yiddish Winterreise*
       Gabriel Kahane, *Craigslistlieder* (anon.)
2009   Mark Anthony Turnage, *A Constant Obsession* (Keats, Hardy, Thomas,
       Graves, Tennyson)

Chapter 1

Concepts

The impulse to gather songs together is probably as old as song itself. Doing so allows us to contemplate particular themes, topics or stories, or the output of certain poets and composers. But what seems at first like a straightforward activity has, in the form of the song cycle, come to represent an altogether more intriguing complex of creative and aesthetic issues. According to Charles Rosen, what began as a modest genre for the unambitious amateur became a major endeavour that in weight and seriousness rivalled opera or the symphony (the string quartet and the piano sonata might be better referents) – a triumph all the more remarkable in that its basis remained the simple lyric, and that its ascendancy has not been challenged.[1] The purpose of this book is to examine the reasons behind the song cycle's rise in status in the late eighteenth and early nineteenth centuries, to discuss its period of great achievement, and to ponder its continued attraction for musicians and audiences during the last century or so. It will not only consider a wide repertoire, but also treat the song cycle as a barometer of music's changing role in culture and society in a number of countries and across many generations, in particular through its relationship to other arts (especially literature) and its participation in the formation of individual and national identities.

But is the song cycle really a genre? Unlike the sonata or symphony, it can boast no conventional pattern of movements; there need only be more than two songs. It might seem that the order in which individual elements are placed should be honoured, and that only the whole work should be taken into account; but to do so would contradict centuries of performance practice. Similarly, one might expect the group to be connected in some way; perhaps that, as a cycle, beginning and end will conjoin. While there are famous song cycles that do just that, there are others (just as famous) that do not. These conundrums, among others, explain why attempts to define the song cycle often end with a throwing up of hands: by describing it as 'the most maddening of genres' or claiming that 'the only requirement is a demonstrable measure of coherence'.[2]

However a song cycle is structured, the 'cycle' element is loaded and the genre's stature is dependent on it. The obvious association with nature – with life cycles, the passing of seasons, and so on – especially during the second half of the nineteenth

1

century conjured up organic metaphors, with attendant ideas of truth, unity, wholeness, progress, even purity (sometimes referred to under the umbrella term organicism). No matter how quaint those words might sound these days, it is vain to ignore
the fact that part of the song cycle's allure is that it can be seen to adhere to those
ideals. Yet at the same time the genre has proved itself capable of questioning our
investment in those values. I'll return to this point in more detail shortly; before
going any further, though, it will be helpful to give a brief preview of how the song
cycle came into being.

   Although almost every European country had its own song-writing tradition by
the start of the nineteenth century, those of Austria and Germany have outweighed
all others in terms of influence. It is there that we must begin. The rise of the song
cycle cannot be separated from significant changes in the way in which, around
that time, music's relationship to words was conceived. Its emergence would not
have been possible without the lyric poem, one of the central forces of literary
Romanticism in the late eighteenth century. Since classical Greece, the lyric had
been associated with an idea of singing. But what was still more important for the
German Romantics was its emphasis on the 'lyric-I'. One important strand of their
poems was typically written in the first person, and typically dealt not so much with
characters and plots as with personal expression. Such focus on inner motivations
encouraged connections between the poem's voice and that of the author – an
association of profound consequence for the interpretation of musical settings of
those texts. The Aristotelian view that poetry should be concerned with mimesis –
imitation – was discarded by Romantic writers such as August Wilhelm Schlegel
and Johann Gottfried Herder; in its place came poetry as a language of feeling.
According to Herder, poetry was 'the music of the soul. A sequence of thoughts,
pictures, words, tones is the essence of its expression.'[3] It was a short step from
likening poetry to music to endowing music with poetic significance. Increasingly,
Romantic writers sensed that the art of tones was a superior vehicle for conveying the
inexpressible, and endowed music – particularly instrumental music – with power
beyond language's grasp.

   It is important to recall, though, that music's new, elevated status was not automatically extended to vocal genres. At the end of the eighteenth century, singing
(apart from that taking place in the opera house or in church) was mostly an amateur pursuit – an entertainment for domestic settings, among family and friends.
Such *Hausmusik* had to be accessible, and arrangements of 'traditional' folk songs
were very popular. Settings of more sophisticated poetry, such as Johann Wolfgang
von Goethe's, also tended towards the folkish: simple and singable. These songs (or
Lieder, as the Germans call them) were usually written for voice and piano (sometimes voice and guitar), and were mostly strophic, meaning that each verse of a poem

(however different in lyrical or narrative content) was sung to the same music. This strophic musical form was used because the words were thought more important than their musical treatment; emphasis was on the poet first, the expressive powers of the singer second, the composer a distant third.

Two social factors need to be taken into account. First, the Lied arose at the same time as, and catered for, a new musical audience: the educated middle classes, who were gradually supplanting the aristocracy as the main patrons of the arts. This shift necessitated a greater commercial awareness on the part of composers and their publishers, who now needed to advertise their wares in a competitive marketplace. Such commodification of music had a direct impact on the development of the song cycle. Because Lieder, like the poems they set, were relatively small-scale, they tended to get published in collections. Gradually – taking their cue from poetic cycles, which emerged from similar circumstances – various terms were borrowed to mark such groupings: *Reihe* (series), *Kranz* (ring), *Zyklus* (cycle) or *Kreis* (circle). These terms might be decided before the poems or songs were composed, or they might be applied afterwards. But in large part they were granted with an eye to making a sellable identity rather than out of any abstract concern to establish a new genre.

The second factor to bear in mind is the close relationship, even in the earliest examples, between Lieder and expressions of national identity. It was in particular the folk-like (the German adjective is *volkstümlich*) aspect to these simple strophic songs, setting German words, which appealed as an expression and definition of national spirit. As this is a point to which we'll return, I will say no more here, apart from to observe that a similar nationalist urge appears in the song cycle traditions of almost every other European country, perhaps because of a tendency to set poems in the native language, often with reverential reference to details of the local landscape.

The umbrella term 'song cycle', when used to describe collections at the beginning of the nineteenth century, thus encompasses many different types. Often they were based around a poetic topic: the seasons or months of the year; a collection of flowers or colours; the experience of wandering; a sequence of emotional states; or an examination of particular imagery, such as the forest. The scholar Ruth Bingham has proposed three basic conceptual shapes for such 'topical cycles' (the circle, the spoked wheel and the spiral), but in few cases does much emphasis seem to have been placed on their precise order – they function more like catalogues, simply collecting diverse items under a common title.[4] A more self-conscious approach to the order of songs developed through the cycle's interaction with narrative literary forms, such as the *Liederspiel* (a play including songs), and through choosing to set poems included in novels, such as Goethe's *Wilhelm Meisters Lehrjahre* (*Wilhelm Meister's*

Apprenticeship, 1795). Because these latter songs were excerpted from larger-scale narratives, they often make no sense as stories in themselves (Bingham calls them 'external-plot cycles'). But the pull of order was great. Poetic cycles were, as the nineteenth century wore on, increasingly constructed to follow their own 'internal plots', encouraging listeners to think of them as closed, complete forms whose order should be respected.

The assertion of underlying coherence was crucial in the upward cultural mobility of the song cycle: it implied that such a collection was worthy of more serious contemplation, in line with larger-scale musical genres, such as symphonies or – more pertinently – cycles of lyrical piano pieces. This impulse to 'higher forms' – evident most clearly to us in Beethoven's one song cycle and in several by Schubert – transformed Lied composition. Increasingly, composers moved away from simple strophic patterns to what is often referred to as through-composition, allowing the music to take its own course rather than being bound by repetitions, and hence aspiring to a more direct response to the meaning of a poem. That formal freedom was matched by a new approach to vocal writing: one which, where appropriate, abandoned tuneful, *volkstümlich* melody in favour of flexible, expressive lines that worked more closely with the piano. The piano's increasing prominence was in keeping with Romantic privileging of instrumental music: soon it tended to define the character of a particular Lied and to suggest an independent interpretation of the text. Another critical change in approach was composers' increasing concern with establishing musical coherence, in terms of treatment of themes and harmony. Early examples include Beethoven's *An die ferne Geliebte* (1816, of which more below) and Carl Maria von Weber's *Die Temperamente beim Verluste der Geliebten* (*The Four Humours at the Loss of the Beloved*, 1816). However, and despite the pre-eminence of these composers, it was not until the late 1830s, with the ballad cycles of Carl Loewe, that critics started explicitly to connect the concept of a cycle with its arrangement of keys.[5]

In other words, the Lied – and, with it, the song cycle – began during the early years of the nineteenth century to become established as a work in its own right, rather than as mere musical accompaniment to a poem. And inevitably that process gradually took it out of the realm of amateur performance. As will be discussed often in this volume, the relationship, never entirely simple and often fraught, between compositional practice and performance practice has had a profound effect on the way in which ideas about the song cycle have been formulated. Once Lieder began to be sung by professionals, and particularly once those professionals began to sing complete cycles in public venues, composers' ambitions soared. The once modest song cycle became a potent vehicle for lofty ideals: for exploring new methods of text setting and modes of musical representation, new vocal and instrumental techniques, new harmonic territories. In this sense, the song cycle interacted more actively with changing conceptions of musical modernity than did any other genre: to trace the history of music through works such as Schumann's *Dichterliebe* (1840), Musorgsky's *Sunless* (1874), Schoenberg's *Das Buch der hängenden Gärten* (1909) and *Pierrot lunaire* (1912), and Boulez's *Le Marteau sans maître* (1955) is to engage with generation upon generation of the avant-garde.

Modernism has never solely been about technical innovations, of course. The song cycle has also continued to attract composers because, through its close relationship with poetry, and its tendency to focus on a single vocal soloist (both as 'author' and 'performer'), it encourages experimentation with notions of self-expression and what might be called constructions of the subject – both of them modernist (and postmodern) preoccupations. At the same time, though, that solitary subject could only be constructed in relation to society; for every daring, radical song cycle there is another that reflects the more conservative outlook of the middle-class audience. This point needs emphasis. Devoting an entire book to the song cycle obviously implies that it is an established genre; but it is very far from the monolith one might assume, a point hinted at by the fact that there has, so far as I could find, never been a volume like this before in English.[6] Although there are many song cycles that nicely illustrate the 'musically composed' model, there are many more that are arranged more loosely, by topic or simply by poet: the different types have continued side by side, and all can be referred to as cycles. To put this another way: it will become apparent during the course of this book that the *idea* of the song cycle has often been more important than whether the cycle itself is a coherent, cyclical structure.

In order to do justice to the varied aesthetic principles behind this complex genre, I do not intend to chart a history of the song cycle, but to make ports of call at what seem significant moments. By way of an introduction, the remainder of this chapter will delve a little deeper into the challenges posed by the concept of the song cycle, by considering some problematic examples. I start where many have started, with what is often called the first 'proper' song cycle: Beethoven's *An die ferne Geliebte*. Following that are two examples by Schubert, ones whose questionable cyclic status raises some interesting issues about the way in which we define cycles more generally: the *Abendröte* cycle (1819–23), and *Schwanengesang* (1828). Then come some responses to perhaps the quintessential Romantic example, Schumann's *Dichterliebe* (1840), which should help clarify what is at stake in attempting to define how cycles work, and perhaps start to answer the much harder question of why they matter. And finally we move into the twentieth century, to three examples that demonstrate how, despite radical reconfigurations in musical language, an idea of the song cycle has continued to capture musicians' imaginations: from Francis Poulenc's *Tel jour, telle nuit* (1936–7) to Serge Gainsbourg's *Histoire de Melody Nelson* (1971) and *A Grand Don't Come for Free* by The Streets (2004).

An die ferne Geliebte (1816)

The first known definition of the song cycle, by music historian and librarian Arrey von Dommer, dates from the early 1860s:

> *Liederkreis, Liedercyclus.* A coherent complex of various lyric poems. Each is closed in itself, and can be outwardly distinguished from the others in terms of prosody, but all have an inner relationship to one another, because one and the same basic idea runs through all of them. The individual poems present different expressions of this idea, depicting it in manifold and often contrasting images and from various perspectives, so that the basic feeling is presented comprehensively.[7]

Two main points emerge, both of significance for our understanding of the song cycle: first, the emphasis on coherence and comprehensiveness; second, the idea of diversity within that unity – that individual poems can stand alone, but also work as components of a larger entity.

Dommer refines his definition with further commentary about the music's technical features, again stressing the idea of parts making up a whole. Typically, he says, the music is strophic. While the melody, musical form and key usually change between poems, the latter are frequently bound together through ritornelli or other instrumental interludes. Although Dommer makes no reference to possible narrative structures, he concludes by claiming that there is little to distinguish the song cycle from the solo cantata, apart from the fact that the former has no recitatives and that it replaces arias with Lieder. The song cycle Dommer seems to have in mind is Beethoven's *An die ferne Geliebte*, in which all the songs apart from the last are strophic (with only minor variations in the vocal melody but with the accompaniment varied between strophes), and in which instrumental transitions unify the parts.

In a letter to his publisher Steiner, Beethoven referred to his 'Liederkreis an die Entfernte', his song cycle to the distant one, and the published score was subtitled 'Ein Liederkreis'.[8] This seems to have been the first time a composer referred to a collection of songs as a cycle (*Kreis*), which is one of the reasons why it has often been taken as the first example. Other defining features are that the six interconnected poems are by a single poet, Alois Jeitteles, and that they sustain a single narrative voice. The theme is separation; the vocal 'character' (or persona) hopes that his love songs will travel over mountains and valleys to reach the ear and heart of his beloved. He asks the clouds, brook, birds and winds to carry his message. But as the month of May comes round again, and he watches a swallow building its nest, he realises that they will never be reunited: all he can do is sing longingly to his beloved, in the hope that the distance between them may recede.

Lost love, distant landscapes and consolation in nature are constant themes in nineteenth-century song cycles. But it is not these that are usually cited as evidence for *An die ferne Geliebte* being their progenitor. Rather, it is a musical trait. Although Beethoven's vocal writing is fairly straightforward, in keeping with the folk-like idiom of contemporary Lieder, it displays a greater concern with formal coherence than any previous example. Because all the songs are linked by the piano, their independent performance is discouraged. What is more, the music of the opening returns at the end, causing *An die ferne Geliebte* to begin and end in the same key, and thus consolidating the sense of harmonic completion. Opening and closing in the same key might seem unremarkable; after all, it was common practice for instrumental works at the time. However, composers tended not to approach the song cycle with similar concern for tonal patterning, probably because they took their lead from the words rather than 'purely musical' concerns. Although individual songs might not be particularly adventurous in harmonic terms, the tonal relationships between them could often be quite wide-ranging (close relationships would be – in descending order – by degrees of a fifth or fourth, or by a change of mode (major to minor or vice versa); modulations of a step upwards or downwards, or by a tritone, are particularly distant). Usually, songs would jump from key to key, as if along stepping-stones. Beethoven's innovation in *An die ferne Geliebte* was in using the piano transitions not only to change the mood and melody, but to modulate, thereby smoothing over the potentially jarring effect of, for example, hearing G major followed by Ab major (the keys of the second and third songs). If you will, he replaced the stepping-stones with a bridge. In other words, this is a cycle not only by virtue of its text, but also by virtue of the consistency and cross-references within its musical design.

However, there are several reasons to query whether *An die ferne Geliebte* should be thought the first or the archetypal song cycle; Dommer chose it for his 1865 definition for reasons we might disagree with. To be sure, citing Beethoven as creator of the model song cycle provided the 'new' genre with an auspicious heritage. But *An die ferne Geliebte* is an anomaly, both for its composer (he wrote nothing else like it) and in the sense that its influence was not immediate. Moreover, in the time between *An die ferne Geliebte* and Dommer's definition, the scale and range of the song cycle had expanded considerably. Strophic forms were no longer *de rigueur*; instead, more varied, often through-composed, structures were favoured. Instrumental interludes between songs were unusual and vocal writing on the whole had become less folk-like. Dommer's reference to the accompaniment's ability to 'portray and paint the situation in a characteristic way, and also supply, in regard to the expression, what the voice must leave unfinished', is good for Beethoven, but was taken much further by later composers. Indeed, while Beethoven casts a long shadow over almost every musical genre in the nineteenth century, song seems to have slipped his grasp; or, as Schumann put it (maybe with his future achievements as a glint in his eye), song was the only genre to have made significant development since Beethoven.[9]

Abendröte (1823) and *Schwanengesang* (1828)

The composer who contributed most to this post-Beethoven phase was Franz Schubert. His development of Lieder as an art form has already been mentioned; his achievements with song cycles were no less profound. His most famous cycles, *Die schöne Müllerin* and *Winterreise*, have a chapter devoted to them later in this book; for that reason, we shall avoid them here, and approach the question of definition using examples that have somehow resisted categorisation: the *Abendröte* cycle to poems by Friedrich Schlegel and, perhaps more surprisingly, *Schwanengesang*.

Abendröte (*Sunset*) is unusual in almost every way. Few composers set Schlegel's lyrical poetry, and Schubert's decision to do so in 1819 probably reflects the sophisticated literary circles in which he moved. Schlegel's *Gedichtzyklus* (cycle of poems) consisted of two sets of ten poems, each set prefaced by an untitled prologue and ending with a sonnet entitled 'Der Dichter' ('The poet').[10] They are bound by mood more than anything else. The first half describes the beauty of the natural world, with poems to the mountains, the birds, the river, the rose, the butterfly, the sun, the wind, and the boy and shepherd who attend to them. In the second half night has fallen. The wanderer walks serenely through darkness, again surrounded by natural wonders – the moon, nightingales, waterfalls, flowers, stars and the night breeze. A lovelorn maiden is the sole other human presence, before the poet steps forth to conclude the cycle.

Schubert produced only eleven songs, although the front page of the fair-copy manuscript indicates that he intended to write a complete cycle under the name *Abendröte*, the title of Schlegel's first prologue. Perhaps Schubert was inspired by *An die ferne Geliebte* to attempt a musically unified cycle when he began his Schlegel settings but abandoned the idea.[11] One obstacle to considering *Abendröte* as a cycle is that the songs are for different types of voice; while all can be sung by a female, the tessitura or 'cruising altitude' of 'Die Rose' is very high, and the end of 'Abendröte' rather low. Another, more considerable, problem has to do with how to order the songs, as Schubert gave no real guidance. If they are given in Schlegel's order, we are left with gaps, which discourages thinking of them as a whole. More importantly, that grouping produces a sequence of slow songs in major keys, and thus lacks the variety we usually expect in a cycle.

What might seem trivial – not least because it ignores the often-startling harmonic journeys of the individual *Abendröte* songs – raises an important issue.[12] Although, after *An die ferne Geliebte*, a cycle's status is often 'proved' in analytical terms by its consistency of harmony and mood, an example that is too uniform risks failing to keep one's interest. For example, Schubert's *Winterreise* was initially criticised because of its monotonous tone. While we might now disagree with that judgement (the monotony of *Winterreise* is surely crucial to its effect), something similar might have been in the back of Schubert's mind as he composed what we now know as his next cycle, *Schwanengesang*, which seems almost deliberately to seek out contrast and diversity.

Indeed, if Schubert's *Abendröte* fails as a cycle because of its incompleteness – it provides neither a coherent narrative nor a sense of musical progression – then so too must *Schwanengesang*, composed in 1828 and published posthumously in 1829. The title, 'Swansong', was devised by the publisher Tobias Haslinger, with a view to selling it as Schubert's 'last work'.[13] Haslinger's role raises some crucial issues about the extent to which we should abide by what, for better or worse, are known as the composer's intentions: it is quite possible that Schubert never meant these songs to be presented as a cycle. Yet this has not prevented several attempts to prove that they should be taken as one, indicating the extent to which the term 'cycle' is somehow thought to bestow added value.

Schwanengesang is made up of two sections, devoted to different poets. It begins with seven songs to poems by Ludwig Rellstab; then come six Heinrich Heine settings; and then, to end, is a setting of Anton Seidl's 'Die Taubenpost'. The final Rellstab song begins the second section, meaning that the poets are not neatly grouped together, and the ordering within the groups, on the surface, makes little sense. Moreover, the two sections are different in form and character. The Rellstab settings have tended to be overlooked in favour of the Heine ones, which are typically treated as a cycle in their own right. (The reason for this might have less to do with Schubert's music than with the reputations of the two poets, Heine being by far the more famous and respected.) Rellstab's poems last between three and six stanzas; Heine's are mostly in three brief stanzas. When setting Rellstab, Schubert adapted his music to the varied structures of the poems; thus some songs are almost exactly strophic, while others are essentially through-composed. With Heine, though, Schubert complemented the simplicity of the text's structure with ternary (or sometimes binary) forms. Neither do the two sections connect on harmonic terms; the whole cycle may begin and end in G major, but only because of Haslinger's inclusion of 'Die Taubenpost'. Otherwise, there are some unexpected leaps from one song to the next, almost to the point where they seem designed to obscure potential connections between them.

It has been argued that when the Heine settings are rearranged in the same sequence as in the poet's *Die Heimkehr* a poetic and musical narrative emerges, thereby forming a 'single coherent work'.[14] But this assumes (on shaky evidence) that there is a distinct narrative to the poems in the first place: the eighty-eight poems of *Die Heimkehr* are merely grouped into loose sub-cycles, around topics such as the sea and returning home. Schubert only once chose successive poems from Heine's collection, otherwise interleaving songs from different sub-cycles.

While there may be associative links between the poems, and perhaps an emotional trajectory, no specific story is told. With regard to musical coherence, the matter is always more complicated. There are some characteristic melodic contours that recur; but if the order in Schubert's autograph manuscript seems deliberately to obscure key relationships between the songs, rearranging them to form a more 'logical' sequence has little to recommend it.[15] What is more, Schubert was prone to transposing songs to suit particular singers, which puts a question mark over any attempt to fix a particular meaning for any given key or key relationship. He does seem to have used tonality to evoke a sense of distance from or closeness between certain songs (for example, the progression from the reasonably hopeful 'Ständchen' to the rejected grief of 'Aufenthalt' is conveyed through the awkward shift from D minor to E minor). But these local connections suggest a concern for immediate contrast rather than abstract design.

It is striking that recently the Heine settings have tended to be considered individually or in pairs, rather than as a group.[16] Moreover, as with all Schubert's cycles, they are often performed independently. In part this probably has to do with their length and, for want of a better word, weight; while there are several complete recordings of *Schwanengesang*, the prospect of singing the whole work live, from beginning to end, is daunting. Yet Haslinger's decision to present these songs as a cycle has, by default, meant that they are known as such, proving the lasting power of labels – and of publishers.

Indeed, it is apparent from the Beethoven and Schubert examples given above that any attempt to define the song cycle as a genre is at the mercy of titles, taking the inclusion of *Liederkreis* or *Schwanengesang* as our guide rather than any formal features. We also need to decide how seriously we should take a composer's arrangement – is it within the scholar's or performer's rights to reorder *Abendröte* or *Schwanengesang*, in order to enhance its claims to being called a cycle? From another angle, we need to decide the extent to which a cycle has to be cohesive, and how much variety is acceptable. Harmonic relationships between songs seem to matter (particularly to scholars, who tend to have the score in front of them), but it would be rather short-sighted to make connections only on 'purely' musical terms. All these questions become still more urgent when we consider one of the most famous of all song cycles, Schumann's *Dichterliebe*.

Dichterliebe (1840)

Dichterliebe, like *An die ferne Geliebte*, deals with lost love, makes explicit tonal connections between songs, and returns to earlier musical material towards its end. These are some of the reasons behind its status as the quintessential song cycle, a work against which all others tend to be measured; however, the full story cannot be addressed without taking into account broader contexts: the relationship between music and text, historical circumstances, aesthetic values and performance history; and, critically, consideration of the method of scrutiny as much as the object scrutinised. It thus seems worth spending some time here with the different approaches taken to *Dichterliebe*: to do so is a means by which to introduce several key issues that will resurface throughout this book.

During the 1830s, Schumann focused compositional energies on piano music, producing collections of short, often literary-inspired pieces such as *Papillons*, *Davidsbündlertänze*, *Carnaval* and *Kreisleriana*. But in February 1840, as he battled in the courts for the hand of Clara Wieck – famous virtuoso and the daughter of his one-time piano teacher, Friedrich Wieck, who was determined that the two should not marry – Schumann began something new: his 'year of song'. His first cycle (op. 24) set poems by Heine, as did *Dichterliebe* (op. 48) composed in just over a week in late May. The rapid escalation in opus numbers between these two cycles indicate at what a rate Schumann was composing; yet out of the nine collections he completed in 1840 only *Dichterliebe* was designated a *Liederzyclus*.[17]

The twenty poems (four were later removed) were taken from Heine's *Lyrisches Intermezzo* (first published in 1823; later editions included new poems, some of which were chosen by Schumann). The title *Dichterliebe* (*Poet's Love*) was not added until 1844, seemingly at the request of the publisher. The theme, once again, was unrequited love: perhaps reflecting Heine's unhappy situation at the time, but an odd choice for the soon-to-be-married Schumann (Wieck's case collapsed over the summer and Robert and Clara married on 12 September 1840). But any sense of self-indulgence, any hubris or hyperbole was effectively punctured by Heine's famous sense of irony. It seems that he mastered the form of the folk song precisely so that, through parody, he could reveal how this supposed route to the German soul was nothing more than an urban literary confection. Equally famously, Schumann responded to Heine's poetry in kind. The eleventh song of *Dichterliebe*, 'Ein Jüngling liebt ein Mädchen' ('A youth loved a maiden'), describes love as a merry-go-round: a boy loves a girl, who rejects him for another; her choice marries someone else and she goes for the next man to come along, leaving the original boy badly hurt. It's an old story, concludes Heine, but remains ever new and just as painful. Schumann undercuts the heartbreak of these home truths by setting them to a relentlessly jolly, if disconcertingly off-beat, mock-folk tune (Example 1.1).

It is what happens next that best illustrates the multiple layers of meaning in *Dichterliebe* when considered as a cycle. Listened to or performed without a break, after the full E♭ major chords that close 'Ein Jüngling liebt ein Mädchen' comes one low note, G♭, gently introducing the tumbling diminished arpeggios that begin the next song, 'Am leuchtenden Sommermorgen' ('One bright summer morning')

Example 1.1 Robert Schumann, *Dichterliebe*, no. 11, 'Ein Jüngling liebt ein Mädchen' ('A Boy Loves a Girl') to 12, 'Am leuchtenden Sommermorgen' ('One Bright Summer Morning'). 'It's an old story, / Yet remains ever new; / And he to whom it happens, / It breaks his heart in half . . . One bright summer morning, / I walk around the garden.' Trans. Richard Stokes, *The Book of Lieder*, p. 471.

Example 1.1 (*cont.*)

(see Example 1.1). Heard without the preceding song, this opening would sound ambiguous enough (the tonic of B♭ major is not clear until bar 3); but heard after those resounding E♭ major chords it is even more so, darkening the major mode with an inflection to the minor (the G♭), much as Heine's poem predicted the young man's heartbreak. It is a neat trick on Schumann's part, not least because the basic tonal relationship between the songs, E♭ to B♭, is the standard tonic to dominant one. By momentarily obscuring that harmonic progression, it might be assumed, the potential connection between the songs would be broken; after all, there is a complete change of mood. Somehow, though, letting that G♭ hook them together creates the stronger link, leading us into the unreal world of 'Im leuchtenden Sommermorgen', where flowers whisper to each other about the sad, pale man.

Later, we discover that 'Am leuchtenden Sommermorgen' extends another tendril through the songs of *Dichterliebe*; the swelling melody of its piano postlude reappears in fuller form at the start of the postlude to the final song, thereby bringing the cycle to a close. As in *An die ferne Geliebte*, then, earlier music returns to end the cycle; but Schumann makes the connection far less explicit, repeating a passage from within the cycle rather than its beginning, and altering its key and melodic trajectory. Moreover, it is far from clear what the return of the postlude to 'Am leuchtenden Sommermorgen' means on a poetic or emotional level. In *An die ferne Geliebte*, the return of the opening melody allows for a sense of reconciliation – the poet/singer hopes at first that his song will reach her; by the end of the cycle he has decided it is enough simply to offer his songs to her. There is no such optimism at the end of *Dichterliebe*; in its final song the poet decides to end his suffering by putting his songs in a coffin, and sinking them in the Rhine.

The problem with cycles, though, is that we automatically assume that in their end is their beginning; that we can reclaim the poet's songs from the riverbed and listen to them again. Whether or not Schumann intended us to think of the cycle in those terms, whether he thought that we would attempt to find a connection between the first and last songs (or indeed, between the others), has caused some strenuous debate in recent times. At stake is the extent to which we should take the composer's intention as our guide; if we are prepared to reorder Schubert's/Haslinger's *Schwanengesang* to establish better claims to poetic or musical coherence, could we not do the same to *Dichterliebe*? There is also a widening rift between those who prefer to approach musical works such as song cycles as unified objects – placing value on the way in which they convey a sense of totality, wholeness, progress, development, maybe even truth – and those who are more interested in ways in which moments in the music query those claims of coherence. In other words, there are some whose methodology is based on a premise of organicism and others who habitually question it; of course, neither approach could exist without the other, which is probably why the debate has been so heated.

Schumann often spent as much energy ordering the songs as he did creating them; however, he typically did so after they were completed, and then frequently *re*arranged them (he composed his Rückert settings, op. 37, in twelve days, but then spent two months putting them in order). That the cyclic arrangement was not premeditated and fixed suggests that Schumann's concept of the cycle was open-ended.[18] For instance, there seems to have been a deliberate clouding-over of the connection between the first and last songs of *Dichterliebe*. The final song begins in C♯ minor and ends in D♭ major, perhaps remembering the C♯ with which the piano tentatively begins the first song, 'Im wunderschönen Monat Mai' ('In the wondrous month of May').[19] However, the link is not secure, not least because the opening of *Dichterliebe* is famous for its ambiguity, both poetic and musical.

The two-quatrain poem itself seems fairly straightforward:

Im wunderschönen Monat Mai,	In the wondrous month of May,
Als alle Knospen sprangen,	When all the buds were bursting into bloom,
Da ist in meinem Herzen	Then it was that in my heart
Die Liebe aufgegangen.	Love began to blossom.
Im wunderschönen Monat Mai,	In the wondrous month of May,
Als alle Vögel sangen,	When all the birds were singing,
Da hab' ich ihr gestanden	Then it was I confessed to her
Mein Sehnen und Verlangen.	My longing and desire.[20]

The vocal melody and piano part are the same for both verses (Example 1.2). To say that Schumann wrote a strophic song, though, does not convey the extent to which the music indicates the complexity of the situation. In Beethoven's *An die ferne Geliebte*, the individual songs themselves were relatively straightforward harmonically; it was the relationship between them that was less clear, but that was rectified by the use of piano transitions. Here, the key of 'Im wunderschönen Monat Mai' is difficult to ascertain and its connection to the subsequent song (not to mention the final one of the cycle) is unsure. The postlude ends on an unresolved seventh chord, meaning that the song itself, harmonically speaking, is incomplete; it has not confirmed a tonic. This fragmentary aspect has several implications. Schumann might be responding to the poem's final reference to yearning and desire, depicting something that can never be satisfied. The piano's repetition of its mysterious introductory figure implies that we are revisiting something that happened to the protagonist in the past. Indeed, the open-endedness of 'Im wunderschönen Monat Mai' might signal that it acts like a taste of Proust's madeleine; recalling the blossoms prompts him to remember his confession of love, beginning a concatenation of memories. Harmonically speaking, resolution might be found in the opening bars of the subsequent song, 'Aus meinen Thränen spriessen' ('From my tears will spring'), which might also be to say that *Dichterliebe* works as a cycle because one song often brings about the next.

Let's pause before the next step, which would be to say that *Dichterliebe* is a cycle because it has to be considered as a whole and that, if it is 'a whole', it must somehow be coherent and unified. For there is one crucial level on which coherence and unity do not consistently coincide: the relationship between the words and the music. It is possible to trace thematic, perhaps even narrative connections between the poems; it is also possible, but harder, to make arguments for small- and large-scale harmonic patterning. Often, though, it seems as if music and words are telling different stories. The text of 'Im wunderschönen Monat Mai' seems to be saying 'Ah yes, I remember

Example 1.2 Robert Schumann, *Dichterliebe*, no. 1, 'Im wunderschönen Monat Mai' ('In the Wondrous Month of May') to 2, 'Aus meinen Thränen spriessen' ('From my Tears will Spring'). Trans. Stokes, *The Book of Lieder*, p. 469.

it well, the first blossoms of young love'. 'But how will it end?' the music enquires. By the final song, the poet wants to send his suffering, with his songs, to a watery grave; the music, though, reminds us that the coffin is not watertight, that memories will seep out.

In other words, we have to decide what we want to listen for: are we interested in the poetry, the music or their combination? Do we want to find an underlying coherence or would we rather concentrate on disruptive moments? Perhaps the reason why *Dichterliebe* has remained so vital an example is that its openness to multiple interpretations allows each generation to fashion its own response, shaping

Example 1.2 (*cont.*)

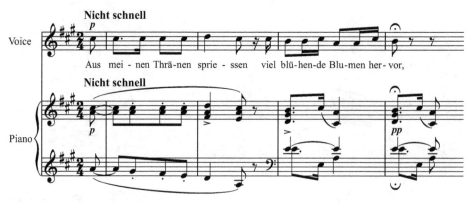

Example 1.2 (*cont.*)

the cycle according to the aesthetic concerns of the day. To borrow an idea from 'Ein Jüngling liebt ein Mädchen', the subject of *Dichterliebe* is old but remains forever new; most of us have experienced unrequited love, along with its feelings of alienation. If we try hard, and if it's our taste to do so, we can probably still feel a pang of it, on reminiscence. The power of the cycle is in that sense of repeating with difference, with the hindsight of experience; so it is perhaps fitting to conclude this chapter by discussing three examples that seem to respond to similar themes to *Dichterliebe*, but that take us far beyond the gloomy world of German Romanticism.

Tel jour, telle nuit (1937)

Francis Poulenc has been called the last master of the French art song, and of his 152 songs about three-quarters were arranged into collections or cycles.[21] In the mid-1930s, around the time he began his duo with the baritone Pierre Bernac, he turned to the surrealist poetry of Paul Éluard. Poulenc claimed that he had been trying to find 'the musical key' to setting Éluard's poetry for years; it was through the combined inspiration of Éluard and Bernac, he explained, that 'lyricism entered my vocal works'.[22]

   It was perhaps the newfound lyricism that encouraged Poulenc to take on aspects of the Romantic song cycle. Of Poulenc's four Éluard cycles, *Tel jour, telle nuit* (*Such a day, such a night*, 1936–7) has been celebrated as 'the most coherent and, in the strongest sense of the term, the most *recueillie* (rapt, contemplative) of Poulenc's works': 'it belongs to the same tradition as *Winterreise* and *Dichterliebe*'.[23] The composer explained that, for him, 'a song in a cycle must have a special colour and architecture... That is the reason why I have opened and closed *Tel jour, telle nuit* with two songs in similar keys and tempi.'[24] In an overtly Schumannian gesture, the last bars of the final song look back to the first. But *Tel jour, telle nuit* is not simply a homage to the past: Poulenc's achievement lies in adapting nineteenth-century structural principles for his own purpose.

The nine poems of *Tel jour, telle nuit* were chosen from Éluard's 1936 collection *Les Yeux fertiles* (*The fertile eyes*). Although Poulenc stripped the poems of their original titles, he maintained the carefully moderated progression found in *Les Yeux fertiles* towards what the poet called *facilité*: simplicity, clarity and unfettered freedom. And while Poulenc reordered the poems, he was sensitive to Éluard's alternations in mood, his 'coherence of opposites': shifts from the positive to the negative were undertaken with the aim of reactivation and regeneration.[25]

To complement Éluard's 'coherence of opposites', Poulenc devised what he called 'mélodie tremplin' or 'springboard songs', whose purpose was to launch into new moods: from despair to drama, desire to ephemerality, denial to resolution. Thus songs three to five were described by the composer as 'strictly songs from a cycle... [they] could not possibly be sung separately'.[26] The last of this group, 'À toutes brides', Poulenc commented, 'has no other pretension than to heighten the effect of [the next song] "Une herbe pauvre"'.[27] With the exception of the fourth song there is not much between songs three to five and the others in the cycle in terms of length, nor are there obvious musical links between them. Indeed, if anything the endings of the 'springboard songs' are more clearly defined, in terms of harmony and phrasing: even the third, which shares the outer songs' tendency to drift into sustained chords in the final bars, closes with a perfect cadence that seems startlingly firm in comparison to the mostly non-functional harmonies of the cycle as a whole. These are not, then, interlinked, fragmentary songs in the sense of Schumann's *Dichterliebe*. Instead, their function within the cycle seems to be to provide contrast: for example, 'À toutes brides' is fast, frantic and loud, whereas 'Une herbe pauvre' is slow, soft and simple. It is as if the 'springboard' songs are the shadows of a chiaroscuro painting, which might seem less interesting when compared to the features bathed in light, but without which the drama and integrity of the whole would be lost.

As mentioned, the piano postlude to the final song of *Tel jour, telle nuit* returns to the key and tempo of the postlude to the first. There are several possible reasons for this move, among them Éluard's principle of reactivation and regeneration: in the cycle, day turns to night. A further reference might be to Poulenc's recent religious reawakening, as these final bars are similar in style to the close of his 1936 choral piece, *Litanies à la vierge noire* (*Litanies to the Black Virgin*). The composer, though, made another connection, acknowledging his engagement with the song cycle's history: 'I endowed this cycle with a piano coda which allows the listener, as in Schumann's *Dichterliebe*, to prolong his own feelings, generated by the songs themselves.'[28] Poulenc's reference to Schumann indicates not only the extended influence of the German tradition, but also how it can be adapted to different ends in very different times. Although an idea of unity still seems fundamental to the concept of the song cycle, what seems as important for Poulenc is the sense that the music which ends *Tel jour, telle nuit* can convey more than has been said, even more than has been sung.

Histoire de Melody Nelson (1971)

Music's ability to mark the passing of time, and its curious hold over our emotional experiences and memories, is made particularly apparent by the song cycle, with its themes of lost love and distant landscapes, and its concern with reminiscence. The genre's continued appeal is evident in the way its main features have been transferred to popular music, as in (to name one of several possible conduits) the concept albums of the late 1960s and early 1970s. How the concept album came into being will be discussed in Chapter 11; here, two examples will demonstrate its indebtedness to the 'concept' of the song cycle already described. Serge Gainsbourg's *Histoire de Melody Nelson* tells the story of a middle-aged man in Paris who loses control of his Rolls-Royce 1910 Silver Ghost and knocks an English teenager off her bicycle. Her name is Melody Nelson. They have an affair but, as in countless song cycles before and after, it does not last: Melody wishes to see the skies of her native Sunderland once more; she leaves and dies in a plane crash. Although Gainsbourg's album is much racier than anything by Schubert or Schumann (there are orgasmic giggles on track six), it is possible to describe *Histoire de Melody Nelson* in terms of nineteenth-century song cycles. The album is stylistically consistent; Gainsbourg's delivery is for the most part half-spoken, half-sung close to the microphone, over funk-like bass guitar. There are only seven songs (the album lasts twenty-eight minutes), meaning that they can be listened to in one sitting, and the connections between them are easy to hear: the songs bleed into one another by maintaining or resolving harmonies, and certain chord progressions recur, as does a distinctive descending four-note bass line. Three songs in praise of Melody's winsome beauty ('Ballade de Melody Nelson', 'Valse de Melody', 'Ah! Melody') are not far removed in spirit from the besotted youth of Schubert's *Die schöne Müllerin*, not least because these are the most openly melodic – there's no other word for it – tracks on the album. Each time Melody's name is spoken it is to the same descending figure; the accompaniment is richer, featuring strings and guitar filigree. Most strikingly, at the end, as the man wishes he could be reunited with his lover, he recalls the first words they exchanged:

Tu t'appelles comment?	What's your name?
Melody	Melody
Melody comment?	Melody what?
Melody Nelson	Melody Nelson

And with these words the music of the first song returns, drawing the album to a close.

Are we dealing here with another *An die ferne Geliebte*? Yes and no. The poetic and aesthetic impulse behind the two 'cycles' seems similar; Gainsbourg undertakes his with greater humour but no less ambition, as is demonstrated by the care taken over the musical relationships between tracks and the use of orchestral and choral accompaniment to build climaxes and make thematic connections (the arrangement was by producer Jean-Claude Vannier, whose own concept album, *L'Enfant assassin des mouches* (*The Child Fly-killer*), appeared the following year). Beethoven may have found his beloved in now-distant meadows, but those rural landscapes are supplanted in *Histoire* by the urban, by technology; their relationship is brought about, but also brought to an end, by a Silver Ghost and a cargo aeroplane. Disentangling composer and character is made trickier in *Histoire* because Gainsbourg sings the main role, with his real-life English partner Jane Birkin providing Melody's voice; the following year they even released a video of the album, in which they more or less acted out the story. Gainsbourg was notorious for playing with the divide between life and art (the original album cover showed a topless Birkin hugging a toy monkey), and pop or rock musicians tend to be associated still more closely with their works than classical composers, partly because they are usually responsible for their music's performance.[29] However, there is as little reason to assume that *Histoire* relates – or, maybe better, confesses to – something that actually happened, as there is to muse that Beethoven was thinking of a particular distant beloved. And the collaborative nature of making an album – shown here by the prominent role of the producer Vannier – in many ways opens up the possibilities for multiple voices, demonstrated by the 2006 live performance of *Histoire de Melody Nelson* by different singers (Jarvis Cocker, Damon Gough aka Badly Drawn Boy, The Bad Seeds' Mick Harvey and Super Furry Animals' Gruff Rhys).[30] An album that can keep its identity intact under such circumstances might fulfil that other criterion of the song cycle; that its independent parts are integral to the larger work. There is also a sense in which the 2006 concert – in London's Barbican Arts Centre, no less – recognised another critical aspect of the song cycle: its aesthetic aspirations. Gainsbourg's album was no commercial success. Its attempt to forge a large-scale narrative, though, has been influential on subsequent artists; there have been similar projects, one of them being by Mike Skinner – aka The Streets – with his 2004 album *A Grand Don't Come for Free*.[31]

Skinner's hard-up twenty-something is a barely recognisable relative of Gains-bourg's louche Rolls-Royce driver, and the album does not share the musical return of *Histoire de Melody Nelson*. Yet its final track is as concerned with cycles as any of the examples discussed above. Mike has lost a thousand pounds and spends *A Grand Don't Come for Free* looking for it, getting together and breaking up with a girl, getting high and gambling. The final track, 'Empty Cans', finds him back home, nursing his wounds: 'If I wanna sit in and drink Super Tennants all day then I will.' Over a drum machine rhythm, repeated broken minor triad on synthesiser, one-note percussive bass line and occasional background sound effects, he explains how he sent his television to be fixed: the repair man tells him he found something in it; Mike thinks he's after more money and they get into a fight. The end. But then there's the sound of a tape rewinding, and a second ending is offered. At first it seems almost identical to the first (although the synthesiser's broken triad is replaced by a sustained tone), but it turns out that in this version his mate fixes his television and, in the back, finds the thousand pounds. The happier outcome is signalled by the piano entering with a repeated sequence of parallel thirds in the major, a thick-ening of synthesiser accompaniment so that it almost sounds like strings, and, most tellingly, Skinner singing:

> The end of something I did not want to end,
> The beginning of hard times to come.
> But something that was not meant to be is done,
> And this is the start of what was.

Each time the refrain is repeated, his voice is ghosted with that of a woman (perhaps meant to be his girlfriend), which takes him out of character (he continues the narrative in his speaking voice), emphasising that his story is drawing to a close. The musical means here might be less expansive than *Histoire de Melody Nelson* and less harmonically adventurous than *Dichterliebe*, but within the context of the album they effectively convey the emotional situation. They also indicate the open ending to the story, letting the listener imagine alternatives or go back to the beginning, repeating with difference. In other words, the ending of *A Grand Don't Come for Free* makes us think about cycles, about how we learn and remember: about how histories – of us, and of music – are shaped. And on that note, it's time we went back to the nineteenth century, to Schubert and 'the start of what was'.

Chapter 2

Wanderers and balladeers

Although separated by only four years, Schubert's two most famous song cycles, *Die schöne Müllerin* (*The Lovely Miller Maid*, 1824) and *Winterreise* (*Winter Journey*, 1828), are very different in character: the first tells the story of a lad's infatuation with the miller's daughter; the second journeys through a winter landscape, when love has long been lost. *Die schöne Müllerin* thus seems to represent youthful flowering while *Winterreise* indicates an existential impasse. Green is the colour of young love and jealousy in *Die schöne Müllerin*; in *Winterreise*, all is white: the protagonist remembers the flowers in May but like his heart they are now frozen over. 'Das Wandern ist des Müllers Lust, Das Wandern!" ("To wander is the miller's joy, To wander!") begins *Die schöne Müllerin*; the miller boy aspires to be that familiar figure of nineteenth-century art and literature, the wanderer.[1] In *Winterreise*, though, the protagonist's footsteps have become heavy – he is ready to bring his travels to a close. These poetic and thematic contrasts are matched by changes in Schubert's musical approach. The melodic, strophic songs typical of *Die schöne Müllerin* are replaced by sparse, declamatory vocal writing in *Winterreise*. Whereas the piano in *Die schöne Müllerin* frequently acts like the often-referred-to brook, burbling in the background, in *Winterreise* it is more adaptable and independent.

Despite the obvious differences, there are points of contact: notably, both set poems by Wilhelm Müller, for whom both cycles were winter tales; the subtitle of *Die schöne Müllerin* advises readers that it is to be read in wintertime. Müller's poetry was very popular in the first half of the nineteenth century. His lyric poems appeared in two volumes of *Sieben-und-siebzig Gedichte aus den hinterlassenen Papieren eines reisenden Waldhornisten* (*Seventy-Seven Poems from the Surviving Papers of a Travelling Horn Player*) in 1820 and 1824; they were grouped into sets and cycles, but mostly by theme – *Die schöne Müllerin* and *Winterreise* were exceptional in being narratives. However, the poetic origins of these two tales were not the same. *Die schöne Müllerin* grew out of a salon entertainment, and thus in some ways represents the hybrid genre of the *Liederspiel*, a narrative play in song and verse. *Winterreise*, on the other hand, belongs to a tradition of *Wanderlieder* composition. The vast literature on Schubert's song cycles might seem to make in-depth discussion here superfluous. But of course they cannot be overlooked: the purpose of this chapter is to place

Die schöne Müllerin and *Winterreise* into context, examining their backgrounds and influence on later composers such as Carl Loewe, Johannes Brahms and Gustav Mahler, in order to explain their significance.[2]

Die schöne Müllerin (1824)

During the winter of 1816–17 the banker, privy councillor and amateur poet Friedrich August von Stägemann, and his wife Elisabeth, an accomplished amateur singer and actress, hosted a series of Thursday-evening salons in their Berlin home. For the sake of their teenaged children, August and Hedwig, the Stägemanns invited a number of promising young artists, including the portrait painter Wilhelm Hensel (who later married Fanny Mendelssohn) and his sister Luise, the poet and pianist Ludwig Rellstab, the poet and publisher Friedrich Förster and his wife-to-be Laura Gedike, the poet Adelbert von Chamisso's fiancée Emilie Piaste and Wilhelm Müller. The older guests included Clemens Brentano, who had produced the collection of folk poetry called *Des Knaben Wunderhorn* with Achim von Arnim, and the composer and piano virtuoso Ludwig Berger.

The eighteen-year-old Luise Hensel must have had something; every eligible male at the salon seems to have been in love with her. Müller duly recorded his infatuation – and her dismissal of him – in his diary around Christmas 1816, and Brentano and Berger both proposed (Luise refused everyone, eventually devoting herself to religious charities and writing Catholic verse). As Susan Youens has suggested, it seems that the decision to stage a *Liederspiel* based on the 'old erotic theme of a miller maid and her various suitors . . . also enacted the archetypal tale of love and rejection in their own lives'; Lawrence Kramer has put this more strongly, arguing that the 'Lied world' of *Die schöne Müllerin* presents an idealised portrait of work, family and society at the mill to satisfy the nostalgic and certainly naive fantasies of the modern bourgeois for whose entertainment Müller's poems and eventually Schubert's songs were written.[3] Despite Luise's obvious qualifications for the role, it was Hedwig Stägemann who originally played the miller maid, with Müller – as befits his name – as the miller, Wilhelm Hensel as the hunter, and Luise as the gardener. Briefly: the miller maid rejects the miller's lad in favour of the hunter; the distraught youth commits suicide. (The version we know now ends there; originally, and perhaps reflecting less-than-entirely-noble wishful thinking on the part of the lovelorn young men in the company, the miller maid is overcome by remorse and drowns herself in the brook; a chorus mourns her passing.)

Liederspiele became popular in German theatres and salons at the beginning of the nineteenth century as a means to provide a native-language, folk-like (*volkstümlich*) alternative to the excesses of Italian opera. The *Liederspiel* was a hybrid form in that it combined the *Liederkreis*, discussed in Chapter 1, with the *Singspiel* – German-language drama, with spoken dialogue and musical numbers. Friedrich Reichardt, an old friend of Elisabeth Stägemann (she had performed in his *Liederspiel Lieb' und Treue* (*Love and Truth*) in 1800), argued that the musical content of the *Liederspiel* should be 'Lied and only Lied'; the words and music should be folk-like and natural.[4] Apart from the personal significance for the salon of the tale of the miller girl and her suitors, the theme was probably chosen to reflect Friedrich Stägemann's interest in German historical literature, and may also have responded to Goethe's famous mill ballads. In its first version there were seven poems, which were mostly improvised and, it seems, accompanied by whatever gestures and vocal inflections were thought fitting. Impressed by the performance, Berger set one of the poems to music; the others approved and so he composed a cycle of ten songs, five of which were to poems by Müller. This was published as *Gesänge aus einem gesellschaftlichen Liederspiele 'Die schöne Müllerin'* (op. 11); songs *from* a *Liederspiel*, rather than as a kind of 'internal-plot' cycle. Poetic and musical unity was primarily achieved by recurring motives – certain colours, the connection between the brook and the miller lad, birdsong and hunting horns. The songs are fairly brief and mostly strophic; there are some tonal links between them but a ruling pattern is hard to discern.[5]

Müller had published a version of the cycle in 1818; two years later, he added ten more poems. The second version became very popular with composers; there are around 500 settings, although Schubert's remains the most complete. But even Schubert did not include all Müller's poems. Apart from omitting three from the main narrative, he dropped the prologue and the epilogue, in which the poet steps forward to introduce and conclude his work. Perhaps such a framing device felt too self-conscious to Schubert; perhaps it made the cycle too long; or perhaps he simply didn't like those poems. What is certain is that the omissions slightly obscure the theatrical aspect of the original *Die schöne Müllerin*, and that this in turn raises an important issue to do with narrative.

By expunging the prologue and epilogue to *Die schöne Müllerin*, Schubert's version makes us experience the story primarily through the protagonist, the miller's lad, rather than through multiple characters. Thus, on one level, we seem to engage directly with the 'lyric-I'. As mentioned in Chapter 1, that emphasis on individual expression has become one of the defining features of the song cycle as a genre; indeed it became so in part through Schubert's Müller cycles, which somehow transcend the 'stock character' status of the miller (and later the wanderer) to imply a deeper investment in the psyche of the individual subject.

At the same time, though, there are other characters in *Die schöne Müllerin*; it is just that for the most part we see them or, better, hear them from the perspective of the miller boy. In other words, their representation is internalised. Famously, the most important secondary character is the brook, which for the first five songs provides a near-constant rippling accompaniment and to which the lad turns for guidance – it helpfully directs him to the mill. Only in the last two songs, though, does the brook move from the piano part to what we might call a speaking role, welcoming the boy into its waters. The miller maid is notable mostly for her absence; her only reported words are the dismissive, 'it's about to rain, goodbye, I'm going home', and a comment about her love for the colour green – a love that bodes ill for the boy, because it becomes associated with his rival, the hunter. Just one song is devoted to the hunter ('Der Jäger'), and it contrasts sharply with its surroundings in mood, style and key. The lad's disdain for the hunter's guns and hounds is expressed in musical terms by the adoption of a bare, brusque texture: what have, with great chronological licence, been called 'jackboot rhythms'. The figure of the hunter, though, continues to plague the boy, in what exemplifies the poetic and musical emphasis on individual experience in *Die schöne Müllerin*. For the hunter does not reappear in person, but becomes associated with symbols such as the colour green; a transference extended musically by references to accoutrements such as hunting horns.

As mentioned, the hunter is also characterised by key. On the one hand, and as mentioned in Chapter 1, it is dangerous to read too deeply into Schubert's choice of keys, if only because he was very willing to transpose songs to suit different voices; certainly, he was not concerned to make his cycles begin and end in the same key, in the manner of Beethoven's *An die ferne Geliebte*. On the other hand, it does seem as if certain songs in *Die schöne Müllerin* make a connection between tonal and emotional areas or, as in 'Der Jäger', use a particular key to convey a sense of distance from other songs or characters. Two songs obviously paired together are the contiguous 'Die liebe Farbe' ('The Beloved Colour') and 'Die böse Farbe' ('The Hateful Colour'), which respond to the hunter's arrival on the scene. In the former, the colour green is still associated with the miller maid, although her new interest in hunting means that the key is a disappointed B minor. In the latter, the colour green has become linked with the boy's rival, causing him to bid her farewell. Apart from occasional minor inflections, the song is in B major. Schubert often used moves from minor to major and vice versa to expressive ends. As is the case here, though, he does not always do so in a conventional fashion (nor does he, to a still greater extent, in *Winterreise*). While on the broadest terms we tend to associate minor keys with sadness and major keys with happiness, these two songs subvert that association, or at least the turn to the major seems to respond to the boy's disappointment, a state other composers may have made unremittingly downcast, in a minor key. Schubert's choice of a major key, though, makes the lad's response bright but tellingly brittle.

With regard to imagery, 'Die liebe Farbe' and 'Die böse Farbe' both make reference to hunting horns. In the first song, horns are hinted at by the tonic–dominant figure that pervades the bass line; within the repetitions of the strophic song they might rise to our consciousness at the reference to the hunter in the second verse, receding to the background – or to the level of subconscious threat – afterwards. The rising arpeggio that features in the vocal melody of 'Die böse Farbe', together with the bass line's triadic movement as we hear of the miller's maid listening to a distant horn in the forest, makes it seem as if the boy almost wishes he were the hunter, so that she would love him. Incidentally, it is in this song that the miller's green – in every sense – dream of love predicts the white of *Winterreise*; his weeping makes him pale as death and he imagines the colour green gloating in triumph over the poor, pale – in German *weißen* – man.

The expressive and representational details of 'Die liebe Farbe' and 'Die böse Farbe' point to Schubert's extraordinary skill at creating links and contrasts within *Die schöne Müllerin*. Although each song can stand alone, they gain significance through association with the other songs in the sequence, by building on the cycle's store of poetic images and by mixing the colours of its harmonic palette. When guided by the brook at the beginning of the cycle, the boy's first four songs remain in major keys (Bb, G, C, G); at the first moment of frustration, in 'Am Feierabend' ('When Work is Over'), there is a move to A minor. Major keys return for the courtship, ending with the frantic and slightly delusional 'Mein!' ('Mine!') in D major. There is then a turn to the flat side, with two songs devoted to his lute in Bb major followed by the arrival of the hunter, which brings about a series of minor keys. The final four songs, beginning with 'Die böse Farbe', demonstrate Schubert's aforementioned unconventional use of the major mode: 'Trockne Blumen' ('Withered Flowers') and 'Der Müller und der Bach' ('The Miller and the Brook') both shift from minor to major as they imagine death's consolation. Thus, while the final song's E major is far-removed from the cycle's opening Bb major in terms of tonal relationships, it manages to convey both the distance travelled by the lad through the cycle and, by grouping songs together by key-types (sharp, flat, major, minor), the various stages of his emotional journey.

Before moving on to *Winterreise* and its relatives a brief detour is in order, to allow us to consider a few further examples of song cycles that can be thought of as hybrid forms. While the theatrical ancestry of Schubert's *Die schöne Müllerin* might have been obscured by its adaptation and by the passing of time, that is not to say that subsequent song cycles have not continued to mix genres: as mentioned in the previous chapter, different types of cycle have continued to exist side by side.

Liederkreise in Balladenform

The so-called 'North German Schubert', Carl Loewe, produced even more songs than his Viennese counterpart, many of which were ballads. Ballads were a long-established type of narrative poem that gained popularity in the late eighteenth century; they told stories in a folk-like style, using simple rhyme schemes, and had an immediate connection with music because they were often intended to be (or at least convey a sense of being) sung or recited. Ballads usually fall into episodes or scenes; this can make them seem on the surface rather like song cycles, but a ballad is a single narrative poem, whereas a song cycle is made up of several lyric poems. Schubert composed a number of ballads – including his famous setting of Goethe's 'Erlkönig' and the more extended *Viola* (D786), to a text by Franz von Schober. It was, though, left to Loewe, in the mid-1830s, to bring the ballad together with the song cycle, in his *Liederkreise in Balladenform: Der Bergmann* (*The Miner*, op. 39) and *Esther* (op. 52), both to texts by Ludwig Theodor Giesebrecht.

While the ballad might seem by nature a more freely structured poetic (and then musical) form, composers frequently gave it more coherent motivic and tonal shape than their song cycles. Schubert's *Viola*, for example, which begins and ends in the same key, uses transitions, modulations and musical cross-references between sections. And several of Loewe's ballads, such as the symmetrically arranged *Gregor auf dem Stein* (*Gregory at the Rock* op. 38), exhibit even more concern with formal design.[6] Loewe maintained this attention to musical structure in his attempt to meld ballad and song cycle. *Esther* consists of five separate songs, which are divided into sections in a ballad-like manner (sections are marked by changes of speaker or subject; they are reflected musically by modulations, changes in time signature and tempo, and new thematic material). They also feature direct speech alien to the song cycle: moments – such as in the fourth song, when the protagonist Esther is told of the death of her son – adopt a recitative-like delivery akin to opera. Neither would her subsequent exhortation to God be out of place on stage. The accompaniment is similarly conceived to convey dramatic tension; as we wait for news of her son, the piano repeats a two-bar figure that, like Esther, awaits resolution. But, at the same time, the way in which Loewe uses these characteristic motives also reinforces the cyclic aspects of the work; at the end of the fourth song an ascending quaver motive that had been heard at the opening of the cycle returns, which serves both to secure the original tonic of A minor and to signify the dramatic resolution of the tale.

Robert Schumann remarked on the tonal return of Loewe's *Esther*, which has led it to be seen as a precedent for his own 1840 song cycles.[7] A better comparison, though, might be to Schumann's choral ballads of the 1850s, which are more obviously sectional and which pursue characteristic motives to a similar degree. Yet there are song cycles which owe an explicit debt to Loewe's hybrid form and, while to do so takes us much later into the nineteenth century, it seems worth exploring one of these to demonstrate the extent to which they can play with the friction between the representational and structural approaches of different genres.

Johannes Brahms began to compose the *Romanzen aus Ludwig Tiecks Magelone* (1861–9) soon after he had accompanied the famous baritone Julius Stockhausen's complete performances of *Die schöne Müllerin* and *An die ferne Geliebte* in Hamburg (see Chapter 3). However, he seems to have taken neither Schubert nor Beethoven as his model; if anything, Loewe's *Liederkreise in Balladenform* are closest in spirit. Brahms chose the lyrical verse interpolated in Tieck's updated *Volksmärchen*, or folk-fairytale, *Wundersame Liebesgeschichte der schönen Magelone und des Grafen Peter aus der Provence* (*The Wonderful Romance of the Beautiful Magelone and Count Peter of Provence*).[8] The songs track the relationship between Count Peter and Magelone: he leaves home; they meet and fall in love, decide to elope, travel, separate; and, finally, they are reunited.

Whereas with Loewe's *Esther* the attention to musical design was surprising, with Brahms's *Magelone Romanzen* it is the avowed lack of emphasis on such matters that upsets our standard view of a composer renowned for thematic transformation. Indeed, Brahms seems not to have encouraged the performance of the songs as a cycle; with self-deprecating wit he claimed that his decision to set almost all of Tieck's poems (apart from the first, sixteenth and seventeenth) was because of 'a certain Germanic thoroughness' rather than an attempt to create a totality.[9] He also resisted Otto Schlotke's connecting narrative, which was intended to link and contextualise his songs for the audience, although some years later he conceded that a few words on the poems to convey the mood in which he had composed the songs might be useful.[10] What is still more unexpected is that Brahms described the *Magelone Romanzen* as 'a kind of theatre'.[11] As in Loewe's *Esther*, there are passages of dialogue. While most of the songs follow what are essentially strophic patterns – indicating that they belong to the Lied tradition – others owe something to the slow–fast model of multi-movement Italian opera arias. And there are further operatic inflections. At the end of 'Wie soll ich die Freude' ('How should I bear the joy'), for example, the tempo increases to *animato*, there are references to material from the opening, and the text is repeated, as if we have reached the culmination of a bravura aria.

If this is operatic writing, though, it is of a fairly old-fashioned kind – more Beethovenian than Verdian, let alone Wagnerian. Given Brahms's predilection for earlier music and his distaste for the so-called New German School of Wagner and Liszt that is not surprising. More out of character is the reference to operatic music of any kind; Brahms has never been known as a man of the theatre. Yet, in the *Magelone Romanzen*, he creates a sense of drama by combining formal elements from opera with those typical of the song cycle in a fashion not dissimilar to that of Loewe's *Esther*. The vocal writing might be more folk-like than virtuosic (or Lied-like rather than operatic), but the relatively large scale of the individual songs gives the whole greater breadth and dramatic reach than if it were a conventional cycle. Indeed, it could be argued that it is in narrative hybrid forms such as these – rather than in what is often taken to be opera's vehicle for interior expression, the aria – that opera and song truly meet.[12]

Example 2.1 Johannes Brahms, *Romanzen aus Ludwig Tiecks 'Magelone'*, no. 15, 'Treue Liebe dauert lange' ('True Love Abides'). 'And whatever held the spirit captive / Then recedes like mist, / And the wide world opens its doors / To the cheerful gaze of spring.' Trans. Stokes, *The Book of Lieder*, p. 86.

Despite Brahms's claims for the theatrical nature of the *Magelone Romanzen*, it seems he could not help devising a thematic scheme and harmonic structure that also makes sense on a musical level. A detailed example will be helpful. The fifteenth and final song, 'Treue Liebe dauert lange' ('True Love Abides'), is in three sections: slow, lively, slow (*Langsam, Lebhaft, Langsam*). While the shift from slow to fast was habitual to solo operatic numbers, the move back to the slow section – creating an overarching ABA form – belongs more to the Lied, which often falls into three-part

Example 2.1 (*cont.*)

forms (a tendency also exhibited by the smaller-scale ABA forms enfolded within the larger sections of this song). However, the more overtly dramatic aspect of the song has to do with the way in which Brahms suggests different voices. Although Tieck's poem does not specify which lines each character should sing, Brahms creates a musical dialogue by presenting us with two themes distinguished by metre: the first is in 4/4, the second in 3/4. At first these alternate but once emotional stability is restored in the third verse the two 'characters' come together; the melodic material of the opening returns, now in 3/4 rather than 4/4 (Example 2.1). The central section is more dramatic and free ranging, but similarly recasts themes in different metres to create contrast and continuity. The end of the song returns to its opening tempo and revisits the first line sung, before the final lines of the poem, which draw on elements from all the different sections to bring the cycle to a close.

It might seem from this example that Brahms's notion of theatre was somewhat abstract, relying as it did primarily on niceties of musical structure. Perhaps the point to emphasise, though, is the composer's openness to a melding of genres or stylistic approaches within the song cycle. From another angle, and probably more importantly, Loewe's and Brahms's concern for musical coherence even within more 'open' texts marks a significant departure for the conception of the song cycle: their approach suggests that poetic and musical forms might take different paths, defining themselves as cycles on their own terms. This is not necessarily to suggest that the history of the song cycle, as a genre, should be seen as a relentless drive towards the 'musically unified' model – as mentioned already, the story is much messier than that. While Schubert might not have been a formal model for Brahms, the folk-like aspect of the *Magelone Romanzen* may have derived from his experience of performing *Die schöne Müllerin*, reminding us that influence can take many different guises. Indeed, a better comparison for the genre's development might be the type of song cycle to which we are about to turn: the *Wanderlieder* – one journey, which may or may not return home, and which along its route reveals several vistas.

Wanderlieder

In the winter of 2004, American tenor David Pisaro undertook the 'coast-to-coast' walk across Northern England (from St Bees in Cumbria to Robin Hood's Bay in North Yorkshire). Along the way, accompanied by pianist Quentin Thomas, he gave thirteen performances of Schubert's *Winterreise*, in churches, halls and farmhouses, to audiences ranging from a few hundred to a farmer and two friends. Pisaro's experiment was partly intended to bring classical music to different audiences and partly a kind of method acting, helping him to get into the role of the traveller. He explained that he was 'trying to make this music relevant to people – people who have been dumped, people who have been dejected, made redundant'.[13]

Pisaro's determination echoes a small but significant adaptation Schubert made to Müller's title for his poetic cycle: he excluded the definite article of *Die Winterreise*, transforming one specific journey into a metaphor for the human condition. But *Winterreise* is not simply a tale of personal loss. Since the late 1820s, both Müller's and Schubert's winter journeys have been interpreted as encoded parables of the sociopolitical conditions then experienced in Austria, of the individual's longing for freedom under the repressive Metternich regime.[14] And beyond their immediate political context Müller and Schubert were not alone in finding the solitary wanderer alluring: from Ulysses to Goethe's Harper, Byron's Childe Harold and the recent writings of W.G. Sebald; from Caspar David Friedrich to Giacometti and Richard Long; from Mahler to Britten, the wanderer has never lacked enthusiastic artistic mediators.

In the early nineteenth century, the most popular *Wanderlieder* were by the German poet Ludwig Uhland. On the surface Uhland's *Wanderlieder* (1815) trace a simple tale: the protagonist leaves his beloved, finds solace in nature, and finally returns home. A more serious task is at hand, though: this is a quest for self-knowledge; is their love true? The further the wanderer gets from home, the darker the night becomes, the colder the winter landscape, the more doubts flood in. That the time and distance travelled is primarily metaphorical is indicated by the final stanza of the seventh song; despite experiencing several seasons, he comments that no one will have lost any sleep since he left home in the morning ('Auch keinem hat's den Schlaf vertrieben, / Daß ich am Morgen weitergeh'). As for Leonard Bast in E.M. Forster's 1910 novel *Howard's End*, who walked all Saturday night to get out of London and escape dreary domesticity, the impulse to wander represents a bid for psychological freedom, even if the reality of life on the road rarely lives up to expectations (the dawn, Bast admits, was merely grey).

Which is also to say that the individual poems of Uhland's *Wanderlieder* are too disconnected chronologically and geographically to present a logical, inviolable narrative. Claims that they are linked by imagery and phrasing are sometimes persuasive, but cannot be pushed too far. It is the wide variety of styles that Conradin Kreutzer achieved in his setting of Uhland's *Wanderlieder* that has been considered his songs' greatest strength (the *Neun Wanderlieder* op. 34 were published in 1818, having already been successful in performance).[15] An early critic described them as forming 'a nearly inseparable cycle, a chain of sweet-smelling flowers'.[16] And, like the links of a chain, each song forms a self-contained unit. As such, they convey as great a sense of travelling as Uhland's poems; they provide snapshots of different scenes rather than a continuous film. It has been argued (along similar lines to discussions of the tonal scheme of *Die schöne Müllerin*) that the relationships between the keys are intended to characterise different stages on the journey. Perhaps the strongest argument for calling the *Neun Wanderlieder* a cycle, though, is that the songs convey the sense of a journey – and if we do not end up where we began (tonally we move from the first song's E minor to a closing D major), then perhaps that indicates the new perspectives discovered while wandering.

Amongst Uhland's and Kreutzer's *Wanderlieder* is a 'Winterreise' whose imagery – cold winds, empty streets, frozen rivers – predicts that of Müller's cycle by the same name, the first twelve poems of which were published in 1823.[17] Müller later wrote an essay about Uhland that described the *Wanderlieder* as leaving 'a long train of imitations behind them'; there were as many composers who took Kreutzer as their model.[18] In musical terms, this meant that each song was self-sufficient; that there were no piano transitions, quotations or other transformations between songs; that the tonal scheme was open; and that keys were determined by poetic content rather than abstract design. In other words, they were definitely not based on Beethoven's *An die ferne Geliebte*, in which the protagonist stays in one, admittedly rural, place, imagining his distant love, and the musician similarly stays if not faithful to then at least mindful of the home key.

Schubert described Kreutzer's *Wanderlieder* as 'very beautiful', even saying that he wished he had written them.[19] The still greater compliment came in his following their example when setting Müller's *Winterreise*. Again, this is as much a journey of the mind as of the winter landscape; unlike Uhland's protagonist, though, Müller's does not return home. We meet him on the road, the constant quaver rhythm in the piano accompaniment and the melodic repetitions of the modified strophic form of the first song, 'Gute Nacht' ('Good night'), conveying his trudging steps and a sense that his journey is inescapable: 'I cannot choose the time for my journey' ('Ich kann zu meiner Reisen nicht wählen mit der Zeit'), he explains (Example 2.2). Once that familiar harbinger of young love, the month of May, favoured him – there was even talk of marriage – now all is covered in snow; rejected, he is leaving town. There is no obvious narrative to the following twenty-three songs (partly because Schubert only half followed Müller's revised order). The poems dwell on the winter landscape and the act of remembering: he dreams of past happiness and contrasts it with his present sadness; symbols of his previous, sociable life (flourishing nature, the arrival of post, barking dogs) are made distant and, literally, cold – the river is frozen over, his once-black hair is sprinkled with frost, and the rustling leaves of the linden tree no longer whisper of love, but of death's approach. At last, he meets a solitary organ grinder ('Der Leiermann'); the continuous drone of whose music seems to encapsulate the endless journey of the wanderer – the cycle that can only end in death (Example 2.3).

Schubert followed Kreutzer's example by creating a series of self-sufficient songs that still, on being considered together, project a sense of belonging to the same journey. He achieved this by using different key areas to convey proximity or distance, and what, for want of a better term, might be called stylistic consistency. There are far fewer strophic forms in *Winterreise* than in *Die schöne Müllerin* and, where they do appear, their repetitive qualities are used for particular affect; 'Gute Nacht' has already been mentioned as an example. Along similar lines, Schubert pays close attention to the imagery of the poems, frequently placing a nugget in the piano part that characterises the whole song. In 'Gute Nacht', it is the plodding quavers; in 'Der Leiermann', it is the drone and the repeated melodic fragment. But it need not be so transparently pictorial. The reach of Jack Frost's fingers in 'Der greise Kopf' ('The Hoary Head') may be suggested by the piano's arching arpeggiated figure over static chords (Example 2.4). This is no singable melody as found in *Die schöne Müllerin*, yet the voice takes it up, not quite matching the top A of the piano's prompt. And the very awkwardness of the vocal line is significant because it demonstrates how, in *Winterreise*, Schubert took a more declamatory, dramatic approach to setting the poetry. The textures are bare: cold, even. The lush, rippling accompaniments that spoke to the miller's lad are frozen over. We are dealing, it seems, with a more distilled version of the internal monologues detected in *Die schöne Müllerin*, with an economy of means that feeds into the relationship between voice and piano, and poem and music, on the deepest level.

Example 2.2 Franz Schubert, *Winterreise*, no. 1, 'Gute Nacht' ('Good Night'). 'A stranger I came, / A stranger I depart. / The month of May favoured me / With many bouquets of flowers . . . I cannot choose the time / For my journey: I must find my own way / In this darkness.' Trans. Stokes, *The Book of Lieder*, p. 363.

Perhaps to an even greater extent than *Die schöne Müllerin*, *Winterreise* has captured the creative imagination of song-cycle composers. At the end of the 1830s, the Leipzig-based composer Carl Banck even produced a continuation and revision of the tale with his *Des Leiermanns Liederbuch* (*The Hurdy-Gurdy Player's Songbook* op. 21).[20] Later composers' tributes came in the form of further *Wanderlieder* and through the adoption of some of the characteristic musical imagery of *Winterreise*.

Example 2.3 Franz Schubert, *Winterreise*, no. 24, 'Der Leiermann' ('The Organ Grinder').
'There beyond the village, / An organ-grinder stands, / And with numb fingers / Plays as
best he can . . . No one cares to listen, / No one looks at him; / And the dogs snarl / Around
the old man.' Trans. Stokes, *The Book of Lieder*, p. 373.

Example 2.4 Franz Schubert, *Winterreise*, no. 14, 'Der greise Kopf' ('The Hoary Head').
'The frost has sprinkled a white sheen / On my hair.' Trans. Stokes, *The Book of Lieder*,
p. 369.

The opening song of Ralph Vaughan Williams's *Songs of Travel*, 'Vagabond' (1904),
for example, uses a tramping rhythm indebted to the trudging footsteps of Schubert's 'Gute Nacht', while Benjamin Britten's *Winter Words* (1954) nods towards
the icy landscape of *Winterreise*: 'The Choirmaster's Burial' and 'At the Railway
Station, Upway (or The Convict and Boy with the Violin)', with their references
to forlorn music played by organ and fiddle, seem like latter-day versions of 'Der
Leiermann'.

The strongest response to Schubert's *Winterreise*, though, was probably Gustav
Mahler's *Lieder eines fahrenden Gesellen* (*Songs of a Wayfarer*, 1883–5). While Mahler
denied any relationship between this, his first song cycle, and Schubert's last, it would

have been an incurious or ignorant musician in late nineteenth-century Austria who was not familiar with Schubert's oeuvre. Mahler's resistance to acknowledging Schubert's influence, however, illuminates some critical points to do with the history of the genre. *Die schöne Müllerin* and *Winterreise* could not be ignored; they were well established by the 1880s as pinnacles of achievement, against which other efforts were measured. Yet Schubert's cycles – whose folk themes already evoked a bygone era – were now themselves historical objects, representative of the end of the century's own nostalgia for earlier, less industrialised, times. What is more, the transfer of the song cycle from the salon to the concert hall in the 1870s (to be discussed in Chapter 3) meant that the 'lyric-I', the subjective voice of *Die schöne Müllerin* and *Winterreise*, could not be heard so clearly. Perhaps partly for that reason, it became more dearly prized at the *fin de siècle* and, as exemplified by Mahler's *Lieder eines fahrenden Gesellen*, metaphorically and literally amplified.

The *Lieder eines fahrenden Gesellen* are undeniably songs of a young man – he might even be the boy of *Die schöne Müllerin*, who wanted so much to be a wanderer. The first song adapts a poem from the early nineteenth-century collection *Des Knaben Wunderhorn*, but Mahler wrote the other three poems himself (this was not entirely without precedent – the Wagnerian Peter Cornelius wrote his own poems – but was still unusual). He explained that:

> The idea of the songs as a whole is that a wayfaring man, who has been stricken by fate, now sets forth into the world, travelling wherever the road may lead him.[21]

The poems are deliberately simple and folk-like, with short lines and a clear rhyme scheme. There is a sense in which they distil some of the key features of *Winterreise*; partly because there are only four songs, rather than twenty-four, but also because Mahler returns to his small repertoire of images – birds, flowers, his beloved's blue eyes – almost obsessively.[22] And, at the end of the final song, 'Die zwei blauen Augen', Mahler's wanderer falls asleep under a blossoming linden tree. Its shadow is also that of Schubert, whose wanderer heard in the linden tree's rustling leaves the approach of death. The young man's journey thus seems to become one with that of *Winterreise*.

But it is not quite that straightforward. The folk-like nature of Mahler's *Gesellen* poems may seem to be matched by the vocal melodies, which fall into short diatonic phrases that move mostly by step or through triadic arpeggios. Also, the harmonic rhythm is slow, each song making use of that routine pastoral signifier, the pedal point (a descendant of the drone). Yet at the same time these are not folk songs, even in the vein of Schubert. They are refracted through a later nineteenth-century musical lens. None of the songs is strophic and, still more significantly, none follows a conventional tonal design. No song ends in the key in which it began, nor does the cycle return to the opening key at its end. This is known as progressive tonality and became a feature of Mahler's music; indeed the key scheme is something he changed on revising the work, suggesting that in the case of the *Lieder eines fahrenden Gesellen* it was a slightly later development.[23] It would be fair to say that Mahler's use of tonality reflected current practices, which at the end of the nineteenth century tended towards greater chromaticism and freer treatment of key relationships. To be sure, composers earlier in the century could not really have conceived such distended harmonic relationships. But it is worth considering whether, at this stage, Mahler's roving keys were in fact an extension of the kind of 'wandering' tonal relationships found in *Die schöne Müllerin* and *Winterreise*; conveying a sense of distance travelled rather than pursuing a particular route. The 1880s were an age of locomotive – and, soon, automotive – travel, which meant that long journeys could be covered at much greater speed than Schubert would have imagined: there's little reason to think that an equivalent, more ambitious *Wanderlust* was not also shared by composers and their invented wanderers.

However, while the wanderer of the *Gesellen Lieder* might have had faster means at his disposal, for now he kept on foot and, as in Schubert's cycles, remained alone. The narrative voice of the *Lieder eines fahrenden Gesellen*, like that of *Die schöne Müllerin* and *Winterreise*, is that of the rejected lover; it has even been said that the wanderer should be considered the young composer himself. Such direct conflation of creator and work is complicated in this instance by Mahler's decision to orchestrate the songs, and to absorb their music into his First Symphony.[24] This transformation has been thought to make what had been personal into something public; as mentioned, songs intended more or less for private consumption were put first on the concert stage, and then – through orchestration and adaptation – amplified still further. As a result, John Daverio suggests that Mahler made explicit 'not only the centrality of the Lied but the centrality of the poet-composer's "I" striving to express itself'.[25] It is a grand claim, for both genre and subject, and one that seems a long way away from the salon entertainment with which we began our discussion of Schubert. Yet, as will be explored through this book, the song cycle has often been a vehicle for poet-composers to explore an individual's relationship to society.

Chapter 3

Performance

The long nineteenth century

So far we have concentrated on the compositional history of the song cycle, but this overlooks the important roles played by other parties. Performers, publishers, instrument makers, critics and, of course, audiences also influenced developments. Driving all was arguably the greatest creative force of the nineteenth century, the engineer. First, improvements in transport systems within and between countries allowed artists and audiences to travel more freely, enabling the wider dissemination of new works and performance styles. Then advances in printing technology facilitated the mass production of cheaper scores and, no less importantly, music journals in which works were excerpted and reviewed, developing ways of thinking about songs and their interpretation. What is more, the newly available repertoire could be played on what was rapidly establishing itself as a standard piece of furniture in middle-class homes – the factory-produced piano.[1]

I mention these factors at the start because they sketch a rather different background for the song cycle than the one typically dispensed. Schubert, Schumann and others did not, in other words, succeed purely on the strength of their music, but with the support of commercial networks (bear in mind that Schubert was one of the first musicians to support himself primarily by his compositions rather than through the aid of a patron or official post). Although, as we will see, over the course of the nineteenth century venues for the song cycle shifted from amateur music-making to professional performance, the genre could not have established itself without strong roots in everyday society and culture. Nor was there a neat migration from private to public realms. Instead, the song cycle continued to inhabit both spheres, in the process illuminating the extent to which concepts about what constitutes private and public, and amateur and professional, changed during the course of the genre's first hundred years.

Before proceeding, an aside on chronology will be useful. This chapter traces the performance practices of song cycles from Schubert's time through to roughly the outbreak of the First World War: what historians would call the long nineteenth century. This causes an overlap with Chapter 9, which starts in the early twentieth century. The distinction between chapters is that our focus here is on the nineteenth century's legacy of increasing specialisation in live performance and listening habits, some of whose culminations were the concert reforms and private performance societies of early twentieth-century Vienna. The later chapter is concerned with the impact of recording on performing and listening habits.

Schubert's singers

Schubert established his fame as a Lieder composer initially through performances rather than publications. There were a number of venues available to him in Vienna, from gatherings of friends, to salon concerts hosted by well-to-do acquaintances, to public concerts for which admission was charged. There were also a number of music societies and charitable associations that arranged evening entertainments, and it was at those that Lieder such as 'Erlkönig' ('Erlking') were first heard. The varied opportunities available to the composer resist categorisation into private or public events: a musical evening, or salon, held at the home of Schubert's friend's father Ignaz Sonnleithner, featuring amateur and professional performers, might be to an audience of ten, or to over a hundred. Often, programmes presented a mixture of genres, and were as much social as musical events, including recitations, eating, drinking and dancing. The same mix was found at public concerts – noisy and often ramshackle affairs, at which audience members talked, applauded and demanded encores during performances as they saw fit. At the other end of the spectrum were the Schubertiades, dedicated to the composer's music. Programmes were not written down, but Schubert and his circle usually performed his smaller-scale works, such as Lieder, partsongs and pieces for four-hand piano.

Some Schubertiades took place in the composer's absence or in distant cities, indicating how popular he was becoming in certain circles. Despite his supporters' calls for his songs to be published, firms such as Breitkopf und Härtel still thought him not sufficiently well known and his music too difficult for most audiences. It was not until 1821 that 'Erlkönig', composed some six years earlier, appeared as his opus 1. Even then, it was printed at friends' expense. It sold swiftly through private salons such as Sonnleithner's, however, and the same system was used to publish opp. 2–7 and 12–14. It was after the latter's success that the publishers Cappi and Diabelli finally offered to take Schubert on.

Individual Lieder were eminently saleable commodities for practical reasons: their size made them easy to transport and affordable. Their dissemination was also aided by their not being too onerous to copy by hand. Indeed, publishers routinely produced multiple versions of songs, either with alternative accompaniments (guitar, for instance) or arranged for other instruments (Liszt's transcriptions of Schubert were promoted much more vigorously than the original songs).[2] It is worth remembering that there was at this early stage little respect for the original source: Diabelli published a heavily embellished version of *Die schöne Müllerin* (of which more later), and Tobias Haslinger's edition of *Winterreise* (1828) transposed two songs ('Mut!' and 'Der Leiermann').[3]

Purchasers of single songs would often have them bound into albums, but selling larger collections of songs – particularly cycles – was a different proposition.[4] *Die schöne Müllerin* was typical in that it did not appear in one volume; instead the songs were grouped into five bundles, the size of which was decided by the number of pages that could be easily bound, and by cost. Even twenty years later Schumann's *Dichterliebe* was published in two volumes, the composer having removed four songs from the original cycle at the request of his publishers. Cycles seem to have been aimed more at collectors, along the lines of albums of keepsakes, to be dipped into rather than sung or played through in sequence (much as the first LP records were treated 150 years later). There is little in the early publication history of nineteenth-century song cycles to suggest they were thought of as complete works, as they often are today.

Schubert's cycles seem not to have been performed in their complete forms during his lifetime. The closest they came was Johann Michael Vogl's version of *The Lady of the Lake*, sung at a private concert at the poet Anton Ottenwald's home in Linz and at a concert in Gmunden in the summer of 1825. As there was no chorus, only the solo songs were presented, and Vogl decided to reorder them, beginning with Ellen's 'Ave Maria' and ending with the rousing 'Normans Gesang'. Of the latter, a listener wrote:

> The warrior with his sacrificial torch, the summons to arms, sings as he fares across the country. Hurrying without respite, he thinks of his errand, of the bride he has left at the altar… The tune and the accompaniment you'll have to imagine. Schubert himself regards this as the best of his Scott songs. Vogl interprets it heavily (a syllable, often a word, to each note), but splendidly.[5]

As is often the case with descriptions of performances, we have to imagine more than just the tune and accompaniment. What can be gleaned from these comments about the way in which Schubert's songs were performed? Vogl's attention to every note and syllable indicates a declamatory style of delivery, and perhaps also resulted from his habit of devising various alterations and ornamental embellishments, as are recorded in the second edition of *Die schöne Müllerin*. These included filling in large intervals with connecting scales, adding turns and trills, altering the pitch of top and bottom notes, using dotted rhythms and inserted rests to make the declamation more dramatic, making changes to dynamic markings, ties and slurs, and even changing harmonies.[6] In Schubert's words, Vogl 'lived on' his songs, making them his own. To do so reflected contemporary musical practice and also, probably, that at the age of forty-five Vogl was making the most of what remained of his voice.

(Apparently 'he merely helped himself out as well as he could, in the manner of the experienced opera singer, where his voice and strength did not suffice'.)

Vogl was not the only interpreter of Schubert cycles during the composer's lifetime, nor the only one of whom the composer approved. The dedicatee of *Die schöne Müllerin*, Baron Karl von Schönstein, was an accomplished amateur singer with 'a beautiful, noble-sounding, high baritone voice'.[7] Having only sung Italian music before meeting Schubert, afterwards he devoted himself to Lieder. Liszt, who heard Schönstein in Vienna in 1838, claimed that he could move the listener to tears: 'Baron Schönstein declaims Schubert's songs with the technique of a great artist and sings them with the simple sensitivity of an amateur who concentrates on the emotions expressed [in the songs], without preoccupying himself with the public'.[8]

The examples of Vogl and Schönstein demonstrate how two seemingly contradictory approaches to Lieder performance became quickly established. On the one hand Vogl, an opera professional, was keen to bring Lieder to public audiences, and even advocated them as replacements for arias on concert programmes. On the other, Schönstein, the accomplished amateur, represents an early instance of Lieder being thought to belong to interior realms and individual experience. Friction between these two approaches to Lieder performance would intensify through the century. Interestingly, what brought them together but also ultimately broke them apart was when professionals began to evoke the internalised expression initially associated with amateur – or, perhaps better, 'private' – interpretation; but that divide would not be fully crossed until the advent of recording in the twentieth century.

Repertoire also had a role to play in the gradual professionalisation of Lieder performance. As already mentioned, the more complex vocal and piano parts, and increasing length, of Schubert's songs made them too difficult for all but the most proficient amateur performers; compositions by the next generation were, if anything, even more technically challenging. Schumann was fortunate to hear some of his collections and song cycles performed in private by famous professionals such as Livia Frege and Wilhelmine Schröder-Devrient. But his experimentation with a mode of song composition designed for professionals in the concert hall, in the *Lieder und Gesänge aus Goethes 'Wilhelm Meister'* op. 98a (1849), was greeted with scepticism by the publisher Johann André:

> I wished mainly for solo songs like your op. 42 [*Frauenliebe und -leben*], songs more for presentation in private circles or appropriate to such musical arenas. I must see that I bring to my press such items as might expect a market with a larger public. Indeed, I purchase all of your songs for myself... but lend many of them out, from which I see that there are only a few amateurs who will sacrifice for the sake of art in order to obtain a vigorously powerful enjoyment.[9]

André's final comment – 'A publisher is ill at ease when an artist . . . values works more highly [than warranted] by their eventual public recognition' – illustrates the widening rift between composer ambition for the song cycle and the traditional domestic associations of Lieder.

It was not until the year of Schumann's death that song cycles were first heard in their entirety on the public stage. The German baritone Julius Stockhausen gave three concerts in Vienna in May 1856. The first was a conventional programme of ballads, Italian and French arias, and Lieder – including 'Wohin?', 'Der Neugierige' and 'Der Müller und der Bach' from *Die schöne Müllerin*. These excerpts were presumably intended to whet the appetite for the next two concerts, each of which presented Schubert's entire cycle (and were sponsored by Diabelli's successor, Spina). Stockhausen modestly credited the success of his *Müllerin* concerts to poor weather and Viennese curiosity. He did, though, detect enough interest in the project to tour it around Germany and Russia (audiences apparently numbered as many as 2,000), and added to his repertoire *Winterreise*, *An die ferne Geliebte* and Schumann's Eichendorff *Liederkreis* op. 39, as well as *Dichterliebe*.

Stockhausen's accompanist was sometimes Johannes Brahms, whose enthusiasm for the venture can be detected in his recommendation to Clara Schumann that she get someone to sing all the songs of *Die schöne Müllerin* to her consecutively: 'Don't be satisfied with one, but do not forget to read the poetry first carefully, so as to get a complete appreciation of the whole.'[10] Clara was not won over, and even divided the eight songs of Schumann's own *Frauenliebe und -leben* in half in an 1866 concert in Vienna, the two parts separated by renditions of Beethoven's C-minor Piano Variations op. 36 and a piano duo by Brahms acolyte Ernst Rudorff.[11] Similarly Eduard Hanslick, the influential Viennese critic, thought that Stockhausen's determination to perform the entire *Müllerin* cycle demonstrated what Susan Youens describes as 'an admirable but skewed fidelity to both the composer and the poet' (at one concert the actress Pauline Rettrich recited Müller's prologue and epilogue as a framing device, perhaps as a nod to the poetic cycle's *Liederspiel* origins).[12] The notion of such fidelity being 'skewed' might raise eyebrows in our era of historically informed performance practice. What is more, Stockhausen's fidelity to the work was hardly such as we would recognise today. In the middle of the first full performance of *Dichterliebe* in 1861, for instance, Brahms played movements from Schumann's piano piece *Kreisleriana*. Even if he did so simply to allow Stockhausen to rest his voice, the interlude confounds attempts to claim that the cycle – as concept – had by this point fully entered performers' consciousness.[13]

Where Stockhausen did come close to a style of performance we might recognise today was in his suppression of theatrical gestures. 'You must not exhibit your personality in the concert hall, for there you are nothing but an interpreter of the poet and composer', he advised students.[14] Attempting to untangle how Stockhausen came to this view of appropriate interpretation reveals the extent to which Lied performance styles intertwined with vocal techniques from very different genres: while a legacy of domestic music-making was retained in the attention to texts and the notion of private interpretation, the more significant touchstones were opera and oratorio.[15] Stockhausen had trained with one of the most famous singing teachers in nineteenth-century Paris, Manuel García Jr (author of the hugely influential *Traité complet de l'art du chant* (1847)), and performed in French and Italian opera. It was from that repertory that he developed the 'rich beauty' of his voice, 'nobility' of style, and 'perfect phrasing'.[16] His 'intimate sympathy and . . . intelligent way in which the words were given' may indeed have derived from his deep appreciation of poetry, but doubtless also from having to project his voice in large spaces, in opera houses and at choir festivals (or, for that matter, those 2,000-strong audiences for his song cycles). Stockhausen himself became a respected teacher; his students were among the first generation to specialise in Lieder. They still, though, adopted techniques and experiences from operatic and choral music. The tenor Raimund von zur Mühlen, for example, studied with Stockhausen in Frankfurt, was tutored by Clara Schumann and worked with Brahms; his first public success was with a performance of *Dichterliebe* in Riga in 1873, but he also explored French and Italian repertoire with Romaine Bussini in Paris. Indeed, Mühlen set out to combine the lyricism of *bel canto* singing with the attention to diction and atmosphere typical of Germanic delivery. In other words, despite being inherently Germanophone works, Lieder in performance were stylistically multi-lingual.

While Stockhausen may have begun to influence how Lieder were interpreted, his first forays into performing complete cycles had no immediate impact. Most continued to devise recitals that jumbled up songs from different cycles. And many appropriated a declamatory-dramatic method, along with theatrical gestures and expressions, derived from the operatic (specifically the Wagnerian) stage. While, in the 1860s, Lieder continued to be marketable commodities and were becoming a fixture in concert halls across northern Europe, many critics and musicians thought the genre had run its course.[17] Stockhausen's recitals of complete cycles were of historical interest, but – as yet – no harbingers of a new performance practice.

The late nineteenth century

Berlin, Paris, London, St Petersburg, New York: the concert life of any of these cities, and indeed many other urban centres, could illustrate how performers brought song cycles into their repertoires in the late nineteenth century. My focus here, though, will continue to be Vienna. This is partly because of its connections to the early history of the Lied but also because it was there that some new trends in performance were initiated.

By the 1870s, a newly built avenue, the Ringstrasse, circled the old city of Vienna, garlanding it with a series of monumental public buildings and private residences.[18] Town planners invested much thought into the way citizens moved around the city and interacted with each other: how the forward movement of the street could be mitigated by plazas where communities could rest, contemplate and mingle; how the architecture of museums, opera houses and apartment blocks could encourage the breaking down of social barriers between aristocracy and bourgeoisie.

Perhaps the invigoration of song-cycle performances should be understood against this backdrop of urban engineering – as a celebration of and education in Viennese musical achievements, and as a means to bridge the divide between high and not-so-high, or at least professional and domestic, art. On his retirement from Vienna's Royal Opera in 1876, tenor Gustav Walter began a series of Lieder evenings, or *Liederabende*, in the city's Bösendorfer Hall. At first few singers followed suit, but his concert manager, the publisher Albert Gutmann, urged Walter to extend his 'monopoly on the Lied' by scheduling still more concerts. The popular success of these enabled Gutmann to add to his stable many opera stars prepared to turn their hand to the Lied. Many became among the first to record Lieder, and also became influential teachers, bridging the chronological divide between the performance traditions of the nineteenth and twentieth centuries. They included Ludwig Wüllner, famed as an actor and reciter as well as a baritone; Stockhausen students Johannes Messchaert (who also studied with Wüllner) and Raimund von zur Mühlen (mentioned earlier); contralto Lulu Gmeiner (a Walter student who briefly taught Elisabeth Schwarzkopf); and Dutch mezzo-soprano Julia Culp, one of the first female Lieder specialists.

Liederabende gained momentum to the extent that by 1887 music critic (and, ironically, song composer) Hugo Wolf claimed that Vienna had succumbed to a Lieder epidemic. They spread to other towns and countries, and became so popular that by the early twentieth century in Berlin there would be at least twenty such concerts offered every week, all of which were likely to be sold out.[19] Walter had interspersed his Schubert concerts with instrumental solos but, increasingly, recitals consisted entirely of Lieder. Emphasis was on the quality of the poem and its interpretation – texts were distributed to the audience, and typically the poem was recited before the song. It became increasingly common to devote recitals to a single composer or to a particular theme, and to perform complete cycles: an attempt, perhaps, for performers to distinguish themselves from the crowd. A further motivation, as always, was commercial: many concerts were sponsored by publishers such as Breitkopf und Härtel who, by the 1880s, had realised their mistake in refusing to take on the composer of 'Erlkönig' and were in the business of producing a complete edition of Schubert's works. Some concerts also had clear pedagogical purpose. For example, Stockhausen student and Brahms scholar Max Friedländer presented *Winterreise* in Müller's order rather than Schubert's, and also added a lecture on the cycle. Amalie Joachim, wife of the famous violinist and a celebrated singer and teacher, presented a series of recitals entitled 'The German Lied from its beginnings to the present day: a song cycle [*Lieder-Cyclus*] in three evenings' at the Vienna Musikverein in early 1893.

Friedländer's and Joachim's programmes demonstrate the extent to which musicians were aware of the cultural history of Vienna. The centenary of Schubert's birth in 1897 was celebrated by exhibitions of paintings inspired by the composer, biographical ephemera or 'Schubertiana' and concerts.[20] A sense of Vienna's rich heritage also filtered into performance habits at concerts. After the death of his mother in 1904, Mühlen decided to retire from his highly successful career. The audience's response to his final recital in Berlin indicates the distance *Die schöne Müllerin* had travelled, in terms of the transfer from the private to the public sphere:

> The hall was filled to overflowing with an audience that loved him … as the cycle developed his powers became superbly intensified, and during the last song ('Der Baches Wiegenlied') a remarkable incident occurred. He began the last verse, 'Gute Nacht', with broad noble tone *f* – diminishing to *p* at the phrase 'Der Vollmond steigt' – building up continuously to the great final climax 'Und der Himmel da oben, wie ist er so weit', singing this *ff* in a heroic timbre; the concluding postlude softened then to a gentle, rocking lullaby, dying away *ppp*. So overwhelming had his expression become that during this last verse the members of his audience, 'drawn by some irresistible power', rose one by one until all were standing with bowed heads as if 'receiving a benediction'. At the climax, where 'a place in Heaven seems possible for the poor suicide miller boy', a deep wave of emotion passed through the hall. Silence reigned as the postlude died away; Mühlen walked slowly from the platform, and then tremendous applause broke out which he returned again and again to acknowledge. The 'Prince of Singers' was heard no more on the public platform.[21]

The transformation of the concert hall into a place of worship is sometimes said to have taken place much earlier in the nineteenth century, in response to the symphonies of Beethoven. But, whether or not that is the case, it became in the early years of the twentieth century a common mode of listening to at least some Lieder recitals.

Finally, and perhaps surprisingly, the reverent response to Mühlen's final performance also had to do with modernism. By the beginning of the twentieth century, Vienna was not only a musical museum, but also a vibrant centre for new music. There were, inevitably, tensions between generations. Audiences were puzzled, even

outraged, by some of the harmonic and timbral experiments of younger composers
such as Mahler, Richard Strauss and, most contentiously of all, Arnold Schoenberg.
Nor were they afraid to say so. Advocates of concert reform were mostly concerned
with encouraging the kind of rapt attention the audience gave Mühlen and Schubert for more challenging works. Some advocated that lights should be dimmed
during the performance; that different coloured stage lights be used to change the
mood between songs; or even that various scents should be used to perfume the
hall, in accordance with what was being sung (it is perhaps in similar spirit that we
should understand Edward Elgar's laconic report of 1899: 'Clara Butt dressed like a
mermaid to sing the Sea Songs [his cycle *Sea Pictures*] at Norwich').[22] Against such
theatrical impulses, other reformers suggested not only that singers should rein in
gesticulation on stage, but even that the musicians should be concealed from view,
behind floral arrangements. We might smile at the idea of going to a concert where a
singer would hide behind an evocatively scented shrub; it is perhaps best understood
along the lines of Wagner's design for the Bayreuth opera house, which concealed the
orchestra beneath the stage, or by taking into account the fact that audiences were
beginning to hear disembodied voices from early gramophones. The desire to sup-
press performers' bodies then seems intriguingly in keeping with music-dramatic
and technological developments.

On a more practical level, Schoenberg requested that the audience at a 1907 concert of his opp. 2, 3 and 6 songs should listen quietly, and not make their views
known by hissing or cheering. He had good cause: on 31 March 1913 in Vienna
he conducted what became known as the *Skandalkonzert*, in which new works by
him and his circle were greeted with laughter, hisses and applause, and the whole
affair descended into an affray between musicians and audience (the president of the
society hosting the event apparently boxed one man's ears!). And this was no one-
off incident: there were reports of stabbings during performances of Berg's songs,
and apparently it was rare to get through Schoenberg's *Pierrot lunaire* in Vienna
without 'violent disturbances'.[23] Some found the negative reactions too much. Following the *Skandalkonzert* Berg withdrew his song cycle *Fünf Orchesterlieder nach
Ansichtskarten-Texten von Peter Altenberg* (*Five Orchestral Songs after Postcard Texts
by Peter Altenberg*) op. 4; they were not published until 1953.[24]

By 1918 Schoenberg had set up a private society for the performance of new
music (*Verein für musikalische Privataufführungen*), accessible only by subscription
(with photo identification). Pieces – often, songs – might be played several times
to enable listeners to get to know them, but there was to be no applause and no
reviews. In a way, we seem to have come full circle – back to the private concerts
for friends known a century earlier as Schubertiades. By the early twentieth century,
however, technology was fundamentally changing musical life. The ability to hear

music through radio broadcasts, or on record, allowed for much wider dissemination of repertoire. At the same time, and as will be discussed further in Chapter 9, the possibility to listen to music repeatedly, and alone, enabled Lieder and song cycles to return to the domestic contexts from which they originated: this time round, however – and it was a significant difference – they were listened to rather than performed.

Chapter 4

Gendered voices

The close relationship between Lieder and domestic music-making in the first half of the nineteenth century had in many ways been defined by gender. While middle-class women enjoyed equal status to men in legal rights and schooling across German-speaking lands by this time, they were directed towards home craft and childrearing rather than more intellectual pursuits. Music was an integral part of the curriculum, as a means to become accomplished in the eyes of society, and because of a long-held belief that a mother's singing voice could help to nurture a child's preschool development.[1] But an excessive interest in musical performance, or in playing 'unfeminine' instruments such as violin, cello, brass or wind, was thought to endanger a woman's moral character. The small scale of Lieder thus provided a suitable vehicle for feminine musical skills within the home; women could sing and accompany themselves on the piano, which was rapidly replacing any other form of instrumental accompaniment. For similar reasons, Lieder were also considered an appropriate genre for female composers (though they produced few song cycles) such as Fanny Mendelssohn Hensel, Josephine Lang, Clara Schumann, Emilie Zumsteeg and Annette von Droste-Hülshoff. In sum, the singing of Lieder in the home became a means by which family relationships could be established and confirmed, be they between mother and child, prospective lovers, or husband and wife.

In is in this context that we can best understand the appeal of a cycle of poems by Adelbert von Chamisso, *Frauenliebe und -leben* (1831). Although Chamisso was male, he wrote in the first person, giving voice to a woman's life experiences from first love through marriage, childbirth and widowhood. The woman describes her feelings on first seeing her future beloved: she feels as if she has been blinded, for he is all she can see. The second poem continues the visual theme; she is happy just to gaze at and admire him from afar, for surely she would not deserve his love (she describes him as a noble star). In the third poem she is ecstatic because he has said he loves her; in the fourth she cherishes the ring he has given her; in the fifth she asks her sisters for help with her bridal attire and bids them farewell. The sixth song is addressed to her husband; can he not guess why she is crying? They are tears of happiness because, according to what her mother has told her, they must soon get a cradle. Poem seven expresses her joy at motherhood. Then, in the eighth poem, the husband's death causes her first pain; she has lost her happiness and her world. The ninth poem shifts perspective: she gives advice to her daughter, now herself a bride.

Many composers set Chamisso's poems to music. But the most famous and enduring cycle has been Robert Schumann's. The root of his attraction to *Frauenliebe und -leben* was obvious: in 1840, after a prolonged legal battle with her father, he was finally allowed to marry Clara Wieck. During their enforced separation, he and Clara had exchanged letters fantasising about what life would be like together, sometimes using similar imagery to Chamisso's cycle.[2] This might have been why Schumann did not set the last poem of the cycle, as it casts everything in the past tense. It might also explain the prominent role the piano plays in the narrative; although it occasionally makes explicit what the words do not (such as her pregnancy), often it can be heard to reveal less the truth of the woman's situation than her hopes and dreams.

For example, the final poem of Schumann's cycle expresses the woman's desolation at the loss of her husband. Yet the chords accompanying her final words – 'you, my world' – end with a major sonority, a shaft of light that prompts the piano to remember music from the first verse of the opening song (Example 4.1). It thereby seems to keep the cycle in the present tense, with the woman finding consolation over her husband's death through replaying memories of happier times together. The postlude also creates a strong musical frame for the cycle itself. The distinctive two-bar figure that opens the whole cycle and now brings it to a close is itself 'cyclic', in that it quickly rotates through a standard cadential pattern (I–IV–V[7]–I), almost as if we have reached the end before we've begun. The device hints that we are dealing with a universal life cycle that might repeat itself, forever.[3]

Of all the works discussed in this book, *Frauenliebe und -leben* has the most clearly cyclic construction. Despite that, it is rarely given as the textbook definition of the song cycle; instead, that position is taken by *Winterreise* or *Dichterliebe*. The reason probably has to do with gender. The subject of Chamisso's cycle keeps it firmly in the domestic realm as, perhaps, do Schumann's musical bookends: there is not the open-endedness of *Dichterliebe* or *Winterreise*'s sense of the open road. Although, as will be discussed later, the protagonists of *Winterreise* and *Dichterliebe* need not be defined by their gender, the domestic sphere was marked as feminine – and it is this distinction that has proved problematic for the status of *Frauenliebe und -leben*. Musicologist Ruth Solie recently claimed that *Frauenliebe und -leben* makes modern listeners uncomfortable because of the emphasis, by a male poet, on woman's role as homemaker.[4] We might counter her argument, as has Kristina Muxfeldt, by thinking of the cycle in nineteenth-century terms: as an opportunity for female readers to imagine their own passionate worlds, without having to adopt a male voice.[5] Here, however, we will explore a slightly different angle on the issue of gender representation, considering the relationship between author/composer

Example 4.1 Robert Schumann, *Frauenliebe und -leben*, no. 8, 'Nun hast' du mir den ersten Schmerz getan' ('Now you Have Caused me my First Pain'). 'There I have you and my lost happiness, / You, my world!' Trans. Stokes, *The Book of Lieder*, p. 443.

Example 4.1 (*cont.*)

and singer alongside the tensions between private and public performance practices discussed in the previous chapter.

The first complete performance of *Frauenliebe und -leben* heard by Schumann was given by soprano Wilhelmine Schröder-Devrient at a soirée in October 1848. We have no way of knowing who, among purchasers of Schumann's score, would have attempted it at home before then; the significant point is that, despite Schröder-Devrient being a professional singer, it was not presented on the public stage. As discussed in the previous chapter, at this stage in the century cycles were mostly for private consumption (or at least the semi-private soirée); it therefore seems unlikely that the decision to perform *Frauenliebe und -leben* was determined entirely by its gender. But it reminds us that the prospect of transplanting Lieder from domestic to public performance contexts raised a number of gender-related issues. Although the concert hall was considered a more respectable venue than the opera house, there was anxiety about the reputation of women appearing on any kind of stage through the nineteenth century.[6] It should perhaps then not be surprising that the first public performance of *Frauenliebe und -leben* was by the baritone Julius Stockhausen, encountered in the previous chapter as the first to give complete versions of *Die schöne Müllerin, Winterreise* and *Dichterliebe*.[7]

Stockhausen's memoirs make it clear that he thought his interpretation of *Frauen-liebe und -leben* a kind of role-playing; in other words, almost as if he were in an opera. Connecting operatic and theatrical practices and Lieder performance allowed for a much looser conception of the correlation between poetic protagonist and singer. In contradiction to the mid-nineteenth-century German composer Robert Franz's claim that 'the Lied belongs to the field of lyricism, and lyricism is, in its sentiments, without gender', singers 'played up' the gender of their parts – even when they were women singing women.[8] For example, the Dutch accompanist Coenraad Bos recalled that the Quebec-born mezzo-soprano Emma Albani intro-duced a new approach to *Frauenliebe und -leben* in the first decade of the twentieth century:

> Up until that time, the singers with whom I played . . . had brought the cycle to a close in a sustained mood of grief. But Albani had a different conception of the finale. At the words 'Der Schleier fällt' ('The veil drops'), she sang with the mournful memory that the husband was dead. At the next phrase, 'Da hab' ich dich' ('There I have you'), Albani placed her left arm as though she were holding a baby, and smiled lovingly toward the imaginary infant. At the following words, 'und mein verlor'nes Glück' ('and my lost happiness'), the mood again, with the memory of the lost dear one, became one of sadness. And, finally, at the closing words, 'Du, meine Welt' ('You, my world'), Albani smiled rapturously at the envisaged child which held the hope of future happiness.[9]

Albani's radical re-reading is striking for its 'happy ending' and overt theatricality. It also indicates how strongly a performer could reinterpret a work. Perhaps under Albani's influence, Bos revised the cycle's musical conclusion: when he performed *Frauenliebe* with the contralto Ernestine Schumann-Heink in Berlin shortly after-wards, he decided to replace Schumann's piano postlude with the music of the first song in its entirety, to 'better convey the vision of future happiness implicit in the final words'.[10] Unwittingly, Bos had returned the score to something very similar to the composer's initial conception; according to the autograph manuscript of *Frauen-liebe*, Schumann originally had the piano recapitulate the music for both stanzas of the first song.[11]

Bos acknowledged that Albani's use of gestures was indebted to her operatic expe-rience; it perhaps also bears the legacy of the expressive culture movement popular in North America at the turn of the century. Yet while he praised the conviction and simplicity with which Albani executed her gestures as 'profoundly moving and eminently appropriate', he claimed that Schumann-Heink's performance was more effective, because it relied not on gesture (despite Schumann-Heink also having been a notable opera singer) but on her superior 'emotional expression and tonal control'.[12] Other critics agreed that Schumann-Heink exhibited 'a fine sense of reserve and of propriety' because 'she indulges in no excesses of facial play or of gestures, nor does she forget that the concert stage and the operatic stage are widely separated'.[13] The use of physical gestures did not really fall out of practice, though, until after the Second World War and the establishment of recording, which encouraged greater specialisation in Lieder performance.[14] As will be outlined in Chapter 9, recording again altered perceptions of the relationship between poetic subject and musical performer: whereas the Lied's arrival on the public stage had made it more theatrical, the disembodiment of recording made it more about the voice, less about the body.

Interestingly, the establishment of recording coincided with – and perhaps even contributed to – a more conservative attitude to gender-appropriate performance. Women had sung songs from 'male' cycles such as *Winterreise* and *Dichterliebe* throughout the nineteenth and for most of the first half of the twentieth century without provoking comment. Elena Gerhardt, Emmi Leisner, Elisabeth Schumann, Lotte Lehmann and Marian Anderson all had songs from the cycles in their repertoire.[15] The question of verisimilitude occasionally came up, but the more significant issue seems to have been whether the songs suited their registers and where their voices sat in relation to the piano accompaniment.[16] For instance, on a 1930 tour one critic in Minneapolis queried whether Lehmann should sing Schumann's 'Ich grolle nicht', which in his view was, if not a man's song, certainly for a contralto.[17]

Since the Second World War, though, a woman singing a 'male' cycle seems to have become a remarkable, even a transgressive, act. While scholars and critics claim discomfort on hearing a cycle such as *Frauenliebe und -leben*, in which male poet and composer speak for a woman, they are no less unsettled by a female performer making 'male' texts her own. Some, such as literary critic Terry Castle, find a sexual frisson in the gender-ambiguity of mezzo-soprano Brigitte Fassbaender's *Winterreise* recording.[18] Others have diverted attention through adding a theatrical aspect to proceedings. For example, Fassbaender revisited *Winterreise* in a film directed by Petr Weigl (1990), which deliberately played with questions of self-identification: she sings the cycle as a nun, against a backdrop of scenes from a doomed love affair between a woman and two men. It is unclear whether we are seeing a recollection of her erotic past, or a reference to Schubert's personal life, or some kind of allegory for failed relationships in general. Angels and devils pose suggestively behind Fassbaender in her convent attic, making this nun far from sexless, and the play-acting process abundantly – some might say absurdly – clear. Oliver Herrmann's film of *Dichterliebe: A Story of Red and Blue* (2002), meanwhile, shifts between soprano Christine Schäfer singing the cycle in a Berlin nightclub and scenes from rehearsal, drawing attention to the event as 'performance', much like Stockhausen's role-playing and Albani's gestures did a century earlier.[19]

It seems, ironically, that attitudes to gender and performance became much less flexible in the late twentieth century. We could blame feminism: heightened awareness of the political implications of women singing male texts – as evident in responses to *Frauenliebe und -leben* – perhaps led to a stricter definition of what constituted gender-appropriate behaviour. There have been, of course, song cycles to texts by female poets, including Schumann's settings of Elisabeth Kulmann (1851), Wagner's Wesendonck Lieder (1857), Aaron Copland's *Twelve Poems of Emily Dickinson* (1950) and Ned Rorem's *Women's Voices* (1975–6) as well as his setting of poems from Sylvia Plath's *Ariel* (1971).[20] The Rorem examples indicate another trend: of trying to establish a distinctly feminine mode of expression. Hungarian composer György Kurtág's *Messages of the Late R. V. Troussova* op. 17 (1981), to texts by female Russian poet Rimma Dalos, stands as a latter-day *Frauenliebe*. On one level the cycle can be heard as a catalogue of music history over the past two centuries; it refers to a variety of miniature song types, from refrains and echoes to traditional Lieder forms, as well as paying homage to Schoenberg (the twelve-tone passages, instances of *Sprechstimme*, and the *Pierrot-lunaire*-like organisation of the cycle into twenty-one movements, each of which regroups the instrumental ensemble). On another level, the *Messages of the Late R. V. Troussova* provides another female life story. She is, however, far more openly libidinous than nineteenth-century mores would have allowed, as is emphasised by Kurtág's writing for the voice.

For example, in the second section, 'A Little Erotic' (Example 4.2), the mounting tension of the singer's semiquavers climaxes in a wordless tumble, evoking physical desire. 'Why should I not squeal like a pig, when all around me are grunting?' she asks in the next song, with appropriate verbal imitations. As with so many song cycles, though, she is disappointed in love: 'I was just a plaything, but I thought I was a heroine', she complains. As she looks back over her experience we might be reminded of the protagonist of *Frauenliebe und -leben*, though Kurtág's cycle ends in more doubt and suffering: 'For everything we did together at some time – I'm paying'.

There have been few female composers of song cycles, despite Lieder's domestic roots, and still fewer that explicitly confront the prospect of what French feminist literary theorist Hélène Cixous called *écriture feminine* – writing that 'inscribes the feminine body and feminine difference in language and text'.[21] An exception that deliberately inserts itself into the *Frauenliebe* tradition is Judith Weir's *woman.life.song* (2000). The seven poems by Toni Morrison, Maya Angelou and Clarissa Pinkola Estés contemplate episodes in a woman's life from youth and motherhood to maturity. Pinkola Estés claims that her point of departure was imagining the body of the singer Jessye Norman and the poems are certainly more playfully

Example 4.2 György Kurtág, *Messages of the Late R.V. Troussova*, no. 4, 'A Little Erotic'.

libidinous than Chamisso would have dared – 'Oh when shall I receive my breasts?' asks the restless adolescent of the second song.[22] Yet despite Estés's claim that almost any time women do something extravagant together it is 'historic' (still? we might ask), woman's life and songs here remain firmly planted in the personal and domestic – encapsulated in the postlude of the first song, as the woman's memories of her grandmother are accompanied by a glockenspiel played with knitting needles.

More extreme examples can be found in the work of Greek-American composer–vocalist Diamanda Galás. It is not insignificant that she performs her own work – indeed, it is hard to imagine that anyone else could. Galás's range is multi-octave, multi-lingual and polystylistic (from shrieks and growls to lullabies and recitation); her poetic preoccupations sexuality and death: it is *écriture féminine* writ large. The song cycle *Defixiones, Will and Testament* (2004) commemorates the Armenian,

Example 4.2 (*cont.*)

Assyrian and Anatolian Greek genocides of 1914–23. It opens with (and subsequently reprises) a section from the Armenian liturgy, 'Ter Vogormia', sung unaccompanied; emphasis is on the solo voice throughout, Galás drawing on Greek vernacular and sacred song. The second part ends with a reworking of the classic blues number by Blind Lemon Jefferson, 'See that my Grave Is Kept Clean'.

Galás could be described as a singer-songwriter (though both her singing and her songs stretch the limits of any genre) and, as is apparent from her incorporation of the blues, her work interacts with popular genres and performance styles. The complicated identity politics of musical performance, discussed here with regard to gender, resulted partly from the separation of poet, composer and singer habitual to classical music: bringing those different roles together, as Galás

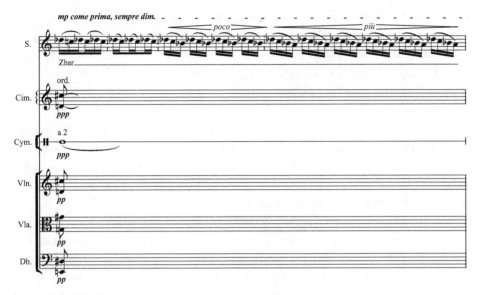

Example 4.2 (*cont.*)

does, might be one way to clarify authorial intention. Yet things are rarely that simple, as is evident from the way gender has figured in performance practices in popular music.

Many of the gender issues discussed with regard to the performance of song cycles recurred, within a more compressed time scale, in popular music. Again, recording played an important part in changing perceptions. Before the Second World War, popular music mostly consisted of dance tunes and numbers from Broadway shows. Notions of authorship were very loosely defined. First, the use of songwriting teams sidelined composer ownership (there were exceptions such as Cole Porter and Irving Berlin). Second, emphasis was on bands, rather than singers, who were viewed for the most part as interchangeable (hence multiple recordings of the same song being made at the same time). Third, while numbers were played on the radio and sold as records they primarily circulated as sheet music, which meant that – as in art song – in theory anyone could sing it. What is more, before the trend for 'integrated musicals' begun by Rodgers and Hammerstein's *Oklahoma!* (1943), Broadway shows rarely included character songs, so numbers could be passed freely between male and female singers. In certain circumstances, then, men might sing lines such as 'can't help loving that man', without acknowledging their sexual implications. Similar practices continued into the 1960s: Elvis covered 'Blue Moon of Kentucky', which had been recorded by Bill Monroe twenty years earlier; Monroe made a new version in response to Elvis's, and Patsy Cline did too, without any sense of one version superseding the other. And Broadway show-tunes were still taken out of context and released as singles by singers of the opposite gender, with varying degrees of self-awareness: Rosemary Clooney simply recorded 'I've Grown Accustomed to your Face' rather than 'her' (or 'his') face, but Frank Sinatra's 1959 version of 'I Could Have Danced all Night', made famous on Broadway by Julie Andrews, was keenly attuned to the song's euphemisms.

Better and cheaper recording technology quashed the market for sheet music. Notions of authorship accordingly became more clearly defined. Making records the primary means of dissemination (they were now played on radio more often than live broadcasts) meant that particular voices became closely associated with particular songs. How popular music was written was also changing; although some record companies still had in-house songwriters who produced numbers for certain artists, the early 1960s saw the emergence of bands like The Beatles and The Beach Boys, who wrote their own material – at first in combination with covers, but then exclusively. Although their use of multiple singers and co-writing of songs suggested a more flexible approach to authorship than the lone-composer model of art song, bands such as The Beatles evinced a strong sense of identity. Perhaps it was only happenstance that that identity was male; it is apparent, though, that the development of rock music in the mid-1960s and the concept albums with which it went hand-in-hand were mostly by men.

There were more female artists among the singer-songwriters of the 1960s. Yet even though the genre implied a much closer relationship between author-composer and performer, songs were often shared between singers of different genders, seemingly with little regard for the interpretative consequences. Joan Baez sang numbers by Bob Dylan, and a song such as Joni Mitchell's 'Both Sides Now' (written in 1967) was recorded by several artists, both male and female, in many different forms: from Judy Collins and Frank Sinatra (1968), to all-female grunge band Hole (1991) and jazz musician Herbie Hancock (2007). Apparently Mitchell's favourite was the version on *Dave van Ronk and the Hudson Dusters* (1967); there is thus no sense of the song belonging to a particular gender; not even the author is prepared to claim her version as the original.

Mitchell has recorded the song twice herself, first on the album *Clouds* (1969) and then on *Both Sides Now* (2000), a concept album that traces the progress of a relationship through Mitchell's rendition of classic jazz songs (and, as well as 'Both Sides Now', Mitchell's 'A Case of You'). The first version is sung in her famous high flutey register to guitar accompaniment: the second is in a much lower tessitura and in keeping with the rest of the album has a more complicated orchestral arrangement (devised by Vince Mendoza).[23] *Both Sides Now* was described by co-producer Larry Klein as 'a programmatic suite documenting a relationship from initial flirtation through optimistic consumerism, metamorphosing into disillusion, ironic despair, and finally resolving in the philosophical overview of acceptance and the probability of the cycle repeating itself'.[24] In other words, we are in similar territory to *Frauenliebe und -leben*, tracing a woman's life story. Musically speaking, the cyclic aspect of *Both Sides Now* depends on awareness of Mitchell's back-catalogue; whereas Schumann used the recurrence of material from the first song in the last to indicate 'the probability of the cycle repeating itself', Mitchell achieves a similar effect by returning to her earlier song: 'I've looked at love from both sides now / From give and take, and still somehow / It's love's illusions I recall'.

It would be crass to stereotype singer-songwriters as female and rock musicians as male. However, the presence of a gender divide between genres of popular music was acknowledged, and criticised, by the all-female post-punk band The Raincoats, who targeted the high production values and indulgent narrative of a concept album by The Kinks: *Lola vs. The Powerman and the Money-go-round Part One* (1970). The album satirises the music industry, from its emphasis on money-making and hit-manufacture to life on tour, and is typical of songwriter Ray Davies in incorporating a number of musical styles – from English music hall to ballads and hard rock. The single 'Lola' was a deliberate, and successful, attempt to regain chart popularity: in this instance, the joke seems to be against the male protagonist, who unwittingly flirts with a transvestite.

The Raincoats covered 'Lola' in 1977. They scratched away the sheen of The Kinks' highly produced original, transforming it into an enthusiastic but unglamorous sing-along (which, to be fair, was how 'Lola' was best known). But The Raincoats' project had a serious purpose. Theirs was a deliberately unpolished style; in typical post-punk fashion, they had only learnt their instruments on joining the band.[25] They also eschewed girly clothes and hairstyles, attempting to point out the extent to which femininity was a social construction, a set of artificial expectations from which women should be liberated. Raincoats singer Ana da Silva explained: 'Being a woman is both feeling female, expressing female and also (for the time being at least) reacting against what a woman is told she "should" be like'.[26] By choosing to cover a song such as 'Lola', which plays with questions of gender identity but ultimately belongs to a male-orientated worldview, and by not subscribing to conventional performance behaviour in terms of musical proficiency or appearances, a feminist band such as The Raincoats could query the rules not only of the music industry but also of the gender game.

A more drastic and extended example of a woman's voice overtaking a man's original is Petra Haden's *a cappella* version of the pirate-radio concept album *The Who Sell Out* (1968; *Petra Haden Sings: The Who Sell Out* was recorded 2000–3).[27] There is no plot. Instead, the album connects its songs with pastiche commercial breaks. It both pays homage to the pirate radio stations that had promoted popular music in England in the 1960s, and criticises their decision to turn commercial. *The Who Sell Out* includes Beach-Boys-style close vocal harmonies and instrumental arrangements alongside psychedelic rock – all of which Haden recreated using only her impressive range of extended vocal techniques and imitative abilities, sung into an eight-track cassette recorder. The album thereby creates a female sound world at odds with the original. For example, a song such as 'Tattoo', which describes two adolescent brothers exploring their masculinity through growing their hair long and getting 'tattoed all over' (risking violence from their parents: 'My dad beat me cause mine said "Mother" / But my mother naturally liked it and beat my brother'), becomes still more tongue-in-cheek as everything is heard through an unquestionably female voice.

One aspect of many of these projects is overshadowed by my emphasis on gender, and also tends to escape description in prose: their sense of humour. Acknowledging that many of these albums or covers are funny, though, seems crucial, particularly on turning to my final example, New-York-based band The Magnetic Fields, who match relatively simple, singable music with lyrics that present sometimes quite complicated accounts of their narrators' gender and, along with that, their sexuality. All the albums are thematically linked, and as such can be considered song cycles of sorts. Songwriter Stephin Merritt seems to have returned to something like the Tin Pan Alley practice of the 1930s, though with far greater self-consciousness about the potential for ambiguity. *69 Love Songs*, for example, spreads its numbers between a group of singers, male and female. Yet the gender assignments do not correspond to the album's narrative, and sometimes reinterpret the narratives within songs. Often, there is no use of a gender-specific pronoun or name until a song is well under way, its sudden insertion gently subverting the listener's assumptions. For example, on volume 2 of *69 Love Songs* (1999), Claudia Gonson sings 'If you Don't Cry' with the refrain 'A year goes by / She doesn't…'; Shirley Sims sings 'Kiss Me like you Mean It', about a man; and Merritt sings not only 'When my Boy Walks Down the Street', with the line 'and he's going to be my wife', but also, on '(Crazy for You but) Not That Crazy' explains 'I made my yard a playground / just in case we had a baby'. The third verse of 'I Don't Believe You' (written in 1998 and rerecorded for *I* in 2004), sung by Merritt, reveals 'You tell me of what once was / And all about Buck, Butch and Buzz'; it's possible he could be talking about a woman, but it seems more likely that it's a man. In 'Drive on Driver' from *Distortion* (2008) a woman complains 'I gave her everything money could buy / I always said that girl / deserved the whole world': and so on. All of these revelations prevent any voice from establishing a consistent subjectivity or sexuality (and in live performance the songs are often given to someone else).

Unlike some of the other song cycles and concept albums discussed in this chapter, where it is tempting to take the creator as the protagonist (Joni Mitchell) or writing with a particular person in mind (perhaps Robert Schumann on his wife-to-be), Merritt almost always catches his listeners out, upsetting assumptions about the songs' target and even narrative voice. This is a slightly different situation from that of the 1950s, or even in the star-making process depicted on recent television shows such as *The X Factor* and *Pop Idol*, in which women often cover songs by men and vice versa, but the difference is barely registered. The slippery approach to narrative voices in the music of The Magnetic Fields, and The Who as covered by Petra Haden, alters the listener's understanding of each song according to the friction between words and voice; pointing out the extent to which gender continues to be constructed and, crucially, performed.

Chapter 5

Between opera and symphony

The orchestral song cycle

One of the most profound transformations of the song cycle during the nineteenth century was caused by what may seem on the surface to be a prosaic technical adaptation: the replacement of piano accompaniment with an instrumental ensemble. The rise of the orchestral song, though, had a deep impact on the scope of the song cycle, in terms of the greater vocal forces that could be harnessed, the range and variety of timbres that could be explored, and the larger scale on which composers could work. As such, the orchestral song became the preferred conduit for many popular poetic and musical themes of the second half of the nineteenth century and so it seems necessary to introduce it as a genre before discussion progresses, although this means that some examples in subsequent chapters will predate the repertoire considered here.

The orchestral song has a complicated genealogy. There were Lieder with instrumental accompaniment by Beethoven and Schumann, but the real spur for development was performance practice.[1] As discussed previously, most nineteenth-century concert programmes were a kind of pot-pourri, consisting of symphonic movements, concertos, pieces of chamber music, operatic arias, and, with time, Lieder. In order to hold their own against the larger-scale works, Lieder needed to be amplified; automatically achieved through the addition of instrumental accompaniment. This would be one way to explain the genesis of what is sometimes called the first orchestral song cycle, but is perhaps better seen as one of its progenitors: Hector Berlioz's *Les Nuits d'été* (*Summer Nights*), composed for voice and piano in 1840–1 and then adapted for voice and orchestra (and published in 1856).

But it was not simply a question of the accompaniment becoming louder; the variety of instrumental timbres available could make it more colourful and, by extension, meaningful. Moreover, for singers to compete with an orchestra, they needed increasingly powerful voices – which basically meant operatic ones. And so we come to the other, more problematic, contender for parentage of the orchestral song cycle, Richard Wagner's *Wesendonck Lieder* (1857–8; published in 1862): problematic because only one song was orchestrated by the composer ('Träume' (Dreams), for violin and chamber orchestra); his disciple Felix Mottl completed the rest much later, in 1910. Yet the *Wesendonck Lieder* can claim some responsibility for the rise

64

of the orchestral song in that two of the songs, 'Träume' and 'Im Treibhaus' ('In the Greenhouse'), Wagner described as 'studies' for his opera *Tristan und Isolde* (1865), one of the most influential scores of the late nineteenth century.

In other words, the orchestral song has dual nationality: the French side coming from Berlioz, the German from Wagner. It would be simplistic to say that from the French came instrumental colour, and from the German came operatic voices, because the orchestral song was nothing if not a successful hybrid. Yet it is true that the French adoption of Lieder in the mid-1830s concentrated on their musical rather than their poetic aspects, 'translating' Schubert's accompaniments for orchestra before they accurately translated the songs' words.[2] And Berlioz's influence as an orchestrator should not be underestimated: it is striking that, when the orchestral song came of age in Vienna in the late 1880s, several of the leading composers had close connections with Berlioz's work.[3]

The orchestration of *Les Nuits d'été* was not simply a 'colouring in' of the piano score; it also affected its organisation as a cycle.[4] Berlioz's selection of poems by Théophile Gautier circle around the theme of love lost. The outer songs, 'Villanelle' and 'L'île inconnue' ('The Unknown Isle'), are marked *Allegretto* and *Allegro spiritoso* respectively, but these lively tempi frame a lugubrious centre: the four inner songs alternate between *Adagio* and *Andantino*. In its first version, for voice and piano, the progression of keys (A–D–G min–F♯–D–F), was fairly conventional. Also, all the songs except the fifth (for tenor only) could be sung by mezzo-soprano or tenor. When Berlioz orchestrated the cycle, though, he arranged the songs for a different sequence of voices (songs 1, 4, 6 for soprano; no. 2 for contralto; no. 3 for baritone; no. 5 for tenor) and, as a consequence, the key scheme was altered to A–B–F min–F♯–D–F.[5] The harmonic shifts made between the first four songs were then much more irregular. What is more, on orchestrating the cycle, Berlioz discarded the timbral continuity that happened naturally in the piano version, by using a different grouping of instruments for each song.

So what was gained by orchestrating *Les Nuits d'été?* Berlioz did not change the material of the accompaniment in any significant way, but by assigning lines to different instruments he was able to clarify harmonic voicing and enhance word painting. For example, in the second song, 'Le Spectre de la rose', about the ghost of a rose sacrificed for a young girl's corsage, reference to the flower's fading fragrance brings about a change in texture. In the piano version there is a change to *pianissimo* tremolando, which builds to full chords in support of the line 'J'arrive du paradis' ('I come from paradise'). In the orchestral version, the *pianissimo* tremolando is given to harp and *sul ponticello* violins, a much lighter sound, joined by the rest of the orchestra to make paradise seem still more luminous. Orchestration can also intensify the songs' sense of drama, because of its greater potential for contrast. At the final lines of 'Le Spectre' – which recount the poet's words, 'Ci-gît une rose /

Qui tous les rois vont jalouser' ('Here lies a rose / That all kings will envy') – the accompaniment thins to a single line; a shift more striking when made from full strings, flute and oboe to solo clarinet than on the piano. Berlioz makes much use of solo instruments, perhaps because their unique timbre complements the solo vocal line; at the same time, his writing for the voice is sometimes more instrumental than lyrical (in this regard he foreshadows Mahler). At the end of the next song, 'Sur les lagunes (Lamento)' ('On the Lagoons (Lament)'), for instance, the recurring step away from one pitch and back again played by second horn and violins is finally taken up by the voice, its wordless exclamation seeming to drift out over the undulating waters of the lower string accompaniment.

Earlier, I referred to Berlioz's *Les Nuits d'été* as a progenitor of the orchestral song cycle. This is partly because it was originally written for voice and piano, and then adapted for voice and orchestra; though if that is to be our criterion most orchestral song cycles would be discounted – they often exist in both versions, and there is rarely a sense that one version should take precedence over another (although, arguably, the orchestral versions demand a different, more powerful, voice type than their piano counterparts). The other reason is that it is hard to trace a direct line between *Les Nuits d'été*, the *Wesendonck Lieder* and subsequent examples: they did not spawn a number of imitators straight away; rather, their seeds took time to gestate, in the process being fertilised by a number of other factors, as Wagner's cycle demonstrates.

Mathilde Wesendonck was married to a silk merchant in Zurich, where Wagner and his wife Minna lived in exile after the Dresden uprisings of 1848–9. Mathilde's husband Otto supported Wagner financially; she, no less crucially, became his muse, particularly once the couples became neighbours in 1857. Wagner had been working on the third of his *Ring* operas, *Siegfried*; in August of that year, though, he put this to one side and began to compose *Tristan und Isolde*, a passionate tale of lovers fated to only be truly united in death. The similarities to his situation with Mathilde may have been obvious, but ultimately the more significant connection between their relationship and Wagner's new opera was musical.

In December 1857, Wagner began to set five of Mathilde's poems, now known as the *Wesendonck Lieder* (he completed the group the following May and they were first performed in public in 1862). All of the songs resemble passages from *Tristan*, in terms of their suspension-laden harmonies, unexpected modulations and tendency to leave chromatic notes unresolved but, as mentioned, 'Träume' and 'Im Treibhaus' were designated studies for the opera. The theme of 'Träume' is sung by Isolde's servant Brangäne, as she keeps watch at the beginning of Act II, foreshadowing the love duet, 'O sink hernieder, Nacht der Liebe' ('Descend, Night of Love'). Song and duet share the same key, A♭ major; their instrumentation is also similar, with strings providing chordal accompaniment and clarinet, bassoon

Example 5.1 a) Richard Wagner, *Tristan und Isolde* Act II, 'Descend night of love, grant oblivion that I may live'.
b) *Wesendonck Lieder*, no. 5, 'Traüme' ('Dreams'). 'Say, what wondrous dreams are these / Embracing all my senses'. Trans. Stokes, *The Book of Lieder*, p. 568.

and horns playing a 'sighing' motive, attached in the song to the word 'Träume' ('Dreams') – an association that may linger over Tristan's and Isolde's impossible desire to lose themselves in their love (Example 5.1). The vocal melody Tristan sings, though distantly related to the *Wesendonck Lieder*, is stretched to become one of Wagner's seemingly endless or 'infinite' melodies. So too is the instrumental introduction of 'Im Treibhaus', drawn on for the thematic material of the Prelude to Act III. Mottl's orchestration of the song refers to Wagner's score while adapting it for slightly reduced forces: the opening bars are for strings, with solo viola again taking the winding second melody.[6] Incidentally, just as 'O sink hernieder' converts the

Example 5.1(a) (*cont.*)

accompanimental rhythm from quavers to triplets, the accompanimental rhythms of 'Im Treibhaus' are more four-square and compact than the opera's (in the Act III Prelude there are syncopations rather than just quavers); it seems as if everything is extended to *Tristan* time.

It is almost impossible to separate the influence of Wagner's songs from that of his operas towards the end of the nineteenth century. This was because the operas were all-consuming, in the sense that *Tristan* absorbed the *Wesendonck Lieder* into

Example 5.1(b)

its musical fabric, and more generally because of Wagner's far-reaching influence in terms both of harmonic and thematic practices, and of vocal and orchestral writing. Yet beyond these abstract notions of musical style, *Tristan* has also been seen to explore 'an *idea* of the Lied . . . the tension between the private character of the Lied and the public face of opera greatly helped to define the opera's sound world'.[7] Wagner, his love for Mathilde Wesendonck unrequited, diverted his private passion, first explored in the intimate sphere of song, into the public space of the opera house.

Wagner's operas were, of course, much better known than his songs: familiar not only from theatres but also in piano reductions to be played at home, and from the concert stage, through the practice of performing in concert what are colloquially known as 'bleeding chunks' – extended passages, even whole scenes, from operas. The rise of the orchestral song in the late 1880s can be seen to compete or at least compare with these operatic excerpts; it is striking that what are sometimes given as the first examples within the Austro-German tradition, Felix Weingartner's *Wallfahrt nach Kevlaar* op. 12 (*Pilgrimage to Kevlaar*, 1887) and Hans Pfitzner's *Herr Oluf* op. 12 (1891), are short dramatic works in the vein of Robert Schumann's choral ballads rather than song cycles; the distinction is that they are for solo voice and accompaniment. For the first orchestral song cycle we probably need to look to Gustav Mahler's *Lieder eines fahrenden Gesellen* (*Songs of a Wayfarer*, 1883–5; 1891–6, discussed in Chapter 2), although there is still some debate about when they were actually orchestrated.[8] Before considering Mahler's motivations for cultivating the orchestral song cycle, though, mention needs to be made of Wagner's influence outside German-speaking lands because, as stated, the genre crossed geographical boundaries; firstly, with France.

To Wagner's frustration, it took some time for his operas to be staged in Paris. The premiere of *Tannhäuser* in 1861 was a famous debacle. However, the main reason his operas were only heard in Paris on the concert stage rather than in theatres was not aesthetic, but political: as nationalism surged in the wake of Napoleon III's defeat by the Prussians in 1870, objections were raised to proposed performances at the Opéra-Comique or the Opéra, which preferred to promote classic French works.[9] By the late 1870s, though, impresarios such as Charles Lamoureux were putting on concerts of the first act of *Lohengrin*, the popularity of which eventually brought them to the stage. By the early 1890s, Wagner was ubiquitous at the Opéra, and pilgrimages to the *Festspielhaus* (Festival Theatre) at Bayreuth were all the rage.

One French composer swept up by Wagner's music was Ernest Chausson, who visited Munich to see productions of *Der fliegende Holländer* (*The Flying Dutchman*), the *Ring* and *Tristan* in 1879–80, and was at Bayreuth for the premiere of *Parsifal* in 1882 (he even went again the following year, for his honeymoon). The impact of Wagner can be heard in the harmonic wanderings of the *mélodie* 'Printemps triste' ('Spring Sadness', 1883), which uses the so-called 'Tristan' chord fifteen times within its forty-two bars (see box opposite). There is also a distinctly Wagnerian flavour to *Poème de l'amour et de la mer* op. 19 (*Poem of Love and the Sea*, 1893), a setting of two long sectional poems by Maurice Bouchor, divided by an instrumental interlude. *Poème* was conceived for voice and orchestra, and the instrumentation owes much to *Tristan* and *Parsifal*, particularly in its tendency to pass melodies 'endlessly' between solo wind instruments, such as oboe or clarinet, against a backdrop of pulsing chords played by strings or occasionally horns.[10] There are no leitmotifs (another famous Wagnerian technique: recurring phrases that link a particular musical theme or sound with a character or symbol), but there are two main themes that – again in a manner reminiscent of Wagner – are generated by the orchestra before being passed to the voice. The dedicatee of *Poème*, Henri Duparc (a renowned song composer), thought that the vocal writing was driven too much by the music rather than the words, but in a way it is the score's least Wagnerian aspect, for the voice sits relatively high above the orchestral parts, giving it a lightness and prominence more in keeping with the French song tradition.

The Tristan chord is one of the most famous and often-referenced sonorities in late nineteenth-century music. It refers to the first chord of the Prelude to Wagner's opera *Tristan und Isolde* (marked 'x' on the example).

X

In harmonic terms the significance of the Tristan chord was that it could not be easily defined. Its ambiguity queried the boundaries of traditional tonal harmony. The Tristan chord also had poetic significance: in Wagner's opera the Tristan chord is associated with the doomed passion of Tristan and Isolde.

Chausson's Wagnerism was a passing phase – during the protracted gestation of his opera *Le Roi Arthus* (*King Arthur*, 1886–95) he decided it was time to 'de-Wagnerise' himself; he became enthralled by the Russian Symbolists (producing the Musorgsky-inflected song cycle *Serres chaudes* (*Hot Houses*) in 1896). *Poème de l'amour et de la mer*, though, stands as a testament to the extent of Wagner's reach, and shows how the late nineteenth-century orchestral song was not simply a Viennese phenomenon. Indeed, because of its length and cohesion, and the fact that it was conceived for orchestra, *Poème* is in many ways a better example of the orchestral song cycle than anything by two composers often mentioned alongside Mahler as at the forefront of the genre, Richard Strauss and Hugo Wolf.

Wolf may have been known at the time as the inventor of 'symphonic song', but the reference was really to the musical scope and complex piano accompaniments of Wolf's songs, rather than their orchestral reworking. Moreover, despite being one of the greatest Lieder composers of the nineteenth century, he did not write any song cycles as such, so sadly cannot be dwelt on here. And as Strauss's cycles will be discussed elsewhere, I will not explore them further at this point, apart from to note that he usually only composed, not to mention orchestrated, his songs for particular performers, and that his songs infiltrated, and were infiltrated by, his works in other genres – from tone poems to operas.

By contrast, it has often been noted as strange that Mahler, renowned as a conductor of operas, did not compose any: perhaps, much as Wagner faced the challenge of Beethoven's symphonies by revolutionising opera instead, Mahler channelled his response to Wagner into his symphonies. For he often included songs in his symphonic music, especially in the first four symphonies, which take numbers from

Lieder eines fahrenden Gesellen and *Des Knaben Wunderhorn* as the basis for some movements.[11] And the later symphonies – typically described as 'purely' instrumental, albeit with the exceptions of the Eighth and *Das Lied von der Erde* – also owe something to the songs; for example, 'Ich bin der Welt abhanden gekommen' ('I Have Become Lost to the World') from the *Rückert Lieder* found its way into the Adagietto of the Fifth Symphony.[12]

Of all Mahler's orchestral songs, the *Kindertotenlieder* are the most self-contained. They were conceived as a cycle and – brief references aside – never appear wholesale elsewhere. Their composition was unusually protracted for Mahler (1901–4) and, as a result, overlapped with the completion of several other works generally agreed to mark the onset of Mahler's musical maturity: the last of the *Wunderhorn* settings, 'Revelge' ('Reveille') and 'Der Tambourg'sell' ('The Drummer-Boy'), the Fifth and Sixth Symphonies and the *Rückert Lieder*.

Mahler's *Kindertotenlieder* set 5 of the 428 poems Friedrich Rückert wrote about the death of children. Rückert's poetic outpouring was in part a memorial to his son and daughter, who died in the early 1830s, but also belonged to a popular tradition of *Kindertoten* poems, reflecting the high infant mortality rates of the nineteenth century, and the era's tendency to romanticise the child as a figure of innocence and hope.[13] Mahler's wife Alma claimed later that her husband's choice of morbid subject matter foretold the death of their eldest daughter a few years later. What seems more likely is that Mahler was attracted to Rückert's poems as a lyrical antidote to the stock characters of *Des Knaben Wunderhorn*, and by their commercial success in the last decade of the nineteenth century.[14] Yet Mahler's (and Alma's) emotional response to Rückert's poems indicates a broader cultural shift in attitudes towards child mortality around this time. As medical care and living conditions improved, so too did life expectancy and, with that, the way in which Rückert's poems were read also changed: bitterness and outrage at losing loved ones began to supplant more stoical responses; although Mahler's cycle ultimately achieves a sense of reconciliation, it travels through some tumult on its way.

Kindertotenlieder begins starkly, in D minor, with solo oboe (marked 'klagend': 'lamenting') in counterpoint with solo horn. The voice's opening phrase seems to be more instrumental in nature than songlike, presenting a thematic fragment immediately repeated by the oboe in shortened form (Example 5.2). With the more positive second line, which describes the sunrise seeming to eradicate the misfortune ('das Unglück') of the night, the texture becomes warmer, though still fairly thin; muted cellos, harp and violas support the voice's tentative lyricism, and there is a glint of the major mode. The final song also begins in D minor, but with full orchestra depicting the unrelenting storm from which the parent would once have had to protect his children. The music only subsides for the final verse: all that remains are the cello harmonics and repeated piccolo a'' that had seemed like the

Example 5.2 Gustav Mahler, *Kindertotenlieder*, no. 1, 'Nun will die Sonn' so hell aufgehn' ('Now the Sun Will Rise as Bright'). Trans. Stokes, *The Book of Lieder*, p. 209.

whistling wind, but now seem to convey a more ethereal atmosphere, summoned by repeated chimes on the glockenspiel. Violins and celesta (a relatively new instrument Mahler would again associate with redemption at the end of *Das Lied von der Erde*) create the sweetest of sweet accompaniments for the voice, which finally rids itself of the angry, urgent linear version of the refrain 'In diesem Wetter, in diesem Braus' ('In this weather, in this raging storm'), discovering a sustained triadic melody in D major, marked 'as if a lullaby' (Example 5.3).

The last song's return to the tonal centre of the first was atypical of Mahler, a habitual user of progressive tonality (meaning that a work begins and ends in different keys). Such harmonic closure here makes poetic sense, though, because the ending provides a moment of solace for the bereaved parent, who realises that the children have now found peace; protected from the storm outside 'they rest, as if in their mother's home' ('Sie ruh'n wie in der Mutter Haus'). Mahler's method of

Example 5.3 Gustav Mahler, *Kindertotenlieder*, no. 5, 'In diesem Wetter'. 'In this weather, this howling gale, this raging storm'. Trans. Stokes, *The Book of Lieder*, p. 211.

Example 5.3 (*cont.*)

Example 5.3 (*cont.*)

returning to the tonic is made all the more effective by its contrast with the preceding musical material, and its different mood is emphasised by changes from minor to major and in orchestration, within this song and the cycle as a whole.

In his preface to the score, Mahler insisted that the five songs of *Kindertotenlieder* 'form a complete and indivisible whole'; in performance 'continuity must be preserved by preventing interruption (such as, for example, applause at the end of each song)'. His instruction may have been determined by musical concerns, but also was in keeping with calls for concert reform at the time. Several Austrian and German critics at the beginning of the twentieth century argued that programmes should not mix genres, nor include too many compositional styles, and that Lieder should be sung in appropriately sized halls.[15] As a conductor, Mahler objected to the practice of including operatic excerpts in concerts, because it destroyed and potentially belittled the integrity of the original. His orchestral song cycles thus were partly intended to replace the 'bleeding chunks'. It is within this context of concert reform that we should consider Mahler's decision to organise a *Lieder-Abend mit Orchester* on 29 January 1905; a programme devoted to his orchestral songs (it featured a number of his *Wunderhorn* settings, two of the *Rückert Lieder* and the premiere of *Kindertotenlieder*).[16] The orchestra, members of the Vienna Philharmonic, was small, as was the chosen hall: a choice made not out of modest ambition, but because of Mahler's instrumentation; as we have seen, despite the vast forces required to perform his symphonies, his orchestral songs often favour single woodwind lines and relatively small numbers of strings.

The innovative chamber-orchestra scoring of *Kindertotenlieder* was the work's most significant legacy. As we will see in subsequent chapters, exploring instrumental timbres in combination with solo voices was a feature of several radical contributions to the song-cycle repertoire in the twentieth century – from Schoenberg's *Pierrot lunaire* (1912) to Brian Ferneyhough's *Études transcendentales* (1982–5). For practical as much as aesthetic reasons, composers have often used relatively modest ensembles. Yet the symphonic and operatic worlds from which the orchestral song cycle emerged continued to engorge compositional ambitions. The premieres of Mahler's 'Lied-Symphony' *Das Lied von der Erde* (*The Song of the Earth*), and Schoenberg's *Gurrelieder* around 1911 seemed to many to be late blooms of Wagnerism: their huge scale and the nature mysticism of their texts had strong nineteenth-century roots. In their use of the orchestra and their treatment of harmony, however, both works nurtured a more modern sensibility. The transformation of *Gurrelieder* from song cycle to cantata involved supplanting two voices and piano with six soloists, four choirs (three four-part male choirs and one eight-part mixed choir), a speaker and a massive orchestra. It also took Schoenberg further from conventional tonality than hitherto achieved. More of that in Chapter 7: *Das Lied von der Erde* seems the better conclusion here, in part because it stands as an elegy for its composer (who died before its premiere) but also because it serves as an introduction to the musical exoticisms discussed in the next chapter.

The poems of *Das Lied von der Erde* were taken from *Die chinesische Flöte* (*The Chinese Flute*), Hans Bethge's 1907 collection of translations of Chinese poems from the eighth-century T'ang dynasty. While very popular amongst composers, the poems were only distantly related to the originals.[17] Indeed, Bethge described them as *Nachdichtungen*, or paraphrase poems; they were based on a German anthology by Hans Heilmann that, in turn, took as its source French translations by Le Marquis d'Hervey de Saint Denys and Judith Gautier.[18] What is more, Mahler, as was his wont, adapted Bethge's verses to bring out certain themes, which often resonate poetically and musically with earlier moments in *Das Lied* or other pieces from his oeuvre. For example, in 'Der Abschied' Mahler added the word *müden*, tired, to the line ('Die müden Menschen geh'n heimwarts'; 'The tired men go homewards'), the reference enabling him to refer melodically to the line 'Mein Herz ist müde' ('my heart is tired') and 'mild aufzutrocken' ('gently to dry up [my bitter tears]') from the second song 'Der Einsame in Herbst' ('The Lonely One in Autumn').[19] And much later in the movement, as the persona describes going into the mountains to seek peace, there is a melodic fragment from the first of the *Kindertotenlieder*.

Despite Mahler's personal editing of the texts, the mountains to which the protagonist retreats were clearly not the Alps. Only one of the songs from *Das Lied von der Erde*, 'Von der Jugend' ('Of Youth'), comes close to a Chinese-style sound world, with its high wind, harp and triangle accompaniment. More often, Mahler's allusions to the exotic are best understood in the manner of Bethge's *Nachdichtungen*; that is, paraphrases rather than direct translations. This is not to say that they simply flavour the music with typical spices; drones, ostinati, unusual percussion instruments (tam-tam, celesta) and pentatonic scales are used, but as means for Mahler to explore new harmonic territories as much as to provide local colour. The arrival of lusty lads on horseback in 'Von der Schönheit' ('Of Beauty'), for instance, spurs an energetic orchestral interlude (Example 5.4). This passage can be understood as bitonal; it compresses together two keys, C minor and A♭ major. However, the same combination of notes also belongs to a Japanese pentatonic (five-note) scale, and within the same passage there are other pentatonic and whole-tone harmonies from Japan and China, indicating the extent to which Mahler was using an undistinguished gamut of 'The Orient', rather than any 'authentic' musical reference.[20]

By distancing himself from conventional tonality in this way, Mahler is not just painting a picture of Asian men on horseback; he is pushing hard at harmonic boundaries. Although *Das Lied von der Erde* draws to a close in C major, this simplest of keys – without sharps or flats – is not presented in a straightforward manner; instead, it acts as a bright background for still more elaborate embroidery. The modulation is unexpected, achieved by a mere thread left from the previous

Example 5.4 Gustav Mahler, *Das Lied von der Erde*, no. 4, 'Von der Schönheit' ('Of Beauty').

passage – a soft e″ in the violins. Meanwhile, the entering vocal melody looks back to a three-note descent heard in the first song, 'Das Trinklied vom Jammer der Erde' ('Drinking Song of the Earth's Sorrows'), at the words 'Das Firmament blaut ewig' ('The firmaments are ever blue').[21] This is known as the 'Ewigkeit' (Eternity) motif and recurs throughout 'Der Abschied' (its lineage extends back to a phrase sung by Brünnhilde in Wagner's *Siegfried*). Its pattern of three whole tones is in keeping with the pentatonic scale, the use of which blurs the pull towards the tonic C, as does the Coda's inclusion of A minor, the opening key of *Das Lied*. 'Ewig, ewig!' ('Eternally, ever!') the voice concludes; but it never descends to C, making it seem – as Benjamin Britten pointed out – that this music could go on forever.[22]

On one level, the melodic and poetic cross-referencing evident in these examples can be understood as an elaborate commentary on Mahler's state of mind: *Das Lied von der Erde* has been explained as a superstitious replacement of a Ninth Symphony (Beethoven and Bruckner both having died after reaching that number), and the themes of farewell and world-weariness seem appropriate to a composer who had recently lost a child and been diagnosed with a fatal heart condition. On another level, they can be understood to contribute towards the cyclic construction of *Das Lied von der Erde*; the recurrence of certain musical ideas throughout the work helps assert a sense, if not of coherence exactly, then of building towards an inevitable conclusion.

At the same time, Mahler's development of thematic materials illustrates the extent to which orchestral song cycles sat between symphonic and operatic music. On the one hand, such tightly wrought motivic working belonged to late nineteenth-century Viennese orchestral music, such as that by Brahms. On the other, its roots might be in the Wagnerian leitmotif. As a 'Lied-symphony' we might decide that *Das Lied von der Erde* is closer to the former than the latter although, in fact, what both trends demonstrate is the nineteenth-century belief in instrumental music's ability to carry meaning. The 'Lied-symphony' moniker also indicates a basic urge to create ever-bigger works. The impulse had been present from the beginnings of the song cycle, as composers conceived not individual songs but groups of them; the introduction of orchestral accompaniment and public concert performances of cycles alongside symphonies and 'bleeding chunks' encouraged further expansion. Mahler's *Das Lied von der Erde* and the final version of Schoenberg's *Gurrelieder* may have been categorised as 'Lied-symphony' and cantata respectively, but they were not cuckoos in the song-cycle nest; they demonstrated the scale of composer ambition.

Chapter 6

Travels abroad

By the First World War, the song cycle had not only developed into an orchestral genre, it had also ventured far beyond the borders of Austria and Germany, to be incorporated into the art song repertoire of most Western countries. This chapter explores how the song cycle travelled abroad in the second half of the nineteenth century, first by considering the impact of Schubert and Schumann on Russian and French composers. The genre's migration depended not simply on how composers responded to Austro-German precedents, but also on the impact of other national traditions. For example, Claude Debussy's encounter with the Schubertian and Schumannian song cycle was filtered through not only the efforts of his fellow Frenchmen Jules Massenet and Gabriel Fauré, but also through the works of the Russian Modest Musorgsky. Such cosmopolitanism is the starting point for the second part of the chapter, which considers how song cycles were used as vehicles for establishing national musico-poetic identities and imagining exotic landscapes. Although we might expect nationalist and exotic projects to inhabit separate spheres, they often went hand-in-hand: for many composers, local folk traditions were as alien as music from other countries. The potential for folk or folk-like songs to convey both the familiar and the unfamiliar (the *heimlich* and the *unheimlich*, in German parlance), often made them attractive as a means for composers to explore new types of melody, harmony, rhythm, metre and timbre.

Russian Schumanns

We have already encountered several song cycles about loss and loneliness, but German Romantic wanderers and thwarted lovers seem almost upbeat in comparison to the song cycles of Musorgsky. The difference has partly to do with narrative voice: whereas Schubert's miller boy, however expressive, can be considered to some extent a stock character, speaking and acting for all who have ever been hurt in love or wanted to escape their parents' home, the first lines of Musorgsky's *Bez solntsa* (*Sunless*, 1874) are more personal:

Komnatka tesnaya, tikhaya, milaya;	A little room, cosy, quiet, dear;

Ten' neproglyadnaia, ten'
  bezotvetnaya;
	An impenetrable darkness, an
	  unanswering gloom;

Duma glubokaya, pesnya unïlaya,	Deep thoughts, a melancholy song;
V b'yushchemsya serdtse nadezhda zavetnaya	A secret hope in a beating heart[1]

Musorgsky responds to these disconnected phrases in kind: every clause – almost every word – is given a new harmonic colour, and is greeted with a resonant pause (Example 6.1). Just as the text includes no verbs, his music contains no functional harmonic relationships: there are few conventional progressions from one bar to the next, although one thread does run through the whole song (a pedal note of D) and the mixture of major and minor somehow feels right. And while the vocal line is more efficient than expansively lyrical, its responsive declamation looks forward to the songs of Debussy, who became obsessed with this cycle later in the century.

At the time it was written, though, the composer of *Sunless* felt he had few friends beyond the author of the poems, his then roommate, Arkad'evich Golenischschev-Kutuzov. Musorgsky's opera *Boris Godunov* had been received poorly by some of his musical allies, beginning the break-up of the so-called *Moguchaya Kuchka* ('Mighty Handful') or the 'Russian Five', who had gathered around the composer Mily Balakirev (the others were César Cui, Nikolai Rimsky-Korsakov and Alexander Borodin). It was in their company that Musorgsky had come to know the songs of Beethoven, Schubert and Schumann. The critic Vladimir Stasov remembered select musical evenings hosted by Liudmilla Ivanovna Shestakova, sister of the composer Mikhail Glinka, or by Cui or opera composer Alexander Dargomïzhsky, at which opera singers such as the Petrovs would perform new pieces by Musorgsky, Rimsky-Korsakov and Borodin alongside the 'great Western composers'.[2] Musorgsky often accompanied, and indeed toured southern Russia to great acclaim with soprano Dar'ia Mikhailovna Leonora in 1879: 'I had never dreamed that an accompaniment could so clearly recreate scenes from nature ... I could really see the rocks, the forest, and the weeping maiden', one audience member recalled of their version of Schubert's 'Zhaloba Devushki' (a setting of Schiller's 'Des Mädchens Klage', 'The Maiden's Complaint'; as we will see again in France, German lyrics tended to be sung in translation).[3]

Schumann's influence is detected in Russian art song primarily through imaginative piano accompaniments and a liking for the poetry of Heinrich Heine (the latter aided by the publication of a new translation in 1858). Yet, despite their admiration for Western composers, Musorgsky and his compatriots also wanted to establish a distinctly Russian manner of composition. In the realm of art song there

Example 6.1 Modest Musorgsky, *Sunless*, no. 1, 'Komnatka tesnaya, tikhaya, milaya' ('A Little Room, Cosy, Quiet, Dear').

was already the *bïtovoy romans*, or domestic romance: a simple strophic song with piano accompaniment, which could be differentiated from its French equivalent by a propensity for minor keys and melodic contours characterised by intervals of a sixth.[4] But instead of the *bïtovoy romans'* artful simulation of folk song, Russian composers increasingly sought the real thing, and Balakirev spearheaded attempts to transcribe local traditions more exactly. The traditions in question were often not familiar or even local to their investigators: Russia's military expansion during the nineteenth century led to its incorporation of the Caucasus and parts of Central Asia that were no less foreign to the inhabitants of Moscow and St Petersburg than they were to Western Europeans. As just mentioned, folk song was thus as much an

Example 6.2 Alexander Dargomïzhsky, 'Vostochniy romans' ('Oriental Romance').

exotic artefact to its urban collectors as it was, as Balakirev put it, representative of 'the soul of Russian music'.

As in other countries, folk music was not approached as something that simply needed to be preserved, but as something that could revitalise creativity. On the one hand Balakirev provided *Sbornik russkikh narodnikh pesen* (*Anthology of Russian National Songs*, 1866) with key signatures and piano accompaniments only he could have devised, perhaps with the intention of facilitating performance in salons. On the other hand, there were folkish elements that could not be 'normalised': rapid changes between time signatures, irregular phrasing (reflected in Glinka's brief 'Gde nasha roza?' ('Where is our Rose?'), the first ten bars of which are in 5/4, the next seven in 3/4), distinctive disjunct intervals and chromatic harmonies were features appropriated by composers to give them the desired 'authenticity'.[5]

The complex layering of folk and art song, and incidentally of the local and the exotic, is apparent in Dargomïzhsky's setting of Alexander Pushkin's 'Vostochnïy romans' ('Oriental Song'). Pushkin, of course, was no folk author but a famous St-Petersburg-based poet and playwright; his texts were sophisticated simulations of the folk rather than copies. The most obviously folkish aspect of Dargomïzhsky's music is its prominent use of the whole-tone scale, visible in the opening bass line (Example 6.2). The harmonic properties of the scale are explained in the box opposite. Dargomïzhsky does not use the scale here to refer directly to folk music; instead, it appears more in the manner of Glinka's opera *Ruslan and Lyudmila* (1842), in which contrasting tonal systems or scale types differentiate between human and supernatural characters: the humans are given diatonic music, while for the dwarf Chernomor Glinka uses greater chromaticism and whole-tone scales.[6] It is this type of codification on which Dargomïzhsky draws: the song's 'oriental' setting is conveyed not only through its text, but also by its use of the whole-tone scale (the harmonisation of which is indebted to Glinka's treatment of Chernomor's motive), and the chromaticism of the vocal part, which begins with descending semitones. The whole-tone scale is thus doubly 'easternised': from a Western European perspective it is associated with Russian folk music; from the Russian perspective it also represents the Orient.

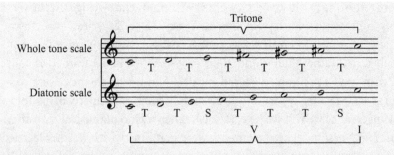

The whole-tone scale does what its name suggests: it moves exclusively in whole-tone steps, rather than the pattern of tones and semitones that make up the diatonic scale on which Western harmony is based. The absence of semitones, particularly between the seventh and eighth degree of the scale, annuls the pull towards the tonic felt in diatonic harmony. The traditional hierarchy within the diatonic system – the privileging, after the tonic, of the fifth (dominant) and fourth (subdominant) scale degrees – is also overturned in the whole-tone scale. Its arrangement is symmetrical; it can be divided exactly in half, at the tritone (an augmented fourth / diminished fifth). The whole-tone scale thus allows composers greater freedom to move between harmonic centres, as no one pulls more strongly than another. Because of the way it is constructed, the whole-tone scale was not only thought to be folkish but also to be 'artificial', and it came to be associated with the magical and exotic, particularly on the Russian operatic stage. (Incidentally, the tritone was traditionally referred to as 'the devil in music'.)

Associating harmonies with particular characters, symbols or moods also encouraged composers to defy formal constraints, such as following conventional key relationships and beginning and ending a song in the same key. This looser approach was matched by a change in text-setting methods. Further investigations into Russian folk lyrics had revealed that metre should be defined not by counting how many syllables make up each line but by stress.[7] This impetus towards following the rhythms, inflections and contours of spoken language is evident in Dargomïzhsky's use of declamation in songs such as 'Vostochnïy romans' and, more famously, in his opera *The Stone Guest* (1866). Dargomïzhsky explained: 'mediocrity seeks out melodies that flatter the ear. I do not choose such. I want music strictly to express the word. I want truth.'[8] He thus set out to establish a kind of musical realism to complement the literary version pursued by Pushkin and Nikolai Gogol, among others (Pushkin's poems in particular were frequently set by Russian composers well into the twentieth century: see Chapter 10). And Musorgsky followed suit, in his Gogol-based opera *The Marriage* (1868) and, most pertinently for our purposes, in his first song cycle *Detskaya* (*The Nursery*, 1872).

Before returning to Musorsgky's works, we should acknowledge that he was almost the only nineteenth-century Russian to compose song cycles. The reason other composers were not interested was probably their emphasis on folk music. Even when fabricated rather than found, their songs seemed better framed as collections; cycles, with their attention to shared musical and poetic themes, were too clearly marked as art. Musorsgky certainly drew on folk song, particularly in his approach to text setting, and as we will see he carefully crafted a kind of musical realism in cycles such as *The Nursery*.[9] These elements were combined with lessons learned from Schubert and Schumann, enabling Musorgsky to create a series of cycles that may have been too few in number, and too idiosyncratic, to establish a Russian tradition, but are among the most compelling results of the song cycle's travels abroad.

Unusually, the songs that make up *The Nursery* are not for or about children, to be sung as lullabies or as exercises in nostalgia; they are songs that seem as if they could have been written by children.[10] Musorgksy wrote – or rather, claimed he 'overheard' – the words himself (alongside adults Dargomïzhsky and Stasov, songs are dedicated to Musorgksy's young nephew and niece, and Cui's daughter). Crucially they enact, rather than describe, scenes in the present tense: the boy is frightened by a fairytale, falls from his rocking horse and encounters the prospect of death (through a cat trying to snag a canary) in the here-and-now, rather than seen from a distance. Similarly the girl gets carried away in her evening prayer, trying to remember a long list of all her relatives, and is reprimanded by her nurse. There is no lyrical conclusion to the song, as we might expect. Instead the girl clumsily copies the nurse's version adding, hesitantly, 'Now, is that right?' In that song, and the first, 'To Nanny', it is clear even to a non-Russian speaker that the vocal writing is closely related to the rhythms and inflections of speech: metre is fluid and pitches are chosen more for emphasis than tunefulness. For the most part the piano has a supportive role, rather like a friend dragged along to corroborate the child's story: in 'To Nanny' it only breaks from the voice's rhythms occasionally, to add brief illustrations; for instance, the threat of the wolf and the children's cries are accompanied by tumbling triplets (Example 6.3).

With his next cycle, the already-mentioned *Sunless*, Musorgsky seemed to turn his back on the irony and realism of *The Nursery* in favour of his own brand of Romanticism. While there are moments in *Sunless* which hark back to his earlier style – the self-conscious evocation of salon music in the fourth song, an illustration of the river in the piano figuration of song six, and occasional passages of declamatory vocal writing – as discussed, on the whole the music is more expressive and introverted.[11] Through its harmonic configuration, though, *Sunless* still exhibits Russian folkish elements such as the whole-tone scale. *Sunless* has no magical or exotic theme, but it does make use of tritone relationships, often to distinguish between references to past happiness and present misery.[12] For example, in the third

Example 6.3 Modest Musorgsky, *The Nursery*, no. 1, 'S nyaney' ('With Nanny'). 'And how those children cried out, wept. Nanny dear! Why did the wolf eat those children?' Trans. David Fanning.

song, 'The Idle, Noisy Day', reference to the 'shadow' (*ten'*) of a May night is marked by a move to a chord of Gb, tritone to the tonic C, a shift which recurs as the next verse refers to turning over the pages of years lost. If these changes of colour seem too subtle, the bigger point to make is that, in Musorgsky's hands, responsiveness to a text is taken to a new level and it is this enhanced freedom – to move beyond lyricism and conventional harmonic relationships – that proved most influential to subsequent song composers.

At the time *Sunless* was published, however, few saw it as anything other than the ravings of 'a neurotically self-absorbed, broken-down aristocrat'.[13] Others have tried to explain its aura of retreat as reflecting Musorgsky's personal life or as expressing a malaise typical of the Russian liberal middle classes in the 1870s. His last years are usually seen as a period of decline, marked by increasing alcoholism and loneliness, the loss of close friends, and an inability to complete the opera *Khovanschina*. If death was sensed around the corner in *The Nursery* (as the cat waited to pounce on the canary), it breathes heavily down the neck of Musorgsky's final cycle, *Pesni i plyaski smerti* (*Songs and Dances of Death*, 1875–7).

The poet, again, was Golenischschev-Kutuzov, who envisioned a vast panorama of Russian deaths – from peasant to Tsar, from poet to priest, from child to aristocratic lady. Despite grander plans, Musorgsky eventually set only four of the poems. Each takes what are usually considered affirmative genres – the lullaby, serenade, peasant dance and triumphant march – and makes them grotesque, by Death's unexpected entrance. Caryl Emerson points out that although Musorgsky did not make many changes to Golenischschev-Kutuzov's poems, those he did make were 'chilling'.[14] Outer frames that commented on each scene, in the manner of a Greek chorus, were omitted, and everything was moved to the present tense, allowing the listener, as in *The Nursery*, to experience emotions directly. These are not songs about death, or sung from the safe distance of recollection. Here Death dances, saving no one.

The second song, 'Serenade', exhibits many of the cycle's characteristic features (Example 6.4). A young woman leans out of her bedroom window, dreaming of love. The piano's right-hand rocking semiquaver figuration belongs to the tremulous atmosphere of conventional romance, as stars glisten against the amethyst sky. But even before it is revealed, at the end of the first verse, that the woman is an invalid and her suitor is Death, we sense that all is not well. The first note of the song is a bare octave B in the piano; it is not clear which key we are in. Instead, it seems as if the piano's semiquavers and the vocal line (supported by the piano's left hand) belong to different harmonic worlds: the piano's B min⁷ chords rub uncomfortably against the C♯s, E and G of the voice. Death's vocal entrance makes the distinction between characters obvious: as he addresses the maiden the harmonies move firmly flatwards, to a stable E♭ minor, and the time signature changes from 2/4 to 6/8, those tremulous semiquavers being replaced by a constant trochaic (long–short/crotchet–quaver) rhythm. His strident melody, with its wheedling triplets, is hard to resist: a brief return to the first verse's sharp side (now F♯ major) and romantic description (tellingly marked *poco capriccioso*, a little playfully) cannot shake off Death's rhythm, and his music soon returns in the ominous key of E♭ minor. 'Your lover is calling, listen . . . Be still', the song ends, dwindling to almost nothing before the final triumphant surge: 'You are mine!'

The clear differentiation between characters by melody, accompaniment, rhythm, vocal style, expressive markings and tonality, as well as their use of direct speech, are features of all Musorgsky's *Songs and Dances of Death*. Many of these musical devices developed out of realism, but they are used to different purposes here: to mock and undercut, to point out – through fantasy – still bitterer truths. Death's harmonies are often irresistibly sweet and his tunes memorable. As he surveys the carnage of the battlefield in the final song, Death declares victory: this is 'death taking its pleasure in death', Musorgsky explained.[15] It was this return to a kind of mellifluousness, whatever its poetic purpose, in the composer's final years that upset defenders of

Example 6.4 Modest Musorgsky, *Songs and Dances of Death*, no. 2, 'Serenada' ('Serenade')
'Magical bliss blue-shaded night, trembling spring twilight . . . "In the darkness of stern and
narrow captivity"'. Trans. David Fanning.

realism. Musorgsky had intended to create an orchestral version of *Songs and Dances*
but death caught up with him, too, before he had the chance.[16]

As mentioned, while there were many Russian song composers, few produced
cycles. One exception was Pyotr Tchaikovsky. In fact, his last substantial work was
a setting of six poems sent to him out of the blue by a law student, Daniil Rathaus,
in August 1892. Like Musorgsky, Tchaikovsky had a predilection for sad songs, and
the cyclic aspect of op. 73 results mainly from the shared theme of lost love.[17] Also

Example 6.5 Tchaikovsky, *Shest' Romansov* (*Six Romances*) op. 73, no. 6, 'Snova, kak prezhde, odin'. 'Again, as before, I am alone, / Once again I am wrapped in grief . . . The poplar is seen at the window, / All lit by the moon.' Trans. David Fanning.

as with Musorgsky, songs often end in a key different from their beginning (the 'progressive tonality' already seen in Mahler). The first song moves from E major to C♯ minor, to mark the passing of years; the third goes from E♭ to A♭ major. We might also sense a Russian inflection to the tritone shift from E major to A♭ major between songs four and five and, in the prevalence of sixths in the piano postlude to song five and introduction to song six, again the legacy of the Russian domestic romance. Tchaikovsky's vocal writing is more lyrical than Musorgsky's, but is still motivically compact: that of the final song, 'Again, as before, alone', is almost exclusively based on a descending third, and is supported for all but six bars by a tonic pedal on A in the accompaniment (Example 6.5). But this is not to say that the melodic figurations at play are without significance: the descending lines heard in the postludes to the first two songs refer to the 'Fate' motif that pervades Tchaikovsky's works from the opera *Eugene Onegin* (1879) through to the *Pathétique* Symphony (1893).[18]

What is decidedly un-Musorgskian about op. 73 is the sentimentality of Rathaus's verse and Tchaikovsky's music, and this raises an important issue about national styles. As Richard Taruskin has pointed out, Tchaikovsky was something of an anomaly among late nineteenth-century Russian composers: he was not an aristocrat, as had been Glinka, Dargomïzhsky and – in an end-of-the-line kind of way – Musorgsky, nor was he a performing virtuoso; he was a conservatory-trained professional who achieved international success.[19] While seen outside Russia as one of the country's finest composers, at home Tchaikovsky's music was considered too Western, too cosmopolitan, to represent 'authentic' national music. But op. 73 still deserves mention here, because it helps explain how its genre managed to survive beyond its first generation: by adaptation. By incorporating different registers – from salon sentimentality to the folk-like, the fantastic or the brutally realistic – and different musical and poetic languages, composers of the song cycle enabled migration beyond borders.

French Schuberts

A scene that could have been painted by Renoir: a flower-filled drawing room with blinds lowered to protect its occupants from the hot sun; our heroine at the keyboard, wearing a fetching summer dress. She sings a new song by a fashionable young musician:

Que l'heure est donc brève	How brief is the hour passed in loving!
Qu'on passe en aimant!	
C'est moins qu'un moment,	It's less than a moment, little more than a dream.
Un peu plus qu'un rêve.	

For the first readers of *Le Nabab: moeurs parisiennes* (*The Nabab: Parisian Mores*), Alphonse Daudet's 1877 roman à clef, the reference would have been obvious; the song is the sixth from Jules Massenet's hugely popular song cycle *Poème d'avril* (*Poem of April*, 1866).[20] The heroine of Daudet's novel – Madame Jenkins – was based on Mrs Charles Moulton, a rich American famous for her Parisian salon. Moulton had engaged Massenet to transcribe some melodies; on hearing strains of *Poème d'avril*, however, she realised she had hired much more than an amanuensis. Her support – along with that of the publisher Georges Hartmann and the composer Ambroise Thomas – secured the success of Massenet's songs in drawing rooms across Paris through the last decades of the nineteenth century, evidenced by their appearance in novels from Daudet's through to Claude Farrère's *Mademoiselle Dax, jeune fille* (*The Young Woman Miss Dax*, 1907), in which the titular heroine describes Massenet as her 'daily bread'.

Massenet's *Poème d'avril* has been deemed the first 'true' French song cycle. The genre's comparatively late emergence in France was due to a number of reasons, not least that the tradition of song-writing was quite different from that in Germany.[21]

French art song has routinely been seen as the poor cousin to the German Lied, more often forsaking higher aesthetic aspirations to pander to domestic, populist markets. In the first few decades of the nineteenth century, the traditional strophic *romance* dominated. The German art-song repertoire was not really known until introduced to Parisian salons by visiting artists such as Franz Liszt, Ferdinand Hiller and Joseph Dessauer. Critically, Schubert's songs were first encountered in instrumental form, as piano transcriptions. Hearing the originals was delayed by French refusal to sing in German, as is evident from the anecdote of how Liszt introduced the famous tenor Adolphe Nourrit to Schubert's 'Erlkönig' in 1837: he explained the basic story and Nourrit then sang the melody to vocalise (wordless singing) – apparently capturing Goethe's spirit, if not his actual words.[22]

Once publishers such as Charles-Simon Richault began to issue translations of Schubert Lieder in the early 1830s, a 'revolution in drawing-room music' came about, one that not only affected what music was performed and listened to, but also had a profound influence on song composition.[23] Richault referred to Schubert's Lieder as *mélodies*, a term that signalled a greater degree of sophistication than the *romance*. As is often the case with labels, *romance* and *mélodie* continued to be used interchangeably (Schubert's songs were sometimes called 'German romances'). But Schubert's influence encouraged interest in serious Romantic poetry, abandonment of strophic forms, and willingness to explore more adventurous harmonies. By 1840, the critic Blanchard was complaining:

> Just like Victor Hugo, who was made the leader of a school of poetry, and who had so many grotesque imitators, Schubert is the focal point of the young musical school who now only dream of Lieder with pretentious, tortuous melodies and harmonies and ambitiously ridiculous modulations.[24]

Another contemporary, Ernest Legouvé, was more sympathetic: 'Schubert killed the romance and created the melody, in which, since his day, Reber, Gounod, Massenet, Delibes and Paladilhe have created a whole series of charming little masterpieces'; to that list we might add Félicien David, Victor Massé and Georges Bizet.[25]

Although individual numbers from Schubert's cycles were sung, no full performance of *Die schöne Müllerin* (heard in Vienna in 1856) can be documented in France until 1898.[26] Beethoven's *An die ferne Geliebte* had been published in 1838 as 'À la bien-aimée absente', but Schubert's admittedly much longer cycles were not made available until Richault's 'complete' edition of Schubert, published in fifteen volumes between 1845 and 1850, which arranged the songs by opus number. The cycles therefore appeared in consecutive order, but there were no title pages to announce their beginnings, nor anything to mark their ends. Nor was the edition a success, although an extracted compendium of forty songs did well, suggesting that there was little interest in cycles *qua* cycles at this stage.

One obstacle to the introduction of the song cycle into the repertoire was the problem of translation; the 'free' approach taken by most translators rendered large-scale narratives virtually meaningless. While alternatives were available from various publishers, it was not until the 1860s that Lieder became readily available in their original language. The reason for this was primarily commercial: German publishers had adopted new printing techniques (offset or 'transfer' lithography) that enabled them to produce music more quickly and cheaply; along with Emperor Napoléon III's series of cuts to import taxes, this meant that they could flood the French market.

One of the composer back catalogues to benefit from the Germans' new hold over the market was Schumann's. Attempts to promote his piano music since the 1830s had not been successful; the songs, though, gradually attracted an audience. Richault had taken the standard path of associating Schumann's music with a famous performer in the *Six Mélodies chantées par Jenny Lind* (*Six mélodies sung by Jenny Lind*, 1855); this was followed a year later by editions of *Myrthen* (op. 25) and the op. 39 Eichendorff *Liederkreis*. But it was the publisher Flaxland's anthology of 'Cinquante mélodies' (1863) that proved more significant, including as it did not only the German words alongside a French translation, but also *Dichterliebe* and *Frauenliebe und -leben* intact (as with Schubert, none of the cycles was given complete public performances until the mid-1890s).

Schumann's influence on French song composition can be felt most strongly in Massenet.[27] *Poème d'avril* was not only the first French cycle to be disseminated as such, it was also one of the first pieces by Massenet to be published altogether, beginning a long and successful working relationship with the publisher Hartmann (also at the start of his career), who did much to improve the presentation of printed music over the next three decades, as well as supporting up-and-coming composers such as Bizet and, later, Debussy. *Poème d'avril* was also the first of several cycles by Massenet to the popular poetry of Armand Silvestre; apparently the two men met on a horse-drawn omnibus, Massenet immediately being inspired to set some of the 'Mignonne' poems from Silvestre's *Rimes: neuves et vieilles* (*Rhymes: New and Old*, published in 1866, with a preface by Georges Sand). In keeping with Schubert's and Schumann's cycles, the nine poems Massenet selected are closely related in style; they revolve around a protagonist and his beloved, and follow the familiar trajectory from springtime romantic revelry to tragic conclusion. The relationship between past and present was made apparent through a web of musical references. Such thematic connections are one of the ways in which Schumann's influence can be detected, but there is nothing like the degree of harmonic interrelatedness between songs found in the German repertoire. *Poème d'avril* also sounds very different in vocal style, primarily because it features spoken recitation as well as singing (a feature of subsequent cycles by Massenet, including his last, *Expressions lyriques*, 1912). And while there are lyrical passages and strophic forms in *Poème d'avril* there are also recitative-like sections, lending these songs a sense of dramatic spontaneity that, in itself, strengthens the relationship between numbers; the 'naturalness' of the delivery encourages movement from one song to the next.

For example, the three recited stanzas of the prelude begin the process of remembrance; the persona is seized again by a gentle madness, to write songs and recall memories ('Et je me sens repris de la douce folie / De faire des chansons et de me souvenir'), prompting a preview in the piano of the opening bars of the second song (Example 6.6; bars 3–6). After the next stanza, in which old flames ask the name of the new, comes figuration taken from the fifth song, whose message – with shades of the Vigil of Venus (AD 2/3) – is that you who never loved will love tomorrow ('vous qui n'aimiez pas / vous aimerez demain!') (bars 7–8). And the prelude begins and ends by an unmeasured ascending arpeggio outlining a cadence on B♭ (bars 1 and 10), which leads into the E♭ major of the next song, and, transposed to C♯, also opens the piano romance following the fourth number, the recited poem 'Riez-vous?' ('Do you Laugh?'). The next recitation comes at the start of the final song, 'Complainte' ('Lament'), and reveals that the affair lasted only three days. There follows a dialogue between the man and woman, he suddenly realising that she is leaving for good: a rather sarcastic and realistic portrait of 'La constance éternelle, / Et les éternelles amours!' ('Eternal constancy, and eternal loves!'). Intriguingly, Massenet slightly altered the text to create a new preface: the final two lines in which she asks him to take care of her memory after she has gone become the more melodramatic 'Je meurs! Adieu, ma chère âme, j'ai gardé ton souvenir' ('I die! Adieu, my dear soul, I have kept your memory'). The music for both farewells is the same, providing a historicising frame that allows for slippage between re-enacting the scene and remembering it – at the same time slightly debunking *la folie d'amour*.

The public appetite for Massenet's songs (he wrote about 260 altogether, roughly the same number as Schumann or Hugo Wolf) was such that sometimes they were published in five keys simultaneously. Yet although *Poème d'avril*, and Massenet's other *Poèmes* were published as cycles, in the nineteenth century they were still often treated merely as collections of individual songs, all of which were quickly anthologised.[28] Similarly, in terms of public performance such as at the Société Nationale de Musique (an institution designed to promote contemporary French

Une rose frileuse, au coeur noyé de pluie,
Sur un rameau tremblant vient de s'épanouir,
Et je me sens repris de la douce folie
De faire des chansons et de me souvenir!

Les amours trépassés qui dormaient dans mon âme,
Doux Lazare sur qui j'ai tant versé de pleurs,
Soulèvent, en riant, leur suaire de fleurs,
Et demandent le nom de ma nouvelle dame.

Ma mignonne aux yeux bleus, mets ta robe et fuyons
Sous le bois remplis d'ombre et de mélancolie
Chercher le doux remède à la douce folie.

Le soleil m'a blessé de ses premiers rayons!

Example 6.6 Jules Massenet, *Poème d'avril*, no. 1, 'Prelude'. 'A chilly rose, its heart drenched with rain, / Has just blossomed on a trembling bough. / And I feel the sweetest folly assail me once more / To create songs and recall the past! / All the dead loves asleep in my soul, / Gentle Lazarus, on whom I shed so many tears, / Laughingly raise their shroud of flowers, / And ask me the name of my new love. / O my blue-eyed darling, dress and let us flee / Through woods filled with melancholy and shade, / To seek a sweet cure for our sweet folly. / The sun has wounded me with its first rays!' Trans. Richard Stokes, *A French Song Companion* (Oxford University Press, 2000), p. 306.

music), while cycles were occasionally heard in their entirety, more often individual songs were sung. There were dozens of song composers in Paris by the end of the nineteenth century. On the whole, few of them wrote cycles, perhaps because there continued to be far more interaction between art song and popular song than in the German tradition, a tendency to crossover perhaps discouraged by the aesthetic aspirations of the song cycle. Among those who did compose cycles, though, were Gabriel Fauré and Claude Debussy, through whose mature works we gain the clearest sense of an approach to the genre that is not simply Schubert or Schumann with a French accent, but French *tout court*.

Fauré, Debussy and Verlaine

Fauré's indebtedness to Massenet is implicit in the title of his first collection of songs, *Poème d'un jour* (op. 21, 1878) and in his many settings of Silvestre (although in this he and Massenet were far from alone). In order to gain a sense of Fauré's impact on song-cycle composition, though, we are better to focus on settings of Paul Verlaine, specifically his famous and influential cycle *La Bonne Chanson*. Apart from the fact that this was one of Fauré's most successful pieces, his choice of poet will allow comparison of *La Bonne Chanson* to two sets of songs by Debussy taken from Verlaine's *Fêtes galantes* (1866–8) to explore in broader terms how these French composers approached song-cycle composition towards the end of the nineteenth century.

First, a brief introduction to Verlaine. He began to associate with the Paris avant-garde and the republicans who would mastermind the 1871 Commune while a law student, gaining prominence on publishing one of the first sympathetic studies of the poet Charles Baudelaire, as well as his own poems. *Fêtes galantes* tend to be thought of as quintessential: they are twenty-two technically brilliant short poems that conjure up scenes from the eighteenth century in the manner of the painter Watteau; a rather fey and nostalgic world of moonlit gardens, marble statues, *commedia dell'arte* characters such as Pierrot and Harlequin, masked lovers and music. *La Bonne Chanson* (1870), his fourth collection, stems from the courtship of his wife (whom he would soon abandon for the young poet Arthur Rimbaud); the twenty-one poems contemplate their love against a Parisian backdrop more squalid than romantic.

Fauré was introduced to the poems by Count de Montesqiou Fezensac (the probable model for Des Esseintes, the decadent protagonist of Huysmans' 1884 novel *À rebours*, and Proust's Baron de Charlus), whom he had met at the salon of Montesqiou's relative, Elisabeth Greffulhe: an indication of how important salons were to intellectual and artistic life at the time. Altogether, Fauré set eighteen poems

Table 6.1 *Fauré*, La Bonne Chanson

Song (order in Verlaine collection)	Key	Date of composition
1. Une Sainte en son auréole (VIII)	Ab	17 September 1892
2. Puisque l'aube grandit (IV)	G	1893
3. La Lune blanche luit dans les bois (VI)	F♯	20 July 1893
4. J'allais par des chemins perfides (XX)	F♯ minor	Autumn 1892
5. J'ai presque peur, en vérité (XV)	E minor	4 December 1893
6. Avant que tu ne t'en ailles (V)	Db	Autumn 1892
7. Donc, ce sera par un clair jour d'été (XIX)	Bb	9 August 1892
8. N'est-ce pas? (XVII)	G	25 May 1893
9. L'Hiver a cessé (XXI)	Bb	February 1894

by Verlaine, including the *Cinq Mélodies 'de Venise'* op. 58 (1891) and *La Bonne Chanson* op. 61 (1892–4).[29] An idea of composing a cycle emerged as he worked on the *Cinq Mélodies*, the songs of which share a musical motif, and alternate textures and tempi. *La Bonne Chanson* takes the notion of cyclic organisation further; the manuscripts indicate that Fauré constantly revised the order of the songs (disrupting Verlaine's arrangement, as can be seen in Table 6.1), eventually creating a sort of suite of poems that form a portrait of the beloved, broken up by paeans to nature (songs 3, 6 and 9). The tonal scheme is unusual but roughly symmetrical; the first six songs progress downwards by step, placing two songs in minor keys at the centre of the work, while the return to G major in the penultimate song refers back to the key of the second song. 'L'Hiver a cessé' ('Winter is Over'), added last, draws together the recurring musical motifs of the cycle; a practice Fauré may have taken from Schumann or Massenet, but which is also present in his symphonic works.

Fauré later tried to claim that there was only one theme in the cycle, taken from his early song 'Lydia' op. 4/2.[30] But while one thematic fragment can be linked to 'Lydia', there are other equally important recurring motifs, as is demonstrated by 'J'ai presque peur, en vérité' ('I Am Almost Frightened, in Truth'). This is the centre-point of the cycle on many levels: it is literally the middle number; the second of the minor-mode pair already mentioned. It is also the emotional core, leading to the crucial shift from a formal declaration of love – 'Je vous aime' – to the more intimate 'Je t'aime'. As he recalls the radiant thought that caught up his soul the previous summer ('la radieuse pensée / Qui m'a pris l'âme l'autre été'), variants of a descending melody first encountered in songs two and four are heard in the brief keyboard interludes between verses (Example 6.7: a further version also appears at the end of the cycle). The fifth verse refers to the contour of the 'Lydia' theme, as he claims that despite all his suffering he still hopes to be with her. With the climactic declaration of love, though, a new arching melody is introduced, which

Example 6.7 Gabriel Fauré, *La Bonne Chanson*, no. 5, 'J'ai presque peur, en verité'. (Transposed to C♯ minor.) 'In truth, I am almost afraid, / So much do I feel my life bound up / With the radiant thoughts / That captured my soul last summer.' Trans. Richard Stokes in Graham Johnson, *Gabriel Fauré: The Songs and Their Poets* (Aldershot: Ashgate, 2009), p. 233.

will appear again in the seventh and eighth songs. The way in which 'J'ai presque peur' draws on previous thematic material and provides ideas for future songs reveals the sophistication of *La Bonne Chanson* as a cycle; it is not simply a question of the first and last numbers connecting, or even of returning to the initial key, but of almost all its songs being subtly embedded within the whole.

The complexity and novelty of *La Bonne Chanson* upset several critics at its premiere (and even composers – allegedly, Saint-Saëns recommended it be burnt). Apparently it even daunted Debussy, yet something of the cycle's expressive power, free and varied vocal style, and prominent piano part can be detected in the songs Debussy composed or revised soon afterwards, including his own settings of *Fêtes galantes*, which appeared in two sets; the first composed in 1892 but not published until 1904, after which the second set soon followed.[31]

The two parts of *Fêtes galantes* have different characters, which can be explained by the years between them. Part I, like most of Debussy's earlier songs, was composed for the light soprano voice of Marie Vasnier; Part II was intended for the lower register of Emma Bardac, who became the composer's second wife (and who, incidentally, was also the dedicatee of Fauré's *La Bonne Chanson*). But Debussy had not just married again in those intervening years; his approach to composition had been fundamentally altered through working on an opera based on symbolist poet Maurice Maeterlinck's play *Pelléas et Mélisande* (the Maeterlinck was premiered in 1892; Debussy started work in 1893 and completed the score in 1902).

Two brothers, Golaud and Pelléas, fall in love with the same woman, Mélisande. A familiar operatic scenario, perhaps, but cloaked by Maeterlinck and Debussy in mystery – the former devising a series of enigmatic encounters between characters, the latter rethinking the relationships between melody, harmony and rhythm, and between voice and orchestra. Critics were divided.[32] While Debussy seemed to have created something entirely new, and distinctly French, *Pelléas* still bears the marks of *fin-de-siècle* Wagnerism touched on in the previous chapter. Quotations and allusions to the score and libretto of *Tristan* are found alongside familiar Wagnerian techniques such as the blurring of formal articulations, a close relationship between text and tonality, and even themes associated with characters or symbols that are leitmotifs in all but name.[33] Wagner was not the only influence on this musical world, though: the whole-tone passages heard in the Prelude refer back to the music of Russians such as Musorgsky, as does the supple declamatory vocal writing.

Traces of *Pelléas*'s 'stammering phantoms', and of the opera's musical world more generally, can be heard in the two volumes of *Fêtes galantes*.[34] 'En sourdine' ('Muted'), the first song in *Fêtes galantes (I)*, is the penultimate poem in Verlaine's collection.[35] It describes a couple in the semi-darkness of a silent forest; one encourages the other to surrender to the sensual atmosphere. The vocal line maintains a fairly limited

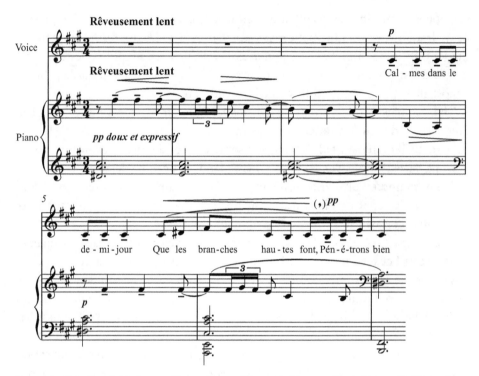

Example 6.8 Claude Debussy, *Fêtes galantes (I)*, no. 1, 'En sourdine' ('Muted'). 'Calm in the twilight / Cast by lofty boughs.' Trans. Stokes, *A French Song Companion*, p. 111.

range and declamatory manner. Even at the end, when the final lines describe the nightingale's song as the voice of the couple's despair, the voice descends, rather than rising to evoke something of the bird's song (as Fauré does in his version). It is left to the piano to convey the nightingale's music, and we realise at that point that we have heard it before, in the syncopated figuration of the opening bars (Example 6.8). Those with ears finely tuned to the Wagner-soaked musical world of Paris at the end of the nineteenth century might also realise that the chord that begins the song references the famous 'Tristan' chord, an unresolved dissonance that embodies yearning within Wagner's music drama *Tristan und Isolde* – which of course fits with the subject matter of Verlaine's poem. But the 'Tristan' chord also links love with death, an association with consequences for the trajectory of Debussy's two-part cycle.

There are other nightingales in *Fêtes galantes (I)*, but the melody of 'En sourdine' does not return until the final song of *Fêtes galantes (II)*, 'Colloque sentimental'. In an old park, cold and deserted, two figures pass by, their eyes lifeless and their mouths slack; their words can barely be heard. These two ghosts are discussing their past:

– Te souvient-il de notre extase ancienne?	– Do you remember our ancient rapture?
– Pourquoi voulez-vous donc qu'il m'en souvienne?	– Why do you want me to remember it?
– Ton coeur bat-il toujours à mon seul nom?	– Does your heart still beat at the sound of my name?
Toujours vois-tu mon âme en rêve?	Do you still see my soul in your dreams?
– Non.	– No.
– Ah! Les beaux jours de bonheur indicible	– Oh! The beautiful days of inexpressible joy,
Où nous joignions nos bouches!	When we would join our lips!
– C'est possible.	– It's possible.
– Qu'il était bleu, le ciel, et grand l'espoir!	– How it was blue, the sky, and how great our hope!
– L'espoir a fui, vaincu, vers le ciel noir.	– Hope has fled, defeated, towards the black sky.

And the couple walk on, heard only by the night. Debussy's setting of 'Colloque sentimental' adds an extra dimension to Verlaine's poem by recalling the descending filigree and syncopated rhythm of the nightingale's music from 'En sourdine' during the ghosts' conversation, though what was once marked 'doux et expressif' (sweet and expressive) is now marked 'très expressif, mélancolique et lointain' (very expressive, melancholy and distant; Example 6.9). A further connection to the earlier song is made through harmony: the Ab underpinning the first speaker is related enharmonically to the G♯ of the nightingale's original music. At the end, the piano cites the nightingale's song three times, each time softer. In other words, Debussy loops a kind of narrative thread around the two volumes of his *Fêtes galantes* by suggesting that the lovers of 'En sourdine' are encountered again in 'Colloque sentimental', now bickering about the past like many old couples: he creates a sense of a life cycle, and with it, perhaps, a song cycle.[36]

Both Fauré and Debussy continued to compose songs and song cycles well beyond the Verlaine settings discussed here. What is apparent in the Verlaine examples is that, as we have seen already with regard to Russian composers, while Fauré and Debussy were influenced by and borrowed from the Austro-German tradition (for example by their use of musical reminiscences), at the same time they were creating something French in terms of the poetry set, their use of harmony, and their vocal and instrumental writing. What is perhaps unusual is that they did so without recourse to folk, or folk-like, music, the path taken by many composers. One reason why Fauré and Debussy did not do so, perhaps, was that they were composing cycles that – as already mentioned with regard to Musorgsky – belonged firmly to the art-song tradition.

Example 6.9 Claude Debussy, *Fêtes galantes (II)*, no. 3, 'Colloque sentimentale' ('Lovers' Dialogue'). 'Do you remember our past rapture?' Trans. Stokes, *A French Song Companion*, p. 120.

Composers around Europe continued to produce collections of folk songs well into the twentieth century (they included Manuel de Falla, Ralph Vaughan Williams and Carl Nielsen). Folkish cycles, however, remained few and far between, and often stood alone in composers' outputs. Norwegian Edvard Grieg's *Haugtussa* op. 67 (*The Mountain Maid*, 1895), for instance, was his only cycle, as was Czech composer Leoš Janáček's *Zápisník zmizelého* JW V/12 (*The Diary of One Who Disappeared*, 1919); a work whose inclusion of two soloists as well as an off-stage chorus adds a theatrical aspect that removes it from the song-cycle tradition we are pursuing here.[37] Two exceptions to the rule were Frenchman Maurice Ravel and Pole Karol Szymanowski, perhaps in part because the folk songs they used came not only from their homelands, but from abroad.

Exoticism near and far from home

Collecting folk song was not simply an obsession of composers; in the age of Empire, it was also state sponsored. Third Republic France (1870–1914) encouraged the gathering of both native *chansons populaires* and *la musique populaire et exotique*; in other words, the fruits of its colonies.[38] The purpose of these projects was to recover – even create, in some cases – a sense of national identity. No less important was the idea of expanding citizens' horizons; making remote territories in Indochina and North Africa seem closer to home. In other words, while economics and politics may have been the driving force of colonisation, governments also needed to find a way to prove to their people what they stood to gain in cultural terms.[39]

The series of Great Exhibitions staged in London and Paris in the second half of the nineteenth century endeavoured to bring the material riches of the British and French colonies to their populations' doorsteps; they were also, crucially, demonstrations of technological progress. The 1889 Exhibition in Paris, marking the centenary of the French Revolution, was perhaps most influential in musical terms, because it introduced composers not only to the modes, repetitive rhythms and layered ostinati of the Javanese gamalan but also to the compositions of the 'Russian Five'. The combination of 'foreign' harmonies (such as those produced by the whole-tone and pentatonic scales) and unusual timbres would come to form the crux of the exotic sound worlds of one young French composer in particular: the then fourteen-year-old Maurice Ravel.[40]

Although Ravel wrote only thirty-nine songs, almost all of them represent the exotic, though it soon becomes apparent that this was almost always at second or third hand. Ravel collected folk songs from Corsica, Greece, Spain, France, Italy, Belgium, Russia and Scotland, even taking down some Hebrew melodies. The three songs of *Shéhérazade* (1903), though, belong to a modern mode of exotic expression, in keeping with Rimsky-Korsakov's earlier Symphonic Suite with the same title (1888), and Léon Bakst's stage designs for the slightly later version by famous Russian ballet company the Ballets Russes (1910). They were based on poems by Léon Leclère (known by the Wagnerian pseudonym Tristan Klingsor), inspired by a recent translation of the ancient Persian fable *The 1001 Nights*, in which the young princess Shéhérazade keeps her life for as long as she can entertain the sultan with her stories. In the first song, Shéhérazade travels the seas to Asia, 'where fantasy sleeps like an empress in a forest full of mysteries'; in the second, she listens to her lover playing the flute; in the third, a young stranger declines her tantalising offer of a glass of wine. Typically, a sinuous melody unfurls itself over undulating, harmonically slow-moving, accompaniment. This is the languorous Orient, where time is suspended. Its sensuality is enhanced by Ravel's orchestral accompaniment, which conforms to orientalist conventions, replete with ouroboric woodwind melodies and shimmering percussion.

Ravel's musical travels also included Spain, a country that perhaps through its associations with North Africa maintained an aura of the exotic and exerted a powerful pull for artists from the rest of Europe. As usual it was more often visited in minds than in reality; already in the previous century the ever ironic poet Heinrich

Heine had asked 'how will you talk about Spain once you've been there?' For Heine's generation the exception was the German Emmanuel Geibel, who visited Spain in the 1840s and subsequently decided to put together (with Paul Heyse) a volume of translations of folk poems, known as the *Spanisches Liederbuch* (1852). Multiple versions of these 'teutonised Spanish songs' appeared, by the famous (Schumann, Brahms, Wolf) and the more or less forgotten, at least as composers (A.B. Marx, Ferdinand Hiller, Anton Rubinstein, Wilhelm Taubert, Gustave Jansen).[41] Ravel's link with Spain should have been closer – his mother was Basque – but despite having written a number of Spanish-themed pieces by the turn of the century he did not visit Spain until 1911, and only made it to Madrid – the home of the Habañera – in 1924. The sources for the Spanish and Basque dance rhythms heard in the song cycle *Don Quichotte à Dulcinée* (1932–3) were second hand: his mother, friends such as the pianist Ricardo Viñes, and Emmanuel Chabrier's orchestral pieces *España* (1883) and *Habañera* (1883).[42]

The political and aesthetic implications of Ravel's exotic adventures are most clearly demonstrated by the *Chansons madécasses*, for flute, cello and piano, commissioned by the American pianist and music patron Elizabeth Sprague Coolidge in the summer of 1925. Ravel's source was a collection of Madagascan poems published by Evariste-Désiré de Parny in 1787. The central song, 'Aoua!' was completed first, and is the dramatic crux, unusually using exotic musical devices to show the aggressive, political face of colonialism. It relates the story of the white man's treachery and defeat by the natives. Ravel's musical characterisation is in many ways simple, but strikingly modern. There are five ostinati in play, taking the notion of 'exotic' repetitive gestures and drones to an extreme, and the two groups are shown by different keys, G major and F♯ major, producing passages of bitonality which are never resolved (Example 6.10).[43] The overall effect was harrowing, as indicated by the protest of an audience member against calls for an encore, after a performance by Jane Bathori: he declared '[I am] leaving as [I] refuse . . . to hear such words again while we are fighting a war with Morocco'.[44]

Ravel's use of bitonality can be considered the fruit of musical exoticism being pushed to its representational boundaries, until it becomes something that in abstract terms is, simply put, new. But he was not the first composer to 'use' exoticism as a means to explore bitonality or other radical harmonies, as we have seen already with the adoption of the whole-tone scale in Russian music, and in the previous chapter with the use of pentatonicism in Mahler's *Das Lied von der Erde*. On one level it is apparent that such technical devices can endow music with cultural, even political, meaning. But it is also obvious that music is a very slippery method of communication: what may sound Austrian to one may sound Chinese to another. (As an aside, some composers in more threatening political environments have found that ambiguity to be a saving grace: Mieczysław Weinberg, for instance, found it

Example 6.10 Maurice Ravel, *Chansons madécasses*, no. 2, 'Aoua!' 'Aoua! Aoua! Beware of white men, dwellers of the shore. In our fathers' time, white men landed on this island; they were told; here is land, let your women work it; be just, be kind, and become our brothers.' Trans. Stokes, *A French Song Companion*, p. 42.

Example 6.10 (*cont.*)

Example 6.10 (*cont.*)

necessary within the Soviet Union to change his 'Jewish Songs' to 'Children's Songs', but in title only.) Few composers, though, exemplify the differences between national styles at the beginning of the twentieth century as clearly as Karol Szymanowski.

Szymanowski was born in the Ukraine in 1882, and moved to Warsaw as a young man. While there he became involved with the 'Young Poland in Music' movement, a parallel to the 'Young Polish Poets', many of whose texts he set as songs. Their purpose in part was to revitalise a sense of national artistic identity in a country that was still under the thumb of its greatest but long-gone musical son, Frederyk Chopin. Szymanowski subsequently felt the need to explore more of the world and spent time in Berlin, Leipzig, Vienna and Paris, also travelling through southern Europe and North Africa before returning to his homeland at the outbreak of the First World War. There followed one of his most prolific periods, during which time he produced the song cycles *Pieśni księżniczki z brsnśi* (*Songs of the Fairy Princess* op. 31, 1915) and *Pieśni muezina szalonego* (*Songs of the Infatuated Muezzin* op. 42, 1918). These, together with the two versions of *Pieśni miłosni Hafiza* (*The Love Songs of Hafiz* op. 24, 1911, and op. 26, 1925), demonstrate the extent to which, despite his first-hand experience of music from other countries,

Szymanowski's exoticism was a product of his imagination rather than the real world.[45]

Although the composer Kaikhosru Sorabji, of Iranian descent, described Szymanowksi's music as being 'permeated with the very essence of the choicest and rarest specimens of Iranian art', there are virtually no examples of Szymanowksi using his first-hand knowledge of Arabic music in his songs.[46] Even the *Songs of the Infatuated Muezzin*, which are framed by calls to Allah and to prayer, bear no trace of the muezzin calls the composer actually heard in Tunis. They do, though, conform to what were now well-established Western portrayals of the exotic: sensual, melismatic vocal writing; instrumental filigree; rhythmic ostinati; and non-functional harmonies, from whole-tone scales to passages of bitonality. Consider the coloratura arabesques of 'The Lonely Moon' from *Songs of a Fairy Princess*, or the languid instrumental opening to 'Das Grab des Hafis' from op. 26, for solo wind, celeste, harps and strings – the flute initiating an arching four-note figure that recurs throughout, taken up by the voice when it first enters, and left echoing on the wine-scented air at the end. As the Muezzin remembers seeing his lover's naked body in the final song, the vocal line slides into chromaticism, supported by the strings, while wind, piano and eventually triangle urgently repeat a short rhythmic figure, the music soon climaxing on a crunch of two key areas, with chords of F♯ over a bass pedal of D major. A harmony, incidentally, beloved of Ravel, although Szymanowski claimed he did not hear *Shéhérazade* until much later.[47]

Following Poland's declaration of independence in 1918 Szymanowski, unlike many of his compatriots, decided to stay. He felt, though, that Polish musical life was 'in a vacuum' and for a while struggled to compose.[48] The example of Stravinsky's *Les Noces* and *The Rite of Spring* persuaded him that, despite having previously resisted using folk materials in his music, they could be a useful way to generate new types of harmonic and rhythmic procedures. He became involved in the Skamander movement, which, as the poet Julian Tuwim explained, believed 'that the greatness of our art does not appear in subjects, but the forces through which it is expressed, in that most light and elusive game of colours, of words transforming a rough experience into a work of art'.[49] To that end, Tuwim invented new words from old Slavic roots, with modified word endings, to create a series of images rich in internal rhymes, assonance, alliteration: a language familiar yet unrecognisable – or, perhaps better, as if reclaimed from an ancient civilisation. (It is virtually impossible to translate.) His 'odd words', as Szymanowski described them, were transformed into some 'odd songs': the cycle *Słopiewnie* (*Word Songs* op. 46b, 1921).[50] Szymanowski devised what he called a lechitic or 'old Polish' compositional style, which drew on folk music from the mountainous Tatra region. The third song, 'St Francis', alternates between stanzas of a melismatic tune, said to derive from the 'Sabała' folk

Example 6.11 Karol Szymanowski, *Słopiewnie*, no. 3, 'Sw. Franciszek' ('St Francis'). 'Little birds, little flowers . . . cheerful alleluia, holy gospels.'

motif, and a short chant-like refrain, accompanied in parallel fifths (Example 6.11). The performance indications also have folk origins: the lines above notes mean they should be lengthened (agogic stresses) and there are numerous tempo indications, as well as fluctuations in metre. But there are artful touches: for example, the 'Sabała' motif returns in the chromatic descents that run throughout the final song. Marked 'monotonnie' and as softly and sweetly as possible, this pays homage to 'Woda wanda wiślana' – the eighth-century pagan princess Wanda, who led her people to victory on the battlefield and then sacrificed herself to the gods in the river Vistula.

The most striking harmonic feature of *Słopiewnie* is Szymanowski's persistent use of the tritone, which we encountered at the beginning of this chapter in Russian music. Its presence is felt especially in vocal contours, and as key areas collide (when A major overlaps with C major and minor on the final chord of song two). Yet according to Jim Samson this is not exoticism for the sake of it or run riot, but disciplined, even conquered.[51] The claim has political and aesthetic implications. Szymanowski declared: 'Let our music be *national* in its Polish characteristics but

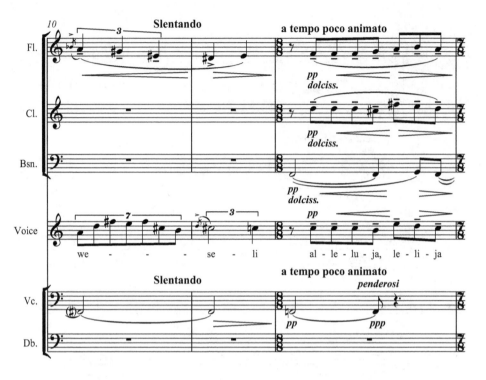

Example 6.11 (*cont.*)

not falter in striving to attain universality. Let it be national, but not provincial.'[52] His call to arms, adapted to different countries, could well have been adopted by many of the composers we have looked at in this chapter, through whose song cycles it becomes apparent that the crossover between exploring foreign realms and discovering new modes of musical and linguistic expression was of vital importance to establishing a sense of identity.

Chapter 7

Modern subjects

Schoenberg often recommended that composers worked on songs when they were stuck for inspiration or needed to solve a particular technical problem. The greatest challenge in the first decade of the twentieth century was how to compose in the absence of functional harmony – without the strong pull towards a tonal centre on which composers such as Beethoven, Schubert and Schumann could rely but that, as we have seen in the music of Wagner, Mahler, Musorgsky and Debussy, was gradually losing its power. This chapter focuses on the way in which Schoenberg in particular dealt with the expansion, we might even say dissolution, of tonality through two song cycles: *Das Buch der hängenden Gärten* (*The Book of the Hanging Gardens* op. 15, 1908–9) and *Pierrot lunaire* op. 21 (1912).

The poetic personae of *Das Buch der hängenden Gärten* and *Pierrot* both exhibit psychological symptoms typical of *fin-de-siècle* Europe's avant-garde – the modern subjects that give this chapter its title. However, Schoenberg's two cycles express the modern condition in contrasting ways; ways that laid divergent paths for song cycle composition through the twentieth century. On the one hand, *Das Buch der hängenden Gärten* perpetuated the nineteenth-century version of the song cycle: it was written for the conventional duo of voice and piano and its musical modernity lay in its harmonic experimentation. Its legacy can be felt in the cycles of Anton Webern, Paul Hindemith, Othmar Schoeck and Benjamin Britten, up to 2009's NMC Songbook project.[1] The roots of *Pierrot lunaire*'s modernism, on the other hand, were theatrical as well as musical. In it, the composer's attention focused on creating unusual timbres through the accompanying instrumental ensemble and a new kind of vocal style between speech and song (*Sprechstimme*). Its impact on subsequent song cycles will be discussed at the end of this chapter. In order to understand how Schoenberg came to write two such contrasting works, both of which can still be understood under the umbrella term of song cycle, we need first to revisit a work he considered 'the key to my whole development': *Gurrelieder*.[2]

In spring 1900, the twenty-six-year-old Schoenberg decided to enter a song cycle contest sponsored by Vienna's *Tonkünstlerverein* (Society of Composers).[3] The notion that the song cycle could be used as a competition piece suggests that it was now well established, even canonic, as a genre – to the extent that the composer

Alexander Zemlinsky advised Schoenberg that his 'truly original' setting would be unlikely to succeed with such conservative judges.[4]

The nine poems of the cycle Schoenberg produced were taken from a German translation of the Danish poet Jens Peter Jacobsen's *Gurresange*, which includes a story set in the medieval kingdom of Gurre. Briefly put, an adulterous liaison between King Waldemar (tenor) and Tove (soprano) results in the latter's murder by the jealous Queen Helwig.[5] In this first version for voice and piano, Schoenberg only dealt with the poems relating to the lovers' nocturnal tryst. The arrangement of the action, such as it is, into scenes lends the whole a quasi-theatrical aspect, increased by Schoenberg's request that the songs alternate between two voices. Still more original, Zemlinsky might have thought, were moments of what has been called 'fluctuating tonality' ('schwebende Tonalität'). For instance, in the first part of the last song, Tove's 'Du sendest mir einen Liebesblick' ('You send me a glance of love'), the actual tonic, G major, is not heard: we are never reassured about which key we are in, and feel we have been left unanchored.[6] Another significant technical development in the cycle was Schoenberg's attention to the development of motivic cells: a pattern of two or three notes sometimes guides the shape of an entire melodic passage, in a manner more typical of instrumental music than vocal writing. Moreover, while there are vestiges of conventional song forms, Schoenberg favoured through-composed rather than strophic forms, as a way to build towards two climaxes within the cycle: the first at the end of song three, when Tove and Waldemar initially make eye contact; the second at the end of song eight, when they kiss. So far, so *Tristan*, you might think – yet the original *Gurrelieder* song cycle did not transgress any boundaries of genre. Ultimately, it was conventional in structure: each song could stand on its own within a carefully arranged tonal scheme, and it began and ended in the same key, Eb major.[7]

Schoenberg eventually decided to abandon the *Tonkünstlerverein* competition and then began to transform the cycle into an altogether more ambitious work. He retained the nine songs of Waldemar's and Tove's romance, but they became the opening section of a massive orchestral cantata.[8] An instrumental introduction and transitions between songs made the cycle continuous. Perhaps most significantly, Schoenberg destabilised the clear sense of Eb major at the beginning and end, replacing the firm final cadence of the cycle with an extended orchestral interlude that both draws on themes from the preceding nine songs and introduces a new character, the wood dove, who relates the news that Tove is dead. The next two parts follow the grief-stricken king on a wild hunt with dead warriors at his side. The rather whimsical hunt of the summer wind ('Des Sommerwindes wilde Jagd') is related by a speaker, using a kind of heightened declamation that perhaps anticipates Schoenberg's use of *Sprechstimme* in *Pierrot lunaire*. The whole closes with a choral celebration of the sunrise in C major.

Although Schoenberg completed the short score of *Gurrelieder* in 1901 he abandoned its orchestration, and it was not until after he had heard his pupil Webern's arrangement of Part I for two-piano eight-hands at a concert in 1910 that he returned to the work.[9] Yet by the time of its premiere two years later, *Gurrelieder* felt to many like a throwback. The grand scale of the orchestral version, with its mythical setting and ill-fated lovers, stood closer to the large-scale symphonic works and music dramas of earlier Romantic generations, of which Mahler's 'Lied-Symphony' *Das Lied von der Erde* (discussed in Chapter 5) had already seemed the last gasp. But Schoenberg claimed that it was through *Gurrelieder* – through its passages of 'fluctuating tonality' and, on its revision, through modifications of the original songs which obscured strong cadences and forged transitions between them – that he conceived the idea of writing music that did not belong to any key or tonality.[10] From 1908 onwards he had produced a series of works that explored what is usually referred to as atonality. One of those was the song cycle *Das Buch der hängenden Gärten*, which had its premiere at the same concert that saw Webern playing his arrangement of *Gurrelieder*.[11]

Das Buch der hängenden Gärten

A man awaits a woman in the hanging gardens of Babylon: the exotic plants around him stimulate the senses, heightening hope that she will return his love. The imagery of *Das Buch der hängenden Gärten* reflects German poet Stefan George's interest in French writers: particularly the symbolists Stéphane Mallarmé and Charles Baudelaire, whose poems George translated. Of all artistic movements, symbolism is among the most elusive to define – indeed, elusiveness was its very essence. The best explanation was given by Mallarmé:

> To name an object is to suppress three-quarters of the enjoyment to be found in the poem, which consists in the pleasure of discovering things little by little: suggestion, that is, the dream. It is the perfect employment of this mystery that constitutes the symbol: little by little to evoke an object, to show a state of the soul, or inversely to choose an object and from it evolve a state of mind by a series of decipherings.[12]

By the first decade of the twentieth century in Vienna the dream had become a gateway not only into poetic realms but also to the psyche. Under the influence of Sigmund Freud, deciphering one's state of mind through the symbolism of the unconscious became of prime concern.

The impact of psychoanalysis is a huge topic that cannot delay us here, beyond noting a change in character of the 'lyric-I' familiar from the nineteenth century.

Although the poetic and musical expression of Schoenberg's song cycles still has roots in preceding romantic generations, they represent a more modern subjectivity. We are dealing with the troubled cousin of the 'lyric-I', prone to breakdown, hysteria and a kind of nature mysticism sharpened by encounters with the increasingly crowded, mechanical and violent age in which it found itself. Significantly that cousin was, if not female, then certainly feminised, the hysteric being etymologically defined by her womb (in Greek *hystera*). Medical, social and artistic – not to mention personal – explorations of sexuality constantly threatened to upset the old-fashioned ideal of love and marriage, as is made explicit in the texts composers chose to set and, occasionally, in their biographies. Schoenberg's *Das Buch der hängenden Gärten*, for instance, was composed around the time of his wife Mathilde's affair with the painter Richard Gerstl, and Gerstl's subsequent suicide. The persona waiting in the exotic garden for his lover to return could be either man. At the same time, it is important not to reduce these works to simple biographical readings. Schoenberg, like other artists of the time (and since), cultivated a particular persona through his works, one that should not be confused with his own personality.[13] In the case of Schoenberg, the persona he established has been described as one of 'public loneliness' – of the modern artist misunderstood by, and striving against, the masses.[14]

One point often misunderstood about Schoenberg was that he did not seek to break with the past; he was committed to furthering musical progress. The scoring of *Das Buch der hängenden Gärten* for voice and piano signals that it belongs to the Lieder tradition. Where the cycle strays onto new terrain is in the symbolism of its text and its harmonic innovations. In some ways text and harmony cannot be separated: Schoenberg's music can be best explained by recourse to the mysterious images of the symbolist poetry it accompanies.[15] Like Mallarmé's pleasure in only partially revealing the name of the object being described, the songs constantly hint at traditional harmonic and formal structures but never present them fully. Triads or diatonic melodies are clouded over with sixths or ninths, or inflected by entirely different tonal areas. The vocal part captures the aphoristic aspect of some of George's texts by forgoing equal or symmetrical phrasing, creating a more flexible form of declamation, sometimes referred to as 'musical prose'.

In the final song reality hits: she will not return. What had seemed paradise at the cycle's opening – flowering meadows, rippling lakes and whispering rushes – becomes rotten grass, stinging plants and heavy night skies. The realisation 'nun ist wahr, daß sie für immer geht' ('It's true, she's gone for good') is sung over a held ninth chord that breaks into fast moving piano figuration that defies harmonic definition: the decaying plants in which the protagonist stumbles (Example 7.1).

Das Buch der hängenden Gärten ends as it began, with solo piano. This is, of course, one of the ways in which the cycle displays its nineteenth-century inheritance. Schoenberg, though, takes the Schumannian model of the piano postlude some steps

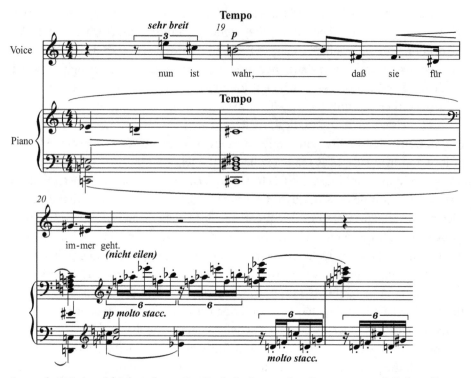

Example 7.1 Arnold Schoenberg, *Das Buch der hängenden Gärten*, no. 15, 'Wir bevölkerten die abenddüstern Lauben' ('We Peopled the Evening-Dusky Arbours'). 'Now it is true she will leave forever.' Trans. Stokes, *The Book of Lieder*, p. 286.

further. The piano here does not only muse on the emotional state of the protagonist, or suggest alternative endings, but throughout the cycle takes on a more independent role. It is not just an accompaniment; instead it is another voice, which speaks over, and sometimes at cross-purposes with, the singer. This greater individuation of constituent parts is one further way in which *Das Buch der hängenden Gärten* represents modern subjectivity. Voice and piano no longer work together as they had in the previous century, their decoupling indicating that they cannot communicate with one another but exist in isolation. The sense of loneliness, of fractures in musical and human relationships, in *Das Buch* points clearly to the cycle which came next, and which remains one of Schoenberg's most difficult works.

Pierrot lunaire

Despite Schoenberg's reputation as arch modernist – the creator of serious, difficult and complex musical works best understood by aficionados – he was not untouched by popular culture. He was briefly employed as Music Director of an avant-garde Berlin cabaret known as the *Überbrettl*, inspired by Parisian bohemian venues such as *Le Chat noir*. Satirical theatrical sketches, recitations of licentious poetry and songs all 'hailed the indecent as the only decent thing'.[16]

It was in such cabarets that the German actor Otto Erich Hartleben recited *Pierrot lunaire*, his free translation of a cycle of poems by the Belgian symbolist Albert Giraud. The *commedia dell'arte* figures of Pierrot, yearning after his Columbine, who gives herself to the heartless Harlequin, were tremendously popular at the *fin-de-siècle*, and spread across countries and art forms. Their appeal lay partly in an ability to puncture the overblown mythologising of Wagnerian aesthetics, through an emphasis on fragmentation, irony, parody and playfulness.[17] For many, the masks of Pierrot symbolised the modern artist.[18]

Schoenberg was commissioned to compose a cycle of Pierrot poems by the actress Albertine Zehme in 1912 (Zehme had already performed Otto Vrieslander's Hartleben settings (1904) on tour). He selected twenty-one poems, and arranged them into three groups of seven, reflecting his interest in numerology (it is no coincidence that this is also op. 21). There is no consistent narrative; it is unclear which character, if any, the voice is meant to represent. Particular poetic images do, though, characterise each section: the moon in Part I (and subsequently); spiritual punishment of sorts in Part II; and nostalgia for home and the past in Part III. It would be difficult to separate any number from the whole; apart from their technical challenges, their brevity and Schoenberg's evident concern for their interrelationships (even down to specifying the length of pauses between numbers) discourage viewing *Pierrot lunaire* as anything other than a cycle.

There are few literal melodic repetitions, but recurring motifs of rhythm and pitch create a degree of musical coherence through the whole, despite the many changes of mood.[19] The harmonic language is mostly atonal, with occasional tonal inflections, such as at the end of 'Eine blasse Wäscherin' ('A Pallid Laundrywoman'). Perhaps in response to the historical roots of the *commedia dell'arte*, the fairytale times or 'Märchenzeit' to which the last number refers, the score is peppered with allusions to other genres and styles, such as the waltz ('Columbine', 'Valse de Chopin', 'Serenade'), the passacaglia ('Nacht') and canons ('Parodie' and 'Der Mondfleck', 'The Moonfleck'). However, rather than an early instance of neoclassicism, these often exaggerated or otherwise distorted references to familiar idioms have been taken to imbue the music with a sense of jadedness and ironic sentimentality.[20]

Still, it is not simply these musical features that have earned *Pierrot lunaire* its notoriety. There is also its emphasis on unusual timbres. Schoenberg devised a unique ensemble of five players: piano, flute/piccolo, clarinet/bass clarinet, violin/viola and cello. Each number introduces a different combination of instruments. Interestingly, the piano is almost always present, maybe as a toehold to traditional Lieder;

more striking, though, are the spotlights that fall on the instrumental soloists. The alienation of voice and accompaniment mentioned with regard to *Das Buch der hängenden Gärten* is here intensified. For instance, in 'Serenade', Pierrot is described scraping grotesquely with a giant bow on his viola. The relatively lengthy instrumental introduction, though, does not feature that instrument, despite it being available. Instead Schoenberg uses the cello. Even then, the cello does not respond to references to Pierrot playing pizzicato or even to his stopping playing; it carries on, the lack of correspondence between words and music making an already strange scenario a little stranger.

It is strange not least because of the kind of vocal delivery Schoenberg required – his famous *Sprechstimme*. The composer specified rhythms, and indicated pitches, but asked for them to be spoken rather than sung; the vocalist should not allow a note to bloom fully (Example 7.2). As seen in Example 7.2, an excerpt from the seventh song, 'Der kranke Mond' ('The Sick Moon') occasionally the instrumental writing took on 'the elusive, wailing character' of the vocal line, as William Austin described it.[21] Here, the semiquaver flurries and rapid changes of dynamic and articulation in the solo flute part resemble the fluctuations in the vocal part throughout.

While the term was newly coined, the technique of *Sprechstimme* was not without precedent. Melodrama, speech performed with instrumental accompaniment or instrumental interludes, had been around since the eighteenth century, and was used as a special effect in popular theatre, in operas by Beethoven and Carl Maria von Weber, and in freestanding works such as Schumann's music for Byron's *Manfred* (1849), Humperdinck's *Die Königskinder* (1897) and Strauss's *Enoch Arden* (1897).[22]

There were also links between the practice of poetic recitation and Lieder, evident in the declamation ballads of Schubert, Schumann and Liszt and, outside of the Austro-German tradition, in the song cycles of Massenet (as discussed in Chapter 6). Although composers seem to have been attracted to speaking voices as a means to achieve a kind of realism, there was little sense that the style in which texts were recited at the turn of the twentieth century was natural or speech-like. Instead, the fashion was for a kind of heightened speech. An actor such as Ernst von Possart (for whom Strauss wrote the melodrama *Enoch Arden*) drew on vocal techniques to help develop resonances and stamina, and deliberately used quasi-musical devices such as portamenti, lengthening of vowels, and exaggerated diction, even advocating reciting on pitches (apparently Possart had a three-octave range).[23] Hartleben's cabaret performances of his *Pierrot* poems and Zehme's concerts belonged to the same strain of performance practice and – without attempting to normalise the impact that hearing Schoenberg's *Pierrot* had on its first audiences – *Sprechstimme* needs to be understood against this historical backdrop.

The theatrical aspect of *Pierrot lunaire* was emphasised at its first performance, in the small Choralion Hall in Berlin on 16 October 1912: Zehme appeared in costume

Example 7.2 Arnold Schoenberg, *Pierrot lunaire*, no. 7, 'Der kranke Mond' ('The Sick Moon'). 'O sombre deathly-stricken moon lying on heaven's dusky pillow, your stare, so wide-eyed, feverish, charms me, like far-off melody.' Trans. Jonathan Dunsby, *Schoenberg: 'Pierrot lunaire'* (Cambridge University Press, 1992), p. 44.

and the musicians were hidden behind screens. While considered audacious, it was immediately recognised as a success and, to the disgruntlement of some, who think other pieces deserve greater recognition, probably remains Schoenberg's most notorious work. There are two possible reasons for its familiarity. First, as will be discussed in a moment, *Pierrot* influenced a number of other compositions. Second, and perhaps more significantly, the music has retained its ability to challenge what we think of as beautiful or normal. In the first chapter of this book I described the history of the song cycle as encompassing generation on generation of the avant-garde: *Pierrot lunaire* exemplifies the extent to which the genre had, by the beginning of the twentieth century, become something rich and strange.

Pierrot's legacy

In the spring of 1913, Maurice Ravel and Igor Stravinsky were in Clarens, Switzerland, working on a commission from the director of the Ballets Russes, Sergei Diaghilev, to revise Musorgsky's opera *Khovanschina*. Stravinsky told Ravel about a work he had just heard in Berlin and found remarkable: *Pierrot lunaire*. The orchestration for soprano and chamber ensemble inspired Stravinsky's *Trois Poésies de la lyrique japonais* (1913). That work and the two composers' memories of *Pierrot* (which was not engraved for publication until 1914), in turn engendered one of Ravel's most difficult pieces, both technically and poetically: the *Trois Poèmes de Stéphane Mallarmé* (1913).[24]

Yet it would be over another decade before *Pierrot* was heard in Paris, London and New York.[25] The delay was caused partly by the First World War and partly by the difficulty of the piece. Schoenberg's stipulations for performance also had an effect. While his onetime teacher Zemlinsky was allowed to put on *Pierrot* in Prague (25 May 1922), using musicians from Vienna, Schoenberg could be very critical of attempts to perform it without his guidance. For instance, although he encouraged singers to perform *Pierrot* in their native language, he objected to French soprano Marya Freund's approach to *Sprechstimme* (she learnt it first as a sung part and then 'slurred' the pitches).[26] He also tried to prevent Edgard Varèse from arranging a concert of it by the International Composers' Guild in New York, fearing it would be insufficiently rehearsed.[27]

Although responses were often divided, *Pierrot* somehow managed to remain on concert programmes to a greater extent than other new works; it has consistently been recognised as a masterpiece – the 'solar plexus' of modern music, according to Stravinsky. Its influence can be detected in cycles as varied as the British composer William Walton's *Façade* (1922) and Hungarian György Kurtág's *Messages of the Late R. V. Troussova* (1981). Walton asked for Edith Sitwell's texts to be recited through a megaphone, accompanied by an instrumental ensemble of flute/piccolo, clarinet / bass clarinet, saxophone, trumpet, percussion and cello. Tellingly, by the composer's final version (1942), *Façade* had accrued twenty-one numbers.[28] Kurtág's *Messages of the Late R. V. Troussova* (discussed in Chapter 4) similarly betrays a debt to *Pierrot* in its varied instrumental groupings, use of *Sprechstimme* and twenty-one movements. More recently, York-based composer Roger Marsh has returned to Giraud's original texts, to create *Albert Giraud's Pierrot lunaire: 50 Rondels Bergamasques* (2006).[29]

Table 7.1 *Structure of Boulez,* Le Marteau sans maître*

1.	BEFORE 'L'Artisanat furieux' [instrumental]
2.	Commentary I on 'Bourreaux de solitude' [instrumental]
3.	'L'Artisanat furieux' [vocal]
4.	Commentary II on 'Bourreaux de solitude' [instrumental]
5.	'Bel édifice et les pressentiments', First version [vocal]
6.	'Bourreaux de solitude' [vocal]
7.	AFTER 'L'Artisanat furieux' [instrumental]
8.	Commentary III on 'Bourreaux de solitude' [instrumental]
9.	'Bel édifice et les pressentiments', Double [vocal]

*Adapted from Pierre Boulez, 'Speaking, Playing, Singing', in *Orientations: Collected Writings of Pierre Boulez*, ed. Jean-Jacques Nattiez, trans. Martin Cooper (London: Faber and Faber, 1990), p. 338.

Two works in particular are always mentioned as homages to *Pierrot*, indeed were deliberately composed as such. Boulez's *Le Marteau sans maître* (*The Hammer Without a Master*, 1953–5), a setting of three short poems by the surrealist René Char for contralto and instrumental ensemble (alto flute, xylophone, vibraphone, percussion, guitar and viola), bears the mark of *Pierrot* partly through its attention to timbre (although Schoenberg stuck to more traditional instruments). Boulez also admitted to a couple of what he called 'abstract quotations': he paired the voice and flute throughout, in reference to *Pierrot*'s 'Der kranke Mond', and he consciously altered the configuration of instruments for each number. As in *Pierrot*, *Le Marteau* plays with the divide between speech and song, though it is more that there are sung passages and others that approach speech, rather than *Sprechstimme* throughout.

Boulez's conception of cyclic structure was, though, different from Schoenberg's. For Schoenberg, *Pierrot lunaire* inaugurated a period of radical experimentation, which would result in the reining-in of free atonality through the development of his twelve-note method of composition in the 1920s. For Boulez, on the other hand, *Le Marteau* came after he had abandoned strict serialism and, while it represented a relaxation in technique, he still retained fairly tight control over the organisation of rhythms, pitches and tempi. Thus, whereas *Pierrot* presented three cycles of seven songs that, even if they do not present a logical narrative, progress in sequence, Boulez devised three cycles that he then interspliced into sections of unequal lengths, as shown in Table 7.1.

Although the text is presented in order, it becomes subsumed into the musical materials, becoming one sound among many. After the final words the score is marked 'bouche fermée' (closed mouth), and the flute takes over from the voice. It is this kind of interchange between parts that has led *Le Marteau sans maître* to be characterised as more lyrical and instrumental in manner than *Pierrot*.

Other composers, though, have been attracted precisely by the theatricality of *Pierrot lunaire* and its radical vocality. In 1967 two British composers, Harrison Birtwistle and Peter Maxwell Davies, founded the The Pierrot Players, an ensemble designed to perform *Pierrot lunaire* and new works.[30] Among the latter was Davies's *Eight Songs for a Mad King* (1969), to a libretto by Randolph Stow that incorporates some of the recorded 'ravings' of King George III – although a music-theatre piece rather than a song cycle, it is worth mentioning here as an example of the reach of *Pierrot*'s influence as well, perhaps, as illustrating the way in which overt theatricality unsettles genre categorisation.

George III apparently had an organ that played eight tunes – hence the eight songs – and he used it to try to teach birds to sing. Maxwell Davies's piece re-enacts those futile lessons by asking for the instrumentalists (flute, clarinet, violin and cello) to be put in cages on stage, with the King (originally sung by actor Roy Hart) kept in check by an addition to the *Pierrot* line-up, a percussionist. The influence of *Pierrot lunaire* can be felt in the vocal writing, which extends the range of *Sprechstimme* to include screams and falsetto, and, in one passage, asks the vocalist to neigh like a horse. Less obvious, perhaps, is the connection between *Pierrot* and Maxwell Davies's inclusion of eighteenth-century musical styles, distorted through pitch clusters and unusual orchestration (among other things, the percussion part asks for railway whistles, chains, sleigh bells and a didgeridoo).

The appeal of *Pierrot* as a model for Maxwell Davies has been located in its exploration of an individual character suffering *in extremis* from some kind of inner conflict.[31] Such a character can be used to confront an audience, or to disrupt conventional narrative structures. *Eight Songs* might be taken as the confrontation, *Le Marteau* as the disruption of narrative. What is most surprising is that, in the second half of the twentieth century, *Pierrot*'s modernity was still intact.[32] At the start of this chapter I suggested that Schoenberg's *Das Buch* and *Pierrot* laid two paths for twentieth-century song cycle composers: as we shall see, neither route proved easy to follow.

Chapter 8

The death of the song cycle

In September 1919, the Austrian-born contralto Ernestine Schumann-Heink returned by boat from Rotterdam to New York with her recently widowed daughter-in-law and two grandchildren. Her companions were detained by immigration; the authorities were suspicious because Schumann-Heink's son had died on a German U-boat. Her other three sons, though, had fought with the American Navy, because Schumann-Heink had become a naturalised American on her third marriage in 1905. Despite her support for her adopted country during the war, Schumann-Heink expressed her dual loyalties through music. Just before the closing group of songs at a concert in Newark, New Jersey, she told the 4,000-strong audience: 'The war is over. The time to sing German songs is here.'[1]

By the time of onetime Brahms collaborator Ludwig Wüllner's final recital in Berlin in 1938, Schumann-Heink's last sentence had taken on an almost completely opposite meaning. Singing German songs was no longer a means for rapprochement between nations, but signalled intensifying hostilities, as the German Chancellor Adolf Hitler and his army annexed Austria and, the following year, invaded Poland, resulting in the outbreak of the Second World War. This chapter, then, doubles back to explore what happened to the song cycle during the interwar years. Its fate was not certain: despite forays into other countries (see Chapter 6) the genre was inextricably linked to nineteenth-century German-language repertoires, and its reception was influenced by the politics and aesthetics of the day. By the 1930s, many thought that art-song composition itself was 'no "modern" affair any longer!' and, to be sure, several of the examples in this chapter are not well known.[2] Yet histories of music are not made up only of great works; in order to understand how we have come to interpret the genre today we must look at its darkest hours as well as its finest.

Lieder migrations

Although many musicians did military service, and creative life was in some ways put on hold, artists moved with surprising ease between Continental Europe, Britain and the United States during and after the First World War. In the wake of the war, inevitably, many were concerned with establishing or re-establishing national traditions; there were also, though, attempts at internationalism. The International Society for Contemporary Music (ISCM) was established in 1922 with the intention of promoting new music, 'regardless of aesthetic trends or the nationality, race, religion or political views of the composer'.[3] It was at the annual festivals organised by the ISCM that many of the song cycles discussed in this chapter, and elsewhere in this book, were first performed.

After the Nazis came to power in 1933, however, Germany withdrew from, and banned membership of, the ISCM. In keeping with its theories about racial purity, the Third Reich cultivated what it considered to be 'true' German art and artists.[4] Many emigrated. Schoenberg and Kurt Weill, persecuted for their Jewish backgrounds, fled to the United States. So too did some non-Jewish composers, such as Paul Hindemith, forced to leave because his music was considered 'degenerate' by the Nazi regime, and Ernst Krenek, who left after Austria was annexed in 1938. Performers were also affected. Elena Gerhardt, who had sung to German troops at the front during the First World War, and was one of the best-known Lieder singers of the age, moved to London in 1934 after her second husband Dr Fritz Kohl, a director of Leipzig Radio, was imprisoned.[5] Although Gerhardt feared her career would be over in England she re-established herself there as a performer and teacher, her students including Benjamin Britten's future partner, Peter Pears.

The tumultuous politics of the interwar years were inevitably reflected in several of the song cycles produced. By 1918, the genre's spiritual home of Vienna had lost much of its cultural capital, not least because several key figures had left (Schoenberg to Mödling and then Berlin; Zemlinsky and Anton Webern to Prague) or died (Mahler). Alban Berg, one of the few to remain, complained that the city had become a 'Café Museum'. What is more, composers of all nationalities seemed determined to distance themselves from the artistic concerns of the pre-war years, especially from the excesses of expressionism, encapsulated in Schoenberg's *Gurrelieder, Das Buch der hängenden Gärten* and *Pierrot lunaire*. Otto Spengler's contentious two-volume tract *Der Untergang des Abendlandes* (*The Downfall of the West*, 1918 and 1923) summed up, for many, a feeling that they had reached a point of no return, and its influence percolated through the following decades. Western civilisation was merely a 'bubble in the stream of world history', one British radio commentator opined in the early 1930s: 'Isn't it most probable that our bubble will burst like the rest?'[6]

Two contradictory trends in Austrian and German music of the 1920s captured the new mood. The first was Schoenberg's development of a twelve-note or dodeca-phonic method of composition, in which the twelve notes of the chromatic scale were arranged into a series (called a set or row), permutations of which could provide the pitch content of a composition – thereby providing an underlying coherence that atonal music had been thought to lack.[7] The second was part of a broader artistic movement referred to as *Neue Sachlichkeit* ('New Objectivity').[8] Taking their cue in part from Les Six in France, some prominent composers began to favour comprehensibility over complexity, using simpler, familiar musical forms whose points of reference were dance and light music, jazz, and classical and baroque idioms.

Neither trend had much to do with the song cycle. Schoenberg's twelve-note works were primarily instrumental and, while his followers Alban Berg and Anton Webern both produced twelve-note songs, they were mostly experimental vehicles and collections rather than cycles.[9] This was perhaps because twelve-note techniques reduced the need for words to provide a structure. The emphasis on popular culture in *Neue Sachlichkeit*, meanwhile, favoured music theatre and opera, such as Kurt Weill's first collaboration with Berthold Brecht, the *Mahagonny 'Songspiel'* in 1927 (subsequently incorporated into the 1930 opera *Aufstieg und Fall der Stadt Mahagonny* (*The Rise and Fall of the City of Mahagonny*)), and Krenek's hugely popular opera following the adventures of a jazz violinist, *Jonny spielt auf* (*Jonny Strikes Up*, 1927).[10]

Against this backdrop the song cycle lost its radical edge. There were a few jazz-inflected Lieder, such as Zemlinsky's *Symphonische Gesänge* op. 29 (*Symphonic Songs*, 1929), and composers sometimes played with the tension between tonal and non-tonal harmonies.[11] The example that best summed up attitudes to the song cycle as a genre that looked backwards rather than forwards was Krenek's *Reisebuch aus den österreichischen Alpen* op. 62 (*Travelbook from the Austrian Alps*, 1929); it both explores musical heritage and critiques modern trends.

Krenek's *Reisebuch* consisted of poems written in response to a journey he had made through Western Austria in June 1929 (the twenty songs were completed the following month). Krenek was pleased to return to the mountains he had loved since childhood (he had recently moved back to Vienna after periods in Paris and Germany), and celebrated the simple rustic life he saw in the villages. We have encountered a desire to reconnect with one's homeland, or *Heimat*, in earlier phases of the song cycle. Many of the titles in *Das Reisebuch* echo routine nineteenth-century themes of travel and homesickness ('Verkehr', 'Heimweh' and 'Heimkehr'), nostalgia ('Rückblick') and nature ('Wetter', 'Gewitter'). However, Krenek made it clear that change was coming. He no longer travelled only on foot, like Schubert's wanderer, but also by electric train, car and bus, surrounded by tourists too busy taking photographs to look at the sights themselves. The twelfth song, 'Alpenbewohner (Folkloristisches Potpourri)' ('Alpine Dwellers (Folkloristic Potpourri)'), is particularly sardonic, complaining about visitors comparing the Alps' offerings unfavourably to churches and golf courses back home, and polluting the atmosphere by cranking out the latest hits on an old gramophone as they drink beer on the veranda, their motorbikes making as much noise as a battlefield. With overtones of Spengler, it ends 'So muß Weltuntergang sein!' ('This must be like the downfall of the world!').

Landscape aside, Krenek's other local reference was musical. His return to tonality with the composition of *Jonny spielt auf*, he maintained, had been inspired by his study of Schubert (the centenary of whose death was celebrated across Austria in 1928). Schubert's ability to make something as simple as a change to the minor 'an unusual musical experience', and his economy of means in terms of developing themes, had encouraged Krenek to attempt to rediscover what he described as the original purpose of tonality.[12] Thus while the songs of *Das Reisebuch* were composed in a deliberately Schubertian manner – lyrical, and relatively modest in scale and form – and exist within a tonal orbit, they are not simply pastiche and are perhaps better thought of as an attempt to imagine how Schubert would have responded had he travelled through the Alps in 1929.

Strauss's *Krämerspiegel*, Hindemith's *Marienleben I*

Richard Strauss almost always composed or orchestrated songs with a particular singer in mind. His wife, the soprano Pauline de Ahna, was an early muse; after her retirement in 1904 Strauss turned his attentions to opera and rarely returned to song. An exception came in 1918, when he found himself obliged to fulfil a contract with the Berlin publishers Bote und Bock (a further impetus might have been the closure of some opera houses towards the end of the war).

Krämerspiegel (*Shopkeeper's Mirror*) op. 66, the work Strauss produced, is his only song cycle intended as such.[13] It is very different in manner from his earlier Lieder, which habitually luxuriate in the upper reaches of the soprano register, bolstered by rich harmonies and sensual poetry. *Krämerspiegel* places the emphasis on the piano, is for male voice, and takes as its texts twelve satirical poems by Berlin critic Alfred Kerr, pieces that pun on the names of the publishers from whose clutches Strauss was trying to escape. The music too is archly referential. Strauss quotes from his own past works and even from Beethoven's Fifth Symphony.[14] Thus, in the second song, the lines 'Einst kam der Bock als Bote zum Rosenkavalier an's Haus' (Once came a goat (*der Bock*) as a messenger (*der Bote*) to the Rosenkavalier's house) prompt allusions to music from Strauss's famous 1911 opera *Der Rosenkavalier*, and so on.[15] There are motivic connections between songs, and a nod to Schumann in the reference to the extended piano introduction to the eighth song as the postlude to the cycle (a passage that would reappear in the moonlight interlude of his final opera *Capriccio*, 1942). Unusually for Strauss, the score was published privately in a limited illustrated edition, furthering the impression that this was a sort of personal vendetta. The self-consciousness of the music – from its quotations to its Schumannian postlude – also implies something about the historical associations of the song cycle as a genre: it was somehow inward looking and conservative.

Hindemith's *Das Marienleben* op. 27 (*Life of Mary*, 1923) was a cycle of much more serious intent. It was the longest work he had written to date, and the last he wrote before turning to composition full time (a development facilitated by a deal with the publisher Schott, which allowed him to give up his job as an orchestral violinist: a further reminder of the important role publishers play in music history). The fifteen poems were by one of the most famous German-language writers of the early twentieth century, Prague-born Rainer Maria Rilke, who had retreated to Switzerland in 1919. They relate events in the life of Mary, mother of Jesus. Unusually, Christ plays a secondary role, his birth, death and resurrection forming the backdrop for contemplation of his mother's life.

Rilke derived his materials from the gospels, apocryphal writings and legends, mixing high and low registers.[16] Hindemith responded in kind. The opening piano melody alludes to the Easter hymn 'Surrexit Christus hodie', perhaps known to Hindemith through seventeenth-century violinist Heinrich Biber's *Mystery* Sonatas, while, at the beginning of 'Mariä Verkündigung' ('Annunication to Mary') there is a quote from the chorale 'Vom Himmel hoch'. The chorale, however, is brutally reharmonised (Example 8.1). There are motivic interconnections between songs ('Mariä Heimsuchung' ('Visitation of the Virgin') takes its material from the preceding 'Mariä Verkündigung') and, as was Hindemith's habit, imagery from the poems even informed musical form. For example, we might liken the passacaglia (a repeated bass-line progression) of the second song to the architecture of the temple Mary visits. Another aspect of the cycle that seems derived from instrumental, rather than vocal, genres is its emphasis on contrapuntal writing, including fugues and canons. Crossovers between instrumental and vocal forms within the song cycle have been touched on in previous chapters.

'I definitely think these are the best things I have yet written', Hindemith stated after the first performance of *Das Marienleben* at Donaueschingen on 17 June 1923, by Beatrice Lauer-Kottlar and the work's dedicatee, Emma Lübbecke-Job.[17] Yet, as mentioned, over the next twenty-five years Hindemith returned to the score a number of times, both revising the version for voice and piano and selecting some songs for orchestration.[18] Before looking at what happened to Hindemith's concept of the cycle, we must consider what happened to the genre in the meantime, beginning with two examples from the year in which the *Marienleben* project began.

Example 8.1 Paul Hindemith, *Das Marienleben* (1923), no. 3, 'Mariä Verkündigung' ('The Annunciation'). 'It wasn't an angel entering (understand), that frightened her.' Trans. Stokes, *The Book of Lieder*, p. 133.

Radical conservatives in 1923

While recovering from an operation in early 1923, the German composer Hans Pfitzner was visited by the newly elected leader of the Nazi party (Nationalsozial-istische Deutsche Arbeiterpartei), Adolf Hitler. It was the only time the two men met; Pfitzner admired Hitler tremendously. Although, ultimately, he was too elitist and close to too many Jews to have an uncomplicated relationship with Nazism, he shared its desire to uphold 'true' German values.[19] He kept almost exclusively to German, or at least German-language, poets rather than working with transla-tions, and his musical points of reference came from the nineteenth rather than the twentieth century. As a young man he had sought to unify Schumann's Eichendorff *Liederkreis* op. 39 by composing interludes to link each song.[20] Of the song cycle he composed after Hitler's bedside visit, *Alte Weisen* op. 33 (*Old Paths*, 1923), he specified that 'These eight songs as a whole have an intimate connection and should only be performed together and in the proper order'.[21] The musical language is not far from Hugo Wolf's, who also set these poems, but Pfitzner's emphasis on the cycle as a whole is new, and its implications are worth pausing over.

Against the stylistic plurality of *Neue Sachlichkeit*, and the new harmonic realms being explored by Schoenberg and his followers, flowed a strong crosscurrent exemplified by the theories of a Vienna-based music theorist called Heinrich Schenker. Schenker was deeply invested in maintaining what he thought was the supremacy of the Austro-German musical canon, and devised a method of graphic analysis that attempted to demonstrate how pieces were unified by their underlying tonality. The intricacies of the method do not concern us here, but what is important is that some of Schenker's song analyses, and his emphasis on the supposed organic coherence of musical masterworks, have strongly influenced some academic interpretations of song cycles such as Schumann's *Dichterliebe*. Current tendencies to think of song cycles as cycles, in other words, stem from approaches to musical form and structure that found their voice in the 1920s, in compositions such as Pfitzner's *Alte Weisen*, and in Schenker's theories.

Another who, as baritone Dietrich Fischer-Dieskau commented, 'took the concept of cycles seriously' was Swiss composer Othmar Schoeck.[22] He had two significant encounters in 1923. The first was in Paris, where his compatriot Arthur Honegger introduced him to fellow members of Les Six (Georges Auric, Louis Durey, Darius Milhaud, Francis Poulenc and Germaine Tailleferre). Schoeck disliked what he considered to be the group's destructive frivolity. The second encounter was at the first festival of the ISCM in Salzburg where, as Schoeck put it, 'the atmosphere was already *verschönbergt*'.[23] The reference is to the influence of Schoenberg, who had just revealed to his circle his new method of twelve-note composition and whose 'destruction of tonality' Schoeck likened to 'an act of Ghengis Khan'.[24]

In several ways *Gaselen* op. 38 (*Ghazals*, 1923), Schoeck's first continuous song cycle, responds to what the composer considered to be the major problems facing musical culture in the 1920s. Like Pfitzner's *Alte Weisen*, it uses texts by the nineteenth-century Swiss poet Gottfried Keller. *Gaselen* begins 'Ours is the fate of the Epigones, who live in the vast halfway world; look, how you squeeze one more drop from old lemon rinds' and ends with the image of a battered old hat, mocked by everyone, although for the poet it still has some wear in it. The decadents, for Schoeck, were those 'destructive' composers he came face-to-face with in Paris and Salzburg; unlike Pfitzner, though, Schoeck's music does not deny modernism. *Gaselen* opens in quasi-serial manner, with solo trumpet and voice presenting a repeated series of notes (Example 8.2).[25] The rhythm of the series alters, however: that for the word 'Epigonen', for example, is different from that for 'einen Tropfen' (bars 5–6). These small dislocations of music and text point towards later cycles such as Boulez's *Le Marteau sans maître* (see Chapter 7), which treat the poems as a kind of absent centre.

Example 8.2 Othmar Schoeck, *Gaselen* (*Ghazals*), no. 1, 'Ours is the fate of the Epigones, who live in the vast halfway world; look, how you squeeze one more drop from old lemon rinds.' Trans. Chris Walton, *Othmar Schoeck: Life and Works* (University of Rochester Press, 2009), p. 124.

If the above features were Schoeck's answer to the decadents, his compositional 'old hat' seems to have been Beethoven's *An die ferne Geliebte*.[26] Keller's ten poems, which move somewhat uncomfortably between satire and expressions of love, are only loosely cyclic. Their one unifying feature is the distinctive alternating rhyme scheme of the ghazal: AA BA CA DA. Schoeck asserts musical connections through thematic reminiscences and connecting interludes; there are also moments of tonal resolution. For example, material from the first song reappears in the last, initially through the use of similar dotted rhythms, then through a lush reworking of the opening melody. A last reminiscence of the dotted theme is scattered across the instruments, and brings the cycle to a close.

Over the next thirty years Schoeck would go on to write over a dozen more song cycles, not to mention hundreds of independent Lieder. He maintained a preference for nineteenth-century poets, with the notable exception of his friend and fellow countryman Hermann Hesse, whose verses Richard Strauss would choose for some of his *Vier letzte Lieder* (1948).[27] The outbreak of war increased Schoeck's sense of isolation (despite Swiss neutrality he kept links with Germany, in part because his wife came from there) and despite his later promotion by Fischer-Dieskau he is rarely remembered today. However, Schoeck is included here not merely as a reminder of the backwaters of music history. His belief in the concept of cycles, approach to text setting, and exploration of tensions between old and new musical styles, would be preoccupations of composers of song cycles for the rest of the century.

English pastoralism

The question of tradition became increasingly urgent for English composers at the beginning of the twentieth century. Some commentators have seen the turn to folk song around this time as an attempt to reassert conservative values, a kind of Edwardian buttoning up after *fin-de-siècle* decadence, cosmopolitanism and urbanism.[28] As in other countries, folk song, or music like it, was taken as a route through which to engage with lost landscapes and past times, and to assert national identity. However, the politics of the pastoral were no more straightforward in Britain than elsewhere, as was apparent in the rise in popularity of a collection of *faux*-folk poems written by a University of London professor of Latin.

The appeal of A.E. Housman's *A Shropshire Lad* (1896) has been credited to its ability to give voice both to nostalgia for a pre-industrial age and to 'a bleak awareness of impermanence in a post-Darwinian, incipiently Freudian, godless and faithless world'.[29] The poems express the city dweller's desire to return to the countryside of his youth, against a tragically – and erotically – charged backdrop of war.[30] The soldiers of Housman's poems were leaving for the Boer War, but quickly became comrades of those enlisted to fight for Britain in 1914: *A Shropshire Lad* was a favourite among educated soldiers in the trenches, a way to keep hold of their corner of England. The poems had already attracted attention from composers: among numerous settings of individual songs there were cycles by Arthur Somervell (1904), Ralph Vaughan Williams (1909) and George Butterworth (1912). Subsequently, composers continued to be drawn to Housman, though with a keener ear to the poems' darker undertones. War had taken its toll: Butterworth had been killed on the Somme, and poet-composer Ivor Gurney, who composed two Housman cycles back-to-back in 1919 (*Ludlow and Teme* and *The Western Playland*), was suffering from shell-shock.

A debate between critics in *The Musical Times* in summer 1918, ostensibly over the relative quality of some *Shropshire Lad* settings, reveals some of the political and aesthetic issues surrounding the cultivation of an English song tradition. On one side was Edwin Evans, who thought Vaughan Williams's *On Wenlock Edge* a landmark piece faithful to Housman's spirit; on the other was Ernest Newman, who accused Vaughan Williams of 'egregious artistic falsities'.[31] Discussion became particularly heated over the setting of 'Is my Team Ploughing?', which Housman considered his best, though 'not the most perfect', poem.[32] The ghost of a young man has returned to his village: he asks his still living friend if they farm and play football as they did before, and whether his girl remains in mourning. Their dialogue is made up of regular rhyming quatrains. As is often the case in Housman's poems, the neatness of the verse structure belies the harsh message of the ending:

> 'Is my friend hearty,
> Now I am thin and pine,
> And has he found to sleep in
> A better bed than mine?'

> Yes, lad, I lie easy,
> I lie as lads would choose;
> I cheer a dead man's sweetheart,
> Never ask me whose.[33]

The challenge for composers was how to distinguish between the living and dead. According to Newman, the most successful version was by Butterworth, who allowed them to speak in the same idiom, 'as two Shropshire lads should do': they both sing folk-like melodies to simple accompaniment but inhabit different registers – the contrast between high and low suggesting 'the ghostly remoteness of one interlocutor and the flesh-and-blood quality of the other' (Example 8.3).[34] On realising the implication of the final lines, the song comes to a harmonically inconclusive end. Vaughan Williams's version, on the other hand, devises what Newman considered a melodramatic conclusion.

Vaughan Williams's cycle was scored for voice, string quartet and piano: for the ghost's verses, the instruments are marked *pianissimo* and to be played with mutes and pedal; the voice is marked to be sung 'quasi da lontano' – as if from a distance. Despite being an avid collector and arranger of folk music, Vaughan Williams's own songs never used a traditional melody. Initially the ghost's verses are folkish, with the answers he receives more full-blooded in harmony and accompaniment. Indeed, according to Newman, the friend's responses are far too agitated, especially at the end, where the expressive setting of 'I cheer a dead man's sweetheart' is 'hurled ... at the ghost's head with a noise and an agitation that would let the most stupid ghost that ever returned to earth into the secret' (Example 8.4).[35]

At stake was whether Vaughan Williams's music could be considered representative of a national musical tradition. His orchestration bore the influence of French composers Ravel and Debussy, but that did not concern Evans or Newman – the

Example 8.3 George Butterworth, *Six Songs from 'A Shropshire Lad'*, no. 6, 'Is My Team Ploughing?'

Example 8.4 Ralph Vaughan Williams, *On Wenlock Edge*, no. 3, 'Is My Team Ploughing?'

former seeing it as healthy cosmopolitanism, the latter unconvinced that any composer belonged to a national tradition; one musician, he claimed, could not speak for an entire population. Although many composers sought solace in pastoral topics during the interwar period, there continued to be anxiety among critics over the appropriateness of expressing English identity through allusions to folk song, which was thought to have little relevance to modern life. In *Music Ho! A Study of Music in Decline* (1934), the critic Constant Lambert complained that combining modal folk tunes with modern harmonies, as Vaughan Williams's setting of 'Is My Team Ploughing?' had done, was like 'an unfortunate yokel in the dock' being prosecuted by a 'cynical barrister'; a London bus conductor, if he sings at all, is more likely to sing 'a snatch of "Love is the Sweetest Thing"' in an imitation American accent than the folk song 'Hugh the Drover'.[36] It would be better for composers, Lambert continued, to escape their 'rustic arbour' to create 'something less nostalgically consoling but more vital'.[37]

The most notable British song-cycle composer to emerge in the 1930s, Benjamin Britten, did not entirely escape that rustic arbour. *Serenade* (1943) for tenor, solo horn and strings, was the first English-language cycle he wrote for Peter Pears, and

Example 8.4 (*cont.*)

the work with which many consider him to have found his voice before the success of his opera *Peter Grimes* (1945). It has also been said to exhibit 'a kind of shadowed pastoralism'.[38] War, again, makes its presence felt. Britten had only recently returned to England from America, and had registered as a conscientious objector, his case supported by statements from Vaughan Williams, among others. The legacy of the older generation of pastoralists can be heard in the orchestration of the *Serenade*, and in Britten's combination of modal and extended diatonic harmonies.[39] 'The shadows now so long do grow', to borrow from the first song (a setting of seventeenth-century poet Charles Cotton's 'Pastoral'), in the recurring theme of death: the bugle's echoes at the end of 'Nocturne' (Tennyson) are left 'dying, dying, dying'; the rose of William Blake's 'Elegy' is sick; the anonymous fifteenth-century 'Dirge' repeatedly hopes 'Christe [will] receive thy saule'; and, finally, John Keats's 'soft embalmer of the still midnight' is asked to 'seal the hushed casket of my Soul'. The horn solo that provides a prologue and epilogue is reminiscent of the military salutes played over soldiers' graves, now heard for the casualties of a second, still more brutal, world war.

Example 8.4 (*cont.*)

Hindemith, *Marienleben II*, Strauss, *Vier letzte Lieder*

Ruins, rubble and burnt-out shells: Europe in 1945 was almost unrecognisable.
The four-storey, fifteenth-century tower in Frankfurt in which Hindemith had lived
while he completed the first version of *Das Marienleben* was severely bombed in
1943. By that time the composer was in the United States, having emigrated there
three years earlier. But he returned to Europe for a concert tour in 1947–8 and it
seems that performances of some of his earlier works, including *Das Marienleben*,
turned his thoughts to revision.

Hindemith had revisited the song cycle soon after its premiere in 1923 and again in
the late 1930s, trying to diminish the stylistic disparity between its parts, and making
small technical improvements.[40] The revisions of the 1940s were more profound.
Hindemith now felt that the first version of *Das Marienleben* lacked what he called
an ethical dimension. In order to create 'a noble music' of serenity he reworked,
and even rewrote, some of his earlier settings; motivic connections were made
clearer and more consistent, and dramatic and expressive highpoints were shifted in

accordance with his rereading of Rilke's verses.[41] The choral quote that began 'Mariä Verkündigung', for instance, had been reharmonised in 1937, to remove some of the harshness of the previous version; in 1941, it was replaced with entirely different music (Example 8.5).[42] The passacaglia of 'Die Darstellung Mariä im Tempel' ('The Presentation of Mary in the Temple') was retained, but the vocal part rewritten and, while the penultimate section of the final song was still designed as a theme and variations, its canonic variations were excised along with other instances of polyphonic writing elsewhere in the cycle.

The only song not to be touched was the twelfth, 'Stillung Mariä mit dem Auferstanden' ('Consolation of Mary with Christ risen'), perhaps because – coincidentally – it chimed with Hindemith's new theory of tonal symbolism. It is in the key of E, which, as Hindemith explained in his lengthy preface to the revised version, represents the essence of Jesus. Hindemith proposed that particular tonal areas could represent emotions and even mental concepts (he admitted that this scheme worked best when listeners were given guidelines by the composer). Thus, in *Das Marienleben II*, Mary is represented by B, providing dominant preparation for the arrival of her son in E; A indicates the presence of the heavenly and divine (mostly angels); C eternity; D trust and confidence; E♭ the 'greatest purity', identical with death; and G the idyllic; C♯, or D♭, embodies what is 'irrevocable, stiff and determined'; F, as the tritone from B, connects with everything fraudulent and short-sighted; F♯ recognises the insignificance of everything when confronted with the sublime and incomprehensible; A♭, or G♯, signifies our inability to grasp what lies beyond our comprehension; and B♭ stands for human resistance to the acceptance of all miraculous events. By aligning tonality and poetic content in this way, Hindemith implied, the cycle gained a still stronger sense of coherence.

The emphasis on tonal organisation in *Das Marienleben II* was a direct attack on the twelve-note compositions of Schoenberg and his followers, from whom Hindemith felt isolated. Although there are not many recordings of the earlier version, many performers preferred its vitality, even its flaws. In comparison the revision felt too abstract, its preface's emphasis on nobility and calm at odds with how the post-war period was being experienced by those who, unlike Hindemith, had not been able to contemplate aesthetics from the safe haven of Yale University. Again, then, we have an example of a song cycle being viewed as a kind of retreat from the world.

Hindemith was not the only composer to find that his onetime home had been destroyed by the war. A British correspondent reported that he had stayed at Richard Strauss's old villa on Vienna's Joaquimgasse: 'the composer's furniture was smashed, his library looted, and we slept on his parquet floor'.[43] The bombing of the German city of Dresden by British and American forces on 14 February 1945 must also

Example 8.5 Paul Hindemith, *Das Marienleben* (1948), no. 3, 'Mariä Verkündigung' ('The Annunciation'). 'It wasn't an angel entering (understand), that frightened her.' Trans. Stokes, *The Book of Lieder*, p. 133.

have hit the heart of the octogenarian composer hard. Dresden had been the site for many high-calibre performances and premieres of his music, from early instrumental works to operas from *Feuersnot* (1901) to *Dafne* (1938). Come the end of the Second World War, Strauss found himself under investigation (and eventually cleared) by the de-Nazification tribunal in Munich. He also busied himself with attempts to reactivate cultural activities in a Europe whose history seemed buried in rubble.

Strauss's son Franz attempted to divert his father's attention back to composition, particularly to Lieder. Eventually he returned to a sketch for an Eichendorff setting, 'Im Abendrot' ('At Twilight'), which he completed by May 1948. In September of that year he presented his daughter-in-law with three more songs, this time settings of the contemporary Swiss writer Hermann Hesse. With characteristic understatement, he told her 'Here are the songs your husband ordered'.[44]

Strauss returned in these songs to the large orchestra he had favoured in his youth. Two instruments stand out: the flute, which brings 'Im Abendrot' to a close with lark trills, and conjures a joyous bird chorus in 'Frühling' ('Spring'); and the violin, featured as a soloist as the soul takes flight in 'Beim Schlafengehen' ('While Going to Sleep'). The violin line dovetails with the voice as it had in Strauss's orchestral Lieder before but, for once, the composer did not have a singer to hand – if he had a voice in mind, it may have been the memory of his wife's glory days. 'We have gone through crisis and joy hand in hand', begins 'Im Abendrot' ('Wir sind durch Not und Freude / Gegangen Hand in Hand'); now the couple will rest. Strauss altered the poem's question 'Ist das etwa der Tod?' ('Is that death?') to 'Ist dies etwa der Tod?' ('Is this death?'). A motive from his 1890 tone poem *Tod und Verklärung* (*Death and Transfiguration*) spreads through the orchestra, perhaps indicating that he was the one asking the question (Example 8.6).

Shortly before he died, Strauss wrote to soprano Kirsten Flagstad asking her to premiere the songs. She did so at the Royal Albert Hall, London on 22 May 1950, accompanied by the Philharmonia Orchestra conducted by Wilhelm Furtwängler. The order then was 'Beim Schlafengehen', 'September', 'Frühling' and 'Im Abendrot'. The publisher Ernst Roth, working for the English firm Boosey and Hawkes, subsequently gave the songs the title *Vier letzte Lieder* (*Four Last Songs*), and put them in their now familiar order, which accentuates their concern with the death of nature. 'Frühling' and 'September' seem to follow the passing of the seasons, with 'Beim Schlafengehen' and 'Im Abendrot' completing a more final journey.

The sense that these four songs were Strauss's farewell to the world cannot be avoided.[45] There is also a strong feeling of nostalgia for a particular kind of music and, with it, a particular Europe. It is no small irony that these very German songs were not premiered in Dresden, Munich or Berlin, but in London. Strauss had been celebrated in that city not long before.[46] The 'pink and upright' composer (as *The Manchester Guardian*'s music critic Neville Cardus rather delightfully described

Example 8.6 Richard Strauss, *Vier letzte Lieder*, no. 4, 'Im Abendrot' ('At Sunset'). 'Could this perhaps be death?' Trans. Stokes, *The Book of Lieder*, p. 563.

him at the time) had attended a festival of his music at the Drury Lane Theatre in 1947.[47] Several critics there were struck by the sense of history evoked by hearing Strauss's music again. This was, after all, a composer who had made his name before the First World War. Now, it was conjectured, he would gain a third generation of admirers: 'boys and girls to whom he is a legend rather than a contemporary figure will with astonishment watch those sparse and unpretentious gestures unloose that slick orchestral opulence which was so shocking and enticing to their grandparents

Example 8.6 (*cont.*)

Example 8.6 (*cont.*)

and so sweetly soothing to their parents'.[48] From shocking and enticing to sweetly soothing: there could be no clearer death toll for an era.

After the Second World War, for understandable reasons, many composers were unwilling to engage with musical genres closely allied to the Austro-German musical tradition: we might even say that the song cycle died with Strauss's *Vier letzte Lieder*. The genre has, of course, enjoyed an afterlife, evident in the many examples to be explored in Chapter 10. Yet it is interesting that, even if we take the question of nationality out of the equation, the majority of song cycles produced in the second half of the twentieth century remained traditional in outlook. They continued the trends established during the 1920s and 30s: the historical awareness demonstrated by Krenek's *Reisebuch*; the emphasis on musical coherence by Pfitzner and Hindemith; the sense that through the song cycle composers could retreat to imaginary landscapes far from the horrors of the modern world (the English pastoralists). A possible reason behind this conservatism, perhaps surprisingly, was technological: the arrival, following the war, of the long-playing record. The LP not only transformed how song cycles were listened to but also, as the next chapter discusses, determined a canon of song cycles drawn from nineteenth-century repertoire. Not insignificantly for general perceptions of the song cycle, the work most often recorded expressed a kind of emotional desolation that now seemed timeless: Schubert's *Winterreise*.

Chapter 9

Performance

The twentieth century

A sense of the rapidity with which recording and broadcasting technology developed during the twentieth century, and the impact those changes had on concert and listening practices, can be gained from the careers of two of the most famous and influential Lieder singers of the time: the mezzo-soprano Elena Gerhardt, whose recording career lasted from 1907 to 1947, and the baritone Dietrich Fischer-Dieskau, who made his first recording of *Winterreise* in 1947 and his last in 1990. Both were German, and both enjoyed international careers, indicating the extent to which not only improved travel and communication networks, but also new modes of musical dissemination such as sound recording and radio broadcasts helped expand audiences.

Spotted during her last year as a student by the conductor Arthur Nikisch, then Director of the Leipzig Conservatoire, Gerhardt gave her debut recital at Leipzig's Kaufhaus Hall on her twentieth birthday, 11 November 1903. She sang a selection of Lieder by Beethoven, Schubert, Schumann, Wolf, Brahms, Liszt, Tchaikovsky, Richard Strauss, Engelbert Humperdinck and now less well-known composers such as Robert Franz and August Bungert. As was typical of the time, she shared the programme with a solo violinist; indeed, on her early tours she was, as she put it, supporting artist to bigger-name instrumentalist-composers such as the violinist Eugène Ysaÿe, or pianists Teresa Carreño or Max Reger. After a few attempts at singing in opera Gerhardt decided on a concert career, and she became one of the first female singers to specialise in Lieder performance (her main rival was the Dutch mezzo-soprano Julia Culp). Her association with Nikisch, who became her sometime accompanist, or conducted the orchestras with which she sang, no doubt accelerated her early career. As a duo they toured Europe, Russia and the United States to great acclaim: an indication of their popularity is the wide range of venues in which they appeared; from city concert halls to provincial music societies, 'at homes' and even seaside resorts.

In 1907 Gerhardt and Nikisch made their first Lieder recordings. Acoustic or mechanical recording, as it became known, had been around for twenty years; while commercial interest was growing, the technology was still extremely limited. Musicians had to perform into a recording horn that funnelled their sound to a mica or glass membrane (a diaphragm), vibrations from which caused a stylus to cut grooves into a disc (subsequently copied onto a resin called shellac for distribution).[1] Voices recorded better than the broader resonances of a piano, though Gerhardt discovered that the technology was not capable of picking up her carefully calibrated dynamic range: softer passages were lost, while singing too loudly could cause the recording apparatus to over-react and damage the master. The relatively short duration of songs made them better suited to recording than longer works: in the first decade of the twentieth century, most discs only lasted around two minutes, and musicians cut works accordingly.

Nikisch died in 1921, by which time Gerhardt had established collaborations with other fine accompanists (Paula Hegner, Coenraad Bos) and a reputation all her own. By the middle of the decade she was regularly recording Lieder for HMV. In 1926 she made her first electrical recording. Electrically amplified microphone systems allowed for a wider range of sounds to be captured, improving the overall quality and sensitivity of recordings. While many recordings were made in studios, music could also be recorded in concert halls, bringing to discs an aura of live performance, even if surface noise from the shellac discs still made playback rather crackly. Until recording to magnetic tape was developed in the 1940s editing was not possible: all recordings were made in one take. They documented a live performance, as evident in the report that Gerhardt's recording of eight songs from *Winterreise* captured 'something of the excitement of those *Winterreise* evenings which she gave at the Queen's Hall [London] in 1928'.[2]

The other means by which a sense of live performance could be conveyed was through radio. Gerhardt made her first broadcast in Leipzig in 1928, meeting her husband-to-be, Dr Fritz Kohl, in the process. Whereas gramophone players and records were beyond the means of most people, and purchasers tended to stick to what they knew (new music was rarely available), wireless sets were more affordable (or could be made at home) and gave listeners access to a broad repertoire. From 1922, national broadcasting networks were set up in North America and across Europe. While there were soon commercial stations, organisations such as the British Broadcasting Corporation (BBC) had noble agendas, setting out to provide a cultural education for listeners. In musical terms, this meant introducing the works of the great masters, devoting programmes to particular composers and, most pertinently for our interests, to specific genres, including song cycles. The lecture-recitals of the late nineteenth century in essence now transferred to the broadcasting studio; meanwhile, volumes of gramophone records such as those issued by the Hugo Wolf Society (whose first discs were made by Gerhardt and Bos in 1932) were accompanied by the equivalent of concert programme notes, as well as the texts of songs and their translations.[3]

Only the most idealistic thought that radio and gramophone records would drastically broaden the demographic of classical music audiences; the aim was more to widen the horizons of the moderately educated listener.[4] Records were typically sold by subscription through composer societies, music magazines such as *The Gramophone*, or by record companies (HMV founded a *Winterreise* Society to sell a limited edition of Schubert's cycle by baritone Gerhard Hüsch and Hanns Udo Müller in 1933). Only when sufficient funds had been contributed would musicians go into the recording studio. It was often a struggle to find sufficient subscribers, however, as is apparent from editorials urging readers to give up two cigarettes a day, so they could 'possess records of the greatest living singers singing some of the world's greatest songs'.[5] Possession was considered a vital part of a gramophone recording's appeal: advertisers encouraged a collector mentality among subscribers, assuring them that they would not be satisfied until they owned every work by a given composer, or every recording by a particular performer.[6] Gerhardt herself tapped into this way of thinking when on the outbreak of the Second World War she was no longer allowed to perform in public in her adopted country of the UK (initially the BBC was banned from transmitting the German language).[7] In the interim she recorded, accompanied by Gerald Moore, Brahms's complete *Zigeunerlieder* and three of his other songs, four songs by Schubert and two by Wolf, selling the set of six double-sided 10-inch records by private subscription. According to her memoirs, she needed 100 subscribers to make the project viable. She was delighted to get double that. Even so, such small numbers do not suggest that in the late 1930s purchasing gramophone records of Lieder was anything other than the province of rich connoisseurs.

Gerhardt's final recording was made in 1947, after her retirement from the concert stage: it was of Schumann's *Frauenliebe und -leben*, again accompanied by Moore. The eight songs were presented on three double-sided 12-inch records, reminding us of the continued limitations of the medium: the maximum length of a side was four and a half minutes. Yet the quality and duration of sound recording was about to change, as companies refocused their attention on commercial markets after the war. Also in 1947, Dietrich Fischer-Dieskau made his first recording of *Winterreise*; taking advantage of new technology developed by the Germans during the war, he recorded the cycle onto magnetic tape rather than directly onto disc.[8] Tape had several advantages: it could be set up quickly; it could record for much longer stretches and, most important, the results could be edited, so musicians were no longer limited to one take. Fischer-Dieskau's 1947 *Winterreise* was only intended for radio broadcast, but the following year came another significant technical advance: the first vinyl microgroove records, which played at $33\frac{1}{3}$rpm (rather than 78rpm). The slower playback and the smaller groove size (made possible by using vinyl instead of shellac) dramatically improved sound quality. These new long-playing (LP) records were more durable, easier to transport and cheaper to produce. What is more, each side of a 12-inch disc could now last up to thirty minutes. All this made them ideal vehicles for classical music – especially song cycles.

Fischer-Dieskau's generation was the first to encounter repertoire as much through recordings as through live performance.[9] He recalled attending recitals by the contralto Emmi Leisner in the 1930s, but also admitted to having listened 'over and over' to her recording of Brahms's *Vier ernste Gesänge*.[10] He was aware that, in presenting 'closed programmes' of complete cycles or the works of one composer, Leisner was perpetuating the legacy of Julius Stockhausen and his students Raimund von zur Mühlen and Johannes Messchaert (see Chapter 3). But Fischer-Dieskau also acknowledged that recording had its own history: that the studios at London's Abbey Road, for instance, had heard tenors Beniamino Gigli and John McCormack, and pianists Artur Schnabel, Walter Gieseking and Edwin Fischer before him.

Recording, in other words, had a profound effect on one's perception of time: it provided hitherto unimaginable access to musicians from the past and, as significantly, enabled one to hear the same performance repeatedly. Both factors fundamentally altered musical interpretation, as is evident from the example of Fischer-Dieskau. Listen to almost any Lieder recording from before the Second World War and you will be struck by what seem like wilful eccentricities: changes of tempo, short-winded breathing, wide vibrato, rubato and portamento (not to mention the kind of rewriting discussed in Chapter 3). Gerhardt may have been judged one of the finest Lieder singers of the age, but her attention to text and atmosphere was counterbalanced by what we would now consider wayward tempi and poor intonation ('Colouring the tone will often mean taking the harmonics out of the voice and sitting on the flat side of the note', one admirer discreetly explained).[11] What Fischer-Dieskau and his cohort began to realise was that recordings have a shelf life: they can be returned to again and again, and errors and idiosyncrasies that would be forgotten in a live performance can grab one's attention and ruin the whole.

One of the remarkable features of Fischer-Dieskau's early Lieder recordings, then, was their consistency and correctness, as well as his beautiful tone and crisp rhythms.[12] Some claimed that his diction was over-emphatic (beyond questions of taste this also caused problems for microphones). The softer end of his dynamic range, though, could now be dealt with much better than by earlier recording equipment. Indeed, Fischer-Dieskau's famous *pianissimo* might even be considered a product of spending time in the studio, crafting performances that could be listened to alone, perhaps even on headphones. His claim 'that only the voice (and therefore the soul) and one's facial expression should speak in a Lied' might also reflect the influence of recording technology on concert practice.[13] Earlier singers (including Gerhardt) had tended to use physical gestures: in the studio, everything had to be conveyed through the voice.

Fischer-Dieskau did, however, perform as frequently in concert halls as he did in recording studios (he also enjoyed a successful operatic career). His attitude to the programming of LPs and live recitals complicates any assumptions we might have about the potential for 'definitive' versions of a particular work. It was also to have a considerable influence on post-war attitudes to song cycles. Echoing earlier concert practices (and gramophone company strategies), Fischer-Dieskau advocated subscription series of recitals, to enable audiences to 'listen their way into the style and programme of one interpreter, achieving a better understanding'.[14] Continuing Leisner's practice, he devised Lieder concerts devoted to the works of one composer. On top of that, he carefully arranged his selection of songs according to tonal relationships between them and with concern for the overall dramatic trajectory.[15] In other words, he crafted such concerts into something akin to the song cycles that had been the focal point of his repertoire from the beginning.

Fischer-Dieskau's first public performance of *Winterreise* had taken place on 30 January 1943. At first the auguries were not good: he omitted two songs he had failed to memorise and was interrupted by a bombing raid: the audience retreated to the basement for a couple of hours, after which they returned to the hall and heard the rest of the cycle. The war would determine Fischer-Dieskau's professional fortunes for many years to come. Drafted into the German army, and captured by the Americans, he first performed *Dichterliebe* to a small group of patients and nurses as a prisoner of war in Italy. By contrast, in 1949, he sang *Die schöne Müllerin* to an audience of 2,000 at the Titania Palast, an old movie house in West Berlin: an early signal that with Western Europe's gradual economic recovery would come a rekindling of interest in high culture. In the 1950s, Fischer-Dieskau's career took off. British audiences first heard him in 1951, at the newly established Edinburgh International Festival; by the early 1960s he was big in Japan; between 1955 and 1980, he reckoned, he made fourteen American tours.

Recitals and opera performances were interspersed with multiple recording sessions. Fischer-Dieskau made seven commercial recordings of *Winterreise* between 1955 and 1990, using five different accompanists (Jörg Demus, Gerald Moore, Daniel Barenboim, Alfred Brendel and Murray Perahia), and recorded *Die schöne Müllerin* with Moore four times (1951, 1955, 1961, 1971). He would also make multiple versions of a cycle for the same record company. For example, there were two takes on *Winterreise* for HMV (1955, 1963), three for Deutsche Grammophon (1966, 1972, 1980), one for Philips (1986), and one for Sony Classical (1990). The usual reason given for recording artists returning to the same work was that they felt they had a fresh perspective to offer – perhaps one developed in concert, continuing the connection between live and studio performance.[16] What seems more remarkable is that record companies felt the market could sustain several versions of the same cycle by the same performer. In this case it was a testament to Fischer-Dieskau's reputation, but it was also proof that record companies continued to play on consumers' collecting proclivities – the desire to own everything.

Among Fischer-Dieskau's most impressive undertakings were his recordings of over 600 Lieder by Schubert (with Moore, 1969–72) and almost all by Schumann (with Christoph Eschenbach, 1975–7). Arguably, rather than with Stockhausen in the 1860s, it was with these boxes of multiple LPs, and the various complete versions of *Die schöne Müllerin*, *Winterreise* and so on, that the idea that song cycles should only be heard in their entirety became established. Only in 1971, at the height of Fischer-Dieskau's reign, could music analyst Arthur Komar have written of *Dichterliebe* that 'a totality is implied by the way the songs are usually performed: the individual songs are rarely heard outside the cycle'.[17] It may only have been coincidence that in that same year Lotte Lehmann's *Eighteen Song Cycles: Studies in their Interpretation* was reprinted but it, too, indicated a shift of perspective: whereas her predecessors would have published general treatises on vocal methods, Lehmann now advised the best way to interpret cycles.[18]

The trick to performing a cycle, according to reviews of Fischer-Dieskau, was to 'allow . . . the emotion to continue between the songs, in the intervals'.[19] Lehmann explained:

> Applause between individual songs would destroy the inner absorption. It is for you to make certain that you are not interrupted by applause by holding your listeners bound as if under a spell.[20]

Other famous exponents of song cycles, such as baritone Pierre Bernac, who performed with French composer Francis Poulenc for over twenty-five years, paid similar attention to the effect of silences between numbers.[21] Quiet reverence in response to a live performance of a cycle had been a feature of concert life since the late nineteenth century, as discussed in Chapter 3. Yet with recording there became available an even more extreme model of silent listening, one that could completely avoid the shuffling of feet, coughs and sniffles heard in the concert hall. The run-in between tracks on an LP, and then the cassette tapes of the 1980s and the compact discs of the 1990s, could hold the mood between songs most effectively. (Incidentally, it is surprising how one remembers those timings: sometimes I have found the most striking thing about hearing a cycle live when I am familiar with it from a recording is the way a singer shortens or lengthens the gaps between songs.)

Fischer-Dieskau did not only perform the nineteenth-century Austro-German repertoire: he worked closely with many living composers, such as Othmar Schoeck, Hans Werner Henze, Frank Martin, Witold Lutosławski and Benjamin Britten. He was, though, primarily associated with the Lieder of Beethoven, Schubert, Schumann, Brahms and Wolf; while not to everyone's taste his mode of delivery became something of a gold standard for the second half of the twentieth century.[22] What is more, Fischer-Dieskau's emphasis on the voice rather than the body, on internalised expression rather than theatrical gestures, came to represent a new view of the repertoire. Schubert lost some of his cosy, Biedermeier associations, and became the lonely, vulnerable protagonist of *Winterreise*; *Dichterliebe* shook off the swooping sentimentality of a thousand renderings of 'Ich grolle nicht', and became a study in neurosis.[23] In Fischer-Dieskau's hands, in other words, the song cycle got serious. Although he retired in 1993, performers and listeners are still dealing with his legacy, on recordings and in the concert hall.

Cycles in the new millennium

In a church converted into a concert hall, a mezzo-soprano in crimson evening gown gives a recital of fifteen Schubert songs, a selection from Dvořák's op. 99 (1894) and his op. 55 (1880). The audience follows the words in their programme booklets, instructed to turn the pages quietly and to reserve their applause for the end of each section. It could be Berlin in the 1890s: it was, though, a coffee concert by Bernarda Fink and Anthony Spiri at the Queen's Hall, Edinburgh, on 2 September 2009. On one level the persistence of this kind of concertising is not surprising, given the rapidity with which nineteenth-century performance practice became tradition. On another level, though, the continuation of such recitals at the Edinburgh Festival, or at London's Wigmore Hall, can seem curious, even quaint. They remain a preserve of high art; in Britain this is partly because of language barriers but, more generally, it is because there is scant sense that this is anything other than music to be listened to: unlike chamber music, which has retained some of its connections to amateur performance, Lieder are rarely tried at home.

With classical music audiences ageing even more rapidly than the general population, the need to engage new listeners is increasingly pressing. It is now rare for single songs from cycles to find their way onto albums, or even concert programmes. The record label Hyperion has produced the complete songs of Schubert, Schumann, Richard Strauss and Gabriel Fauré, going further than Fischer-Dieskau by including works for female and multiple voices. However, technological developments have again changed the way we listen to music. Digital modes of recording and dissemination are eroding the complete works ethos of the late twentieth century (to be discussed further in Chapter 11). Listeners can now easily download individual tracks, rather than having to buy complete albums. Shuffle, which makes a random selection from a collection of tracks, has become the play-mode of choice for many individual listeners and on music sharing websites. Internet sites such as YouTube.com provide free access to a huge range of performances – old, new, amateur and professional recordings, videos of live concerts and television broadcasts – but, much like early recordings, these are of limited duration and low quality. All this puts the emphasis back on songs rather than cycles.

There has also been a trend towards reinterpreting song cycles through live performance, dismantling those carefully set-up concert conventions by collaboration with theatre, film, dance and even puppetry.[24] Lovelorn and alone in a wintry landscape, in the late twentieth century the wanderer of *Winterreise* has become an embodiment of isolation and timelessness. Some have underscored the universality of the wanderer's experience by making their own winter journeys: David Pisaro's coast-to-coast version was discussed in Chapter 2; in 2003 the artist Mariele Neudecker made a film to accompany the cycle that traces a journey along the latitude of 60 degrees north, stopping at the Shetland Islands, Helsinki, Oslo and St Petersburg. Snow-covered natural beauty is overtaken by banality: 'a sense of non-arrival, of ongoing movement on a descending escalator or those big, passing ferries'.[25] Schubert's protagonist has also been understood in more symbolic terms. Baritone Thomas Guthrie, for example, stayed in shadow on stage behind a puppet, the purpose of which apparently was to convey the distance between the singer and the character of the wanderer (on tour with guitarist Matthew Wadsworth since 2004), while Simon Keenlyside worked with choreographer Trisha Brown to devise a version of the cycle incorporating three modern dancers (2003). *A Yiddish Winterreise* (2009, bass-baritone Mark Glanville and Alexander Knapp) takes Schubert's work itself as a symbol for the destruction of home and family. A *badkhn* (wedding singer) flees the Holocaust through a winter landscape. With the exception of a translation of 'Der Lindenbaum', the twenty-four songs are taken not from Schubert's cycle, but from Yiddish folk and popular repertoires.

Others have picked up on *Winterreise*'s status as one of Schubert's last works. Opera director David Alden's filmed version (1997) took place in a deserted mental asylum, with tenor Ian Bostridge – in nineteenth-century dress – implied to be increasingly delusional, haunted by images and figures from his past and eventually straitjacketed. The cycle has also been intercut with other works. In 2005, the Long Beach Opera Company spliced *Winterreise* (sung by Erik Nelson Werner) with scenes from Goethe's novel *Die Leiden des jungen Werthers* (*The Sorrows of Young Werther*, 1774). Still more anachronistically, two 2009 productions, working independently, have paired *Winterreise* with poetry by Samuel Beckett. Their motivation in part has been Beckett's own appreciation of Schubert's music, but also the affinities between the cycle and Beckett's desolate landscapes and characters. The Rotterdam-based company Muziektheater De Helling performed *Winterreise* alongside Beckett's poetry, and video installations (voice Gerrie de Vries, piano Ellen Carver). So too did Katie Mitchell's 'One Evening', performed at the National Theatre and the Aldeburgh Festival by tenor Mark Padmore singing a new translation of Müller's poems by Michael Symmons Roberts, accompanied by Andrew West; the actor

Stephen Dillane read poems by Beckett. Mitchell explained that she wanted to use sound effects and film to bring audience and singer closer: '[f]rom six rows back you can't see the subtleties, the flickers of expression'.

Few singers would seem to agree with Mitchell's judgement: on the documentary accompanying Alden's *Winterreise* Bostridge and his accompanist Julius Drake are openly unconvinced by the director's vision while, when left to his own devices, Keenlyside presents the cycle as if 'the audience were not invited', avoiding eye contact.[26] Yet Mitchell's desire to 'see the subtleties' is interesting, for it brings us back, once again, to the tension between theatricality and interiority that divided Schubert's interpreters in the nineteenth century. The question of venue remains important. Director Oliver Herrmann said of his film *Dichterliebe: A Story of Red and Blue* (2000), which stages a performance of Schumann's cycle by soprano Christine Schäfer in a plush Berlin nightclub, that he wanted to return to the salon context of the nineteenth century: in a similar way to Mitchell, to bring singer and audience closer together. In some ways film is the most effective medium to do that, as close-ups give us greater proximity to the musicians than is possible in concert halls or theatres. But there is another, perhaps more important, way in which films such as Herrmann's (and Alden's *Winterreise*) change the circumstances in which we view song cycles. They were not released in cinemas. Instead, they were made available through television broadcasts or on DVD: to be consumed as small-screen home entertainment. It is in this form that the theatrical, experimental song cycle projects of the new millennium most resemble nineteenth-century salon performances.

However, unlike in the nineteenth century, few of these adaptations sample from or curtail the work, or rearrange the sequence of songs. This fidelity indicates just how established the cycle is as a concept nowadays. For all the radical reinterpretations of *Winterreise*, it is more often performed and recorded straight. In the UK in 2009 there were concert recitals of the entire cycle by Matthias Goerne and Christoph Eschenbach, Thomas Quasthoff and Daniel Barenboim, and Wolfgang Holzmair and Andreas Haefliger, among the most famous. With the exception of the last, the accompanists had all played with Fischer-Dieskau, indicating the reach of the baritone's legacy. Similarly, while there were several new recordings there were also two remasters of Fischer-Dieskau (with Alfred Brendel on Philips and Klaus Billing on Audite), and reissues on DVD of concert performances by Christa Ludwig and Hermann Prey.[27] The prestige and popularity of the song cycle in the twenty-first century cannot be separated from the strong performance tradition established, in tandem with recording technology, in the decades after the Second World War.

Chapter 10

Afterlife

The late twentieth century

Oxford, 1972. Britten and the poet W.H. Auden have met for the first time in twenty years. Both are now near the end of their lives and they talk about their reputations. 'I've never wanted to shock', Britten confides: 'I just want an audience to think that this is music that they've heard before and that it's a kind of coming home – even when they're hearing it for the first time.'[1] His words, and the reunion with Auden, are fictional; they come from Alan Bennett's play *The Habit of Art* (2009). The sentiment expressed, however, rings true for Britten's song cycles, and for others from the second half of the twentieth century.

The death of art song had been proclaimed at least twice before (see Chapters 3 and 8); after the premiere of Strauss's *Vier letzte Lieder* in 1950, composers who continued to produce song cycles really seemed to be working in the genre's afterlife. Art song and modernism had already begun to part ways during the 1920s and 30s. Their separation was furthered by the post-war recording industry, which focused on nineteenth-century repertoire, rather than new works. In many ways, cycles by Schubert and Schumann were ideal ambassadors for Austrian and German culture; their relatively small scale, and their focus on the individual psyche (particularly feelings of loss and alienation), aptly contrasted with the symphonic and operatic works that had been used for Nazi propaganda. It is unsurprising that the cycle that seemed to resonate most strongly with musicians and audiences in post-war Europe was Schubert's desolate *Winterreise*.

There is a problem for composers, though, when the strongest model for a particular genre is well over one hundred years old. History had long haunted song cycles: Schubert's legacy troubled Mahler back in the 1880s, and was a motivation for Krenek's return to tonality in the 1920s. Yet after the Second World War song-cycle composition seemed to become, almost exclusively, about dealing with history: musical, political and personal. To borrow Bennett's words for Britten, it became about coming home; or, no less importantly, about where that home might be.

Many song cycles have been written since the mid twentieth century, but the basic principle has not changed: 'song cycle' still refers to a group of songs with a coherent identity usually established by textual and/or musical features. The broadness of the definition perhaps accounts for its persistence. One word stands out, though:

coherence. It is not an attribute commonly associated with late twentieth- or early twenty-first-century artworks. As discussed in previous chapters modernist poets and composers began to fragment representations of subjectivity, of the 'lyric-I'; in the process, the formal limits of works were stretched and, in many genres, snapped; not with the song cycle, however. While, as we will see, radical texts and techniques were incorporated, the idea of the cycle – its 'concept', to look forward to the next chapter – maintained an unfashionable tendency towards coherence. In so doing, the genre kept one foot in the past.

The history of late twentieth-century music as told through song cycles does not, in other words, read as a modernist trajectory, striving onwards and upwards to ever more complex innovations. Instead it consists of troughs and eddies; of composers looking backwards, forwards and sometimes sideways. If a genre were capable of having a late style, the song cycle is in it. The problem is that this means there can be no magic-carpet, forward narrative here; nor can any claims be made for the future of the song cycle. Instead, we have to move back and forth between decades, to consider examples of the old, the new and the late side by side.

A road map will be helpful. We will start with the song cycle's Austro-German tradition, then consider what constitutes the radical branch of song cycles, including the impact of technology on vocal performance, and expanded forms. Finally, we will examine why some cycles produced towards the end of composers' careers deserve the label late style, and how that reflects more generally on the current status of song cycles. Choosing such selective, thematic viewing points means that not every composer of song cycles is represented here. For instance, there has not been space for Elliott Carter's contributions or for those by the prolific Ned Rorem, among many others. Readers may well take issue with what has been included as well as excluded, which is as good a starting point as any for discussion about the position of song cycles today.

Ancient voices

Those who continued to produce song cycles in the early 1950s tended to have begun their association before the War (Hindemith, Schoeck, Poulenc, Britten) or were somehow removed from the Austro-German tradition. The most notable arrivals among song-cycle composers of the early 1950s were British (Michael Tippett) and American (William Grant Still, Aaron Copland, Samuel Barber and Ned Rorem).[2] The language divide was significant and political: few braved setting German texts; those that did were self-conscious.

For example, it was only after having essayed cycles in French (*Les Illuminations*, 1940) and Italian (*Seven Sonnets of Michelangelo*, 1943), as well as several in his native language, that Britten set his first German texts: the *Sechs Hölderlin-Fragmente* (*Six Hölderlin Fragments*, 1958). His choice of poet was revealing. Few nineteenth-century composers had chosen Hölderlin's poetry as sources for Lieder; their reputation was tainted by his prolonged mental illness – a factor that, no less crucially for post-war generations, had also made him unacceptable to the Nazis. The fragmentary qualities of Hölderlin's later poems in particular also had affinities with twentieth-century modernists such as T.S. Eliot and Samuel Beckett.[3] Hölderlin thus fitted the bill for composers searching for a German poet who had connections with Romanticism but was also somehow set apart from it.

Interestingly, on setting Hölderlin Britten adopted what musicologist Philip Brett describes as a 'severe Lieder-like style'.[4] Despite the different characters of each song, there are evident motivic and tonal connections. The floating recitative of the third song, 'Sokrates and Alcibiades', is accompanied by chords incorporating all twelve notes of the chromatic scale, while the last number opens with a crunchy canon in the piano.[5] Schoenberg- or Hindemith-like features such as these suggest that the Austro-German legacy was on Britten's mind as he composed the *Sechs Hölderlin-Fragmente* in a way not apparent in his non-German works. The same is true of a number of other cycles written to German poetry, including Hans Werner Henze's multi-genre cycle *Kammermusik 1958* (*Chamber Music 1958*), which incorporates *Drei Fragmente nach Hölderlin* (*Three Fragments after Hölderlin*).

Henze dedicated *Kammermusik 1958* to Britten; its premiere was by Peter Pears and guitarist Julian Bream. Nationalities are worth mentioning here: they indicate the important role musicians played as cultural ambassadors and the complex relationships artists had with their native traditions. Henze had left his homeland of Germany for Italy in 1953, for political and personal reasons. Until *Kammermusik 1958*, he composed according to serialist methods: the technique of choice among post-war composers keen to write music that did not bear the mark of German Romantic history in its harmony or expression. But with the Hölderlin settings Henze began to revisit earlier music: his points of reference with *Kammermusik 1958* were John Dowland, Claudio Monteverdi, Schubert, Schoenberg and Webern. Perhaps in response to the tonal associations of some of those allusions, but also as a further means to reconnect with the past, Henze also began to explore tonality.

The feeling of history breathing down the neck of Britten's and Henze's Hölderlin *Fragmente* goes some way to explain the challenges song-cycle composition posed for those close to the Austro-German tradition. Gradually, more composers began to re-engage with the past: to set poets such as Hölderlin and to refer to earlier harmonic practices, styles and works.[6] However, they found it hard to shake off the feeling that song cycles were museum pieces: attitudes explored in Mauricio Kagel's 'Lieder Opera' *Aus Deutschland* (*From Germany*, 1980), which functions as a (somewhat naive) commentary on the political and sociohistorical reception of song cycles by Schubert and Schumann, interweaving them with, and even morphing them into, jazz and blues.[7] The twenty-seven tableaux are staged as a sort of surreal Schubertiade, with the main characters doubled according to gender, race and sometimes age: *Winterreise*'s hurdy-gurdy man is accompanied by a hurdy-gurdy woman; Goethe is shown as poetess and blackface actor; Schubert is paired with Duke Ellington.

The continuing challenge of how to respond – never mind contribute – musically to the canon of Schubert and Schumann is evident in attempts to recast famous cycles in modern dress. Hans Zender's *Schubert's Winterreise: A Composed Interpretation* (1996) and *Dichterliebesreigentraum* (*Dream of the Round of the Poet's Loves*, 1995) by Belgian composer Henri Pousseur function as both analyses and recompositions of Schubert's and Schumann's works. In each, the original music is clearly present. Zender leaves the vocal line basically intact, but reconfigures the accompaniment for orchestra, which occasionally takes on a life of its own: providing musical commentary by extending passages and making stylistic allusions. The cries of 'Mein Herz' in 'Die Post', for example, are slowed down, repeated, and given luscious orchestral support.

Pousseur's 'paraphrase' of *Dichterliebe*, as he described it, has none of the technicolour beauty of Zender's *Winterreise*.[8] It seems less like a conservation project than a palimpsest: a reworking of the score that obliterates and replaces parts. 'Ich hab' im Traum geweinet' becomes a rhythmic chant for spoken chorus, with references to Schumann's melodies constantly at risk of being dragged into an atonal vortex. The famous postlude is played at first by piano, seemingly with a novice hammering away in the upper register; the orchestra gradually joins in but this is not to be a reconciliatory ending: their reiterations of Schumann's final, languishing phrases are unsettled by a whispered chant from the chorus: 'verschleiert, verweht, verziehn' ('blurred, scattered, forgotten'). The words are not from *Dichterliebe*: they do, however, describe both the sinking of the coffin in the final song and, in broader terms, the musical and historical processes to which the song cycle has been subject.

New voices

'Blurred, scattered, forgotten' might also describe the treatment of texts by some composers from the late 1950s onwards. It is probably unsurprising that the lyric voice of the song cycle did not seem to speak to younger generations; it had already begun to fragment fifty years earlier, most famously in the works of Schoenberg. The legacy of *Pierrot lunaire* was mentioned in Chapter 7; here, we will take up the story, to consider how extended vocal techniques and new sounds expanded the musical language, if not always the form, of the song cycle.

In the early 1950s composers found fresh material through technology: in studio manipulation of recorded sounds such as train whistles, known as *musique concrète*, or in electronic music. Karlheinz Stockhausen's *Gesang der Jünglinge* (*Song of the Youths*, 1955–6) was one of the first works in this vein to incorporate the human voice, although it does so in a very different way from any song cycles so far encountered. The seven-part text was a biblical song of praise by three youths thrown into the fiery furnace. It was read and sung by a boy, whose recorded voice was subject to a number of electronic manipulations, decided according to serial methods: in some sections syllables and words remained clear; in others they were overlapped and distorted, becoming part of a sonic spectrum that ranged from pure sine tones to white noise.[9] *Gesang der Jünglinge* was diffused through speakers around the concert hall, subverting the traditional concert model of directing the audience's attention towards a solo live performer on stage. The audience was surrounded by what seemed to be multiple fragmented voices – a disturbing auditory experience that would be exploited by many composers to come.

Crossover between music produced in studios and that composed for live performance proved particularly fruitful for composers of vocal music in the late twentieth century. On one level, the fixity available through recording seemed to encourage a rethinking of the relationship between score and performance. Composers such as Stockhausen, Pierre Boulez and John Cage sometimes left decisions about when and how to play particular passages to be decided by chance – by the throw of a dice (hence the term 'aleatoric music') or by performers. The central movements ('Improvisations') of Boulez's Mallarmé settings *Pli selon pli* (1957–65), for example, give the musicians increasing amounts of interpretative freedom, until eventually the conductor is instructed to choose between various segments of score. On another level, the manipulation of voices made possible by studio technology fed back into live performance practices, as demonstrated by the extended vocal techniques of Armenian-American singer Cathy Berberian. There have often been creative partnerships between composers and particular singers; think of Poulenc and Bernac, Britten and Pears, William Grant Still and Leontyne Price. But the input of a singer such as Berberian was different: she often determined texts as well as music. What is more, composers' interest in chance and improvisation (which was often accompanied by graphic rather than conventional notation, of which more shortly) gave her much more freedom to choose how she might shape a work – a freedom that had the potential to overturn ideas of cycles altogether.

Cage met Berberian while he was working on a tape piece at Milan's electronic music studios. The work he produced, *Fontana Mix* (1958), cut up and randomly spliced recorded street sounds. There was nothing particularly special about that; Cage had used a similar technique in his *Williams Mix*. He was amused, though, by

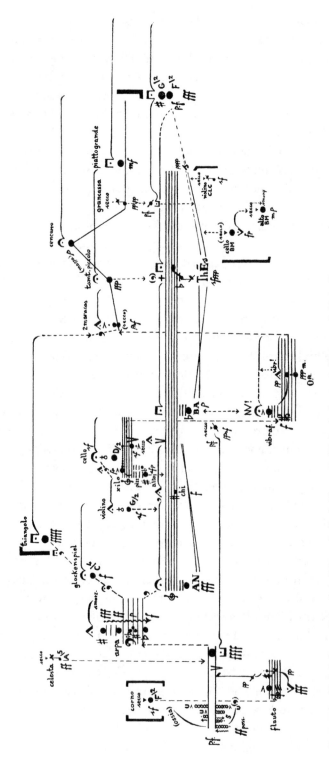

Example 10.1 Sylvano Bussotti, *Pièces de chair II*, no. 7, 'Voix de femme' ('Woman's Voice').

the ability of Berberian – then wife of the studio director, composer Luciano Berio – to mimic the tape montages the composers at the studio produced and devised a piece for her in similar vein: *Aria*. Berberian provided texts in five languages (Armenian, Russian, Italian, French and English), which Cage broke into fragments, then allocated to ten different singing styles, to be chosen by the performer, who was also expected to create sixteen noises.[10] The score represented pitches but did not specify how they were to fit with the text. *Aria* could be performed with or without *Fontana Mix.*

Aria spawned a number of vocal works for Berberian in similar vein. Two among them were self-declared song cycles: Italian Sylvano Bussotti's *Pièces de chair II* (*Pieces of Flesh II*, 1958–60) and Luciano Berio's *Circles* (1960). The categorisation of Bussotti's piece is problematic: it is multi-genre, with a graphic score that does not always specify pitch, rhythm, duration or dynamics (Example 10.1). It is difficult to determine, as a result, what musical qualities define this work as a cycle of fourteen songs, not least because, to my knowledge, there has never been a complete performance (the most often heard sections are 'Voix de femme', a multi-lingual stylistic collage for Berberian, and, for piano, the *Five Pieces for David Tudor*).

Berio's *Circles*, on the other hand, was composed for Berberian's American debut and became one of the most influential models for the late twentieth-century song cycle. The score of *Circles* displays aspects of Berberian's 'new vocality' within an arch-like structure. Berberian chose the poems, by American e.e. cummings: the two outer movements set 'stinging', and the second and fourth 'riverly is a flower'. At the centre is 'n(o)w', a poem that, as the parentheses in the title demonstrate, makes idiosyncratic use of typography, the inflections of which are carefully followed in the score. The setting of the line 'Whoshout(Ghost)atOne(voiceless)O', for example, asks for some words to be sung approximately at pitch (the square-head quavers on 'Whoshout . . . atOne'), for '(Ghost)' to be 'on the breath', and for '(voiceless)O' to move swiftly from whispered *ppp* to a *fff* sung high g (incidentally, the cut circle at '(voiceless)' also means the singer should clap) (Example 10.2). The disintegration of the words into their phonetic components brings them closer to the sounds played by the accompanying instruments.[11] The merging of voice, harp and percussion becomes the keystone of the arch; at the end of 'n(o)w' the singer starts to sing some of the preceding phonetic material in reverse order, prompting the return of material from the second and first songs – in other words, the textual arch is set askew by the music. The structure of *Circles* was also reflected through its physical performance. The two percussionists were instructed to encircle themselves with the three families of instruments (wood, skin and metal); the harp should be stationed between them. At the start of the piece, the singer should stand some way in front but then gradually move to join them – reflecting the integration of their sound worlds.

Example 10.2 Luciano Berio, *Circles*, no. 3, 'n(o)w'.

The virtuosity and theatricality showcased by *Circles* filtered into many subsequent cycles. Berberian's influence can be detected in Italian composer Giacinto Scelsi's *Canti del Capricorno* (1962–72) – twenty songs that grew from improvised collaborations with Japanese soprano Michiko Hirayama – and perhaps even in the extended techniques of Peter Maxwell Davies's *Eight Songs for a Mad King* (1968; see Chapter 7). Its influence was also felt in the United States; in cycles such as George Crumb's *Ancient Voices of Children* (1970), which combined the virtuosic abilities of mezzo-soprano Jan DeGaetani with an ensemble that included amplified piano, toy piano, musical saw, detuned mandolin and exotic percussion (Tibetan prayer stones, Japanese temple bells and tuned tom-toms). The range of stylistic reference is similarly broad: from the eastern-inflected melodies borrowed from Mahler's *Das Lied von der Erde* heard in the final song to the bolero rhythms of 'Dance of the Sacred Life-Cycle'.

Despite their novel timbres, neither *Circles* nor *Ancient Voices* is particularly radical in terms of form: the arch-shape of the Berio, even the retreat of the singer to join the instrumentalists, underlines beginning, middle and end. Nor does their vocal writing fragment the 'lyric-I' to any greater degree than we heard in *Pierrot lunaire*. *Ancient Voices* begins with a poem about a boy who has lost his voice ('El niño mudo', 'The Little Mute Boy') and ends with what Crumb claimed was the 'creative germ' of the project: the words: '. . . and I will go very far . . . to ask Christ the lord to give me back my ancient soul of a child'. At this point the soprano's voice is ghosted by that of a boy, but the point is their union, not their separation.[12] We might even say that the focus on the soprano's performance abilities in works such as *Circles* and *Ancient Voices* emphasises the singularity of the subject: that it is one body creating all these sounds.

Perhaps works that include such unusual sounds simply need clear narrative trajectories, a sense of a final resolution that draws everything together. Yet, as mentioned at the start of this chapter, the way these examples still lean on notions of coherence links them back to traditional aspects of song cycles. Even a work such as Gérard Grisey's *Quatre Chants pour franchir le seuil* (*Four Songs for the Crossing of the Threshold*, 1997–8) for soprano and fifteen instruments, which sounds unlike any other song cycle discussed in this book, has a conventional structure. A 'spectral' composer, Grisey was interested in analysing the acoustic properties of sound, to understand how particular timbres were constructed and perceived. The pulses and microtones thus discovered were then taken as the basis for music made, as Grisey explained, 'with sounds, not notes'.[13] *Quatre Chants* begins with the hiss of brush on bass drum – also the marker of breaks between movements – that becomes unpitched air blown through brass and wind instruments, followed by repeated descending (melting seems a better word) microtones. The initial soprano line (a recurrent, nervy, mordent figure) sits high above the instruments, but their worlds merge when the ensemble imitates the sonic spectrum of her long notes on significant words such as 'mort' ('death'). The *Quatre Chants* all contemplate the approach of death: of an angel, of civilisation, of the voice, of humanity. Civilisation's doom is conveyed by lines from an archaeological catalogue listing texts from Egyptian sarcophagi: '811 and 812: (almost entirely disappeared) / 814: "Now that you rest for eternity..." / 809: destroyed'. The voice sings the entries in a monotone, against a repeated three-note cell played by the harp; its initial consonance is gradually deformed by microtones, as if realising the implications of the inscriptions and their disappearance. The first and last songs are about equal in length, and much longer than the inner two; the solidity of the cycle's structure is weakened by an epilogue with gently rocking berceuse rhythms, but then an open-ended postlude has been practically routine for song cycles since Schumann.

The most novel approach to cyclic form in the second half of the twentieth century, it might be argued, comes from a group of compositions not conceived as song cycles: early minimalist tape pieces. Steve Reich's *It's Gonna Rain* (1965) and *Come Out* (1966) revealed a new way to hear voices that depended on a kind of cyclic listening, sensitive to the development of material from beginning to end. *It's Gonna Rain* was created from a street recording of an African-American pentecostal preacher talking melodiously about Noah and the Flood, played back on two tape loops. Initially the recordings were in unison, but they gradually began to shift out of phase with one another, each distorting the clarity of the other until the sound of a pigeon taking off in the background resembles a drum and, as Reich explains, 'you seem to hear all kinds of words and sound that you've heard before, and a lot of psychoacoustic fragments that your brain organises in different ways'.[14] A clearer example of the connection between such tape pieces and the song cycle is British composer Gavin Bryars's *Jesus' Blood Never Failed Me Yet* (1971), made from a repeated tape-loop of a homeless man singing the title phrase, put to simple instrumental accompaniment. The cumulative emotional effect of the repetitions can make it difficult to leave this music without hearing it through to the end, hoping for a conclusion to its eternal returns.

The length of *Jesus' Blood* varied according to the playback format: Bryars extended it for LP, cassette and CD respectively (eventually it was performed live by singer Tom Waits). The work's open-endedness, the sense of the cycle being continued forever, is not a feature shared by the examples by Berio, Crumb and Grisey, providing further evidence that song cycles are conceived as closed works. There have, though, been attempts to expand concepts of cycles, to create what I call 'meta-cycles' that absorb or are absorbed by other cycles, sometimes in other genres. A nascent version was Olivier Messiaen's *Harawi* (1945), a twelve-song cycle for voice and piano that became the first work in his *Tristan* trilogy (the others were the *Turangalîla* Symphony and the choral work *Cinq Rechants*, both from 1948). Then came Boulez's *Le Marteau sans maître*, with its interleaving of instrumental and vocal cycles (see Chapter 7) and Henze's *Kammermusik 1958*, which includes as well as the *Drei Fragmente nach Hölderlin* for tenor and guitar, *Drei Tentos* (*Three Attempts*) for guitar, three octet movements and three movements for the whole ensemble. The complete version mixed up all the different genres, but Henze also allowed for groups of works from *Kammermusik 1958* to be performed.

It is this last point that is most interesting. Providing multiple versions of a cycle so that it functions as a large-scale work but can also be divided into smaller groupings might seem little different from a singer selecting songs from a nineteenth-century cycle. What is new is that the composers are not encouraging single numbers to be selected, but cycles from within cycles. In other words the cycle may be opened up to incorporate other forms, but it retains a strong sense of its identity as a work: rather like a Russian doll, each group resembles or reminds one of the others.

The 'meta-cycle' thus demonstrates the extent to which memory is built into the form of cycles. Composers have played with this idea through references to music by others (as Henze does in *Kammermusik 1958*) or by alluding to their own earlier works. British composer Harrison Birtwistle first combined instrumental and vocal cycles in *Entr'actes and Sappho Fragments* (1964) – his model, apparently, was Boulez's *Le Marteau* – and has since done so in *Pulse Shadows* (1989–96), which plaits together *Nine Movements for String Quartet* and *Nine Settings of Poems by Paul Celan* (again, they can also be presented separately). More recently *Semper Dowland, Semper Dolans* (2009) alternates settings of John Dowland's seventeenth-century poetry for voice and harp with interludes for string quartet, while *Bogenstrich* (2009) follows a setting of Rilke's 'Liebeslied' with three instrumental movements (a *Lied ohne Worte*, variations and a fugue). 'From two strings draws one voice', Rilke's poem concludes; again privileging this idea of unity.

The conceptual formal expansion of the 'meta-cycle', the exploration of unusual timbres and vocal writing, and an awareness of history are brought together in Brian Ferneyhough's *Études transcendentales* (1982–5), the core of a cycle of seven pieces called, after Piranesi, *Carceri d'invenzione* (*Dungeons of the Imagination*); three of the others were for larger chamber ensembles, and the rest were for solo instruments.[15] As with other 'meta-cycles', while *Carceri d'invenzione* could be performed in one concert, Ferneyhough also sanctioned smaller groupings of the pieces.

Like Birtwistle, Ferneyhough took his inspiration for the structure of *Carceri d'invenzione* from Boulez. The other work that looms in the background is *Pierrot lunaire*. *Études transcendentales* itself is divided into three groups of three songs, each characterised by different instrumental groups taken from an ensemble of oboe/cor anglais, cello, harpsichord and flute. Ferneyhough also exhibits a Schoenbergian predilection for canons, such as the high-pitched one between winds and cello, heard at the opening of the final number. It is the vocal writing of *Études*, though, that best demonstrates how far composers have pushed the timbral experiments begun by the use of *Sprechstimme* in *Pierrot*.

There is little to distinguish voice and instruments by the ninth song. First only the consonants of the text are heard, the singer enhancing their percussive quality by accompanying herself with claves. Each instrument then plays an impossibly virtuosic cadenza before all join together, *fff* and heavily accented (Example 10.3). When the vocalist next enters she sings only vowels, and during the course of her melismatic vocalise the dynamic levels dwindle. Eventually she is reduced to speech. The music becomes increasingly fragmented, its parts uncoordinated. Recollections of earlier songs are separated by pauses that become ever longer until the cycle implodes.

The dismantling of language that takes place in Ferneyhough's song suggests that the composer was not invested in making the texts' meanings clear. I have touched on the connection between radical vocal writing and the potential for it to fragment representations of subjectivity before in this chapter; Berio and Crumb, I argued, did not do more than chip away at the 'lyric-I'. Perhaps Ferneyhough achieves more here. His is some of the most overtly complex music of the late twentieth century; in his hands, the song cycle can have its modernist moment. Well it does, but not to the degree we might expect, for Ferneyhough maintains an idea of the cycle: despite the 'absurdist discontinuity' of the text setting he admitted that he wanted, through the songs, to create 'some sort of broken continuity'. Moreover, he was interested in a 'circle of [poetic] themes … of death, the resonance potential of stones; precious, gravestones, natural stones'.[16] Beneath it all, then, the concept of the cycle holds true. The moribund German poems chosen may be another allusion to the song cycle's heritage, or reveal, according to some commentators, that the composition of *Études* coincided with a period of personal crisis for Ferneyhough.[17] Mortality is a familiar topic for song cycles: there have been examples marking the passing of time, of life cycles, since the nineteenth century.[18] As the next section shows, it is yet another reason why song cycle composers more often look back- than forwards.

Late voices

Benjamin Britten and Peter Pears spent New Year's Eve 1966 in Moscow, with Russian composer Dmitri Shostakovich, his family and friends. After twenty-four hours of eating, drinking, watching Charlie Chaplin's *Goldrush* and playing card games, Britten, 'in furious despair', according to Pears, 'called for *Winterreise*. I saw what he meant, and it was a very good cleanser for the palate and the mind; we sang the first half through to our dear Galya, Aza and Slava [Shostakovich had already

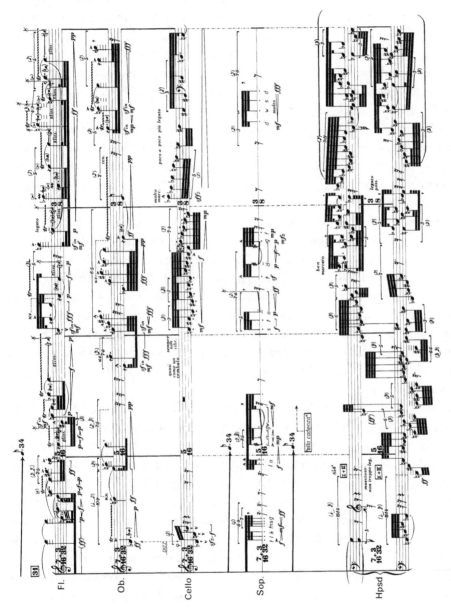

Example 10.3 Brian Ferneyhough, *Études transcendentales.*

gone to bed]. This was as much as I could manage, without practice and with a furious tummy-ache.'[19]

A less than ideal performance situation, then, but nobody was getting any younger or healthier, as Pears's digestive trouble and Shostakovich's early night attest. By this stage Britten had composed his penultimate song cycles, drawing to a close his associations with a genre to which he had contributed prolifically since the 1930s (see Chapter 8). *Songs and Proverbs of William Blake* and *The Poet's Echo* (both 1965) encapsulated some key characteristics. Englishness, and the importance of particular singers, was represented by the Blake settings. The texts were chosen and arranged by Pears but, unusually, the cycle was not for him: instead, it was for Dietrich Fischer-Dieskau. As already apparent in the discussion of the *Sechs Hölderlin-Fragmente* (1958), Britten's engagement with the Austro-German tradition was not only through performance, but also creative. In *Songs and Proverbs*, for example, he continued to develop his own brand of twelve-tone composition (a process begun in his 1954 chamber opera *The Turn of the Screw*); one distinct from Schoenberg's in that the row was used within a tonal context, and often had a symbolic purpose (in *Songs and Proverbs* its only melodic statement occurs at the line: 'To see the world in a grain of sand'). *The Poet's Echo*, on the other hand, reflected Britten's affinity with Russian culture. The six poems were by Pushkin and were set in the original language. Pears recalled that when the final song – 'the marvellous poem of insomnia, the ticking clock, persistent night-noises and the poet's cry for meaning in them' – was performed in the Pushkin house and museum, '[h]ardly had the little old piano begun its dry tick tock tick tock, than clear and silvery outside the window . . . came ding, ding, ding, not loud but clear, Pushkin's clock joining in his song'.[20]

Time was pressing for Shostakovich too. He suffered a series of heart attacks in the mid-1960s: while recovering in hospital his thoughts turned to a request from the soprano Galina Vishnevskaya (who premiered *The Poet's Echo*) and her husband Mstislav Rostropovich, for a vocalise for voice and cello. The song cycle he eventually produced, *Seven Verses of Alexander Blok* op. 127 (1967), has been said to mark the beginning of Shostakovich's late style.[21] The label is more easily applied in hindsight than during a composer's lifetime; there was, though, a clear change between the seriously minded Blok cycle and Shostakovich's previous songs in more popular vein. Each of the seven songs makes evocative use of the instrumental accompaniment (Shostakovich added violin and piano as well as words), alternating between voice and strings for gentler passages (songs 1, 3 and 7: 'Ophelia's Song', 'We Were Together' and the end of 'Music'; the exception is the somnambulant passacaglia for cello and piano in song 4, 'The Town Sleeps') and full ensemble for more dramatic numbers (songs 2 and 5: 'Gamayun, Bird of Prophecy' and 'The Storm'). Interestingly, although Shostakovich resorted to the octatonic scale to create the distinctive profile of the piano line in 'Gamayun' (the octatonic scale alternates tones and semitones), the sixth song, 'Secret Signs', makes use of twelve-note rows. The point of reference here, it seems, is Britten, for the row's function is symbolic – it is one of the poem's secret signs – rather than structural.

Before his death in 1975 Shostakovich composed three more song cycles, and a Fourteenth Symphony often classed as such. With the exception of the final cycle, the *Four Verses by Captain Lebyadkin* op. 146 (1974), which in typical Shostakovich fashion provides a satirical coda to the group, their poetic themes continued along shady paths familiar to many artists in their late period: the cruelty of nature; the challenge of creation. What is interesting for our purposes is the way notions of lateness were inherently associated with the genre of the song cycle. In part those associations were structural: as we have seen several times over, the cycle was an ideal vehicle for reminiscence. The penultimate song of the *Suite on Texts by Michelangelo Buonarroti* op. 145 (1974), for example, recapitulates the cycle's opening statement. Subsequently 'Immortality' – a late-style preoccupation if ever there was one – incorporates a theme Shostakovich claimed to have composed as a nine-year-old. Its jauntiness sits oddly with the remainder of the cycle, probably with ironic intent. However, the childish theme also represents a more personal kind of reminiscence: the composer looking back over his life.

The confessional aspect of late style is contentious: typically, there are those who want to read works through an artist's life, or what they might have felt about the end of their life, and those who prefer to sideline personal issues to focus on creative concerns. Shostakovich's predilection for gloomy texts in the above examples has provided grist for the biographers' mills. His turn to the song cycle has also been taken as significant. The increased interest in solo vocal writing he demonstrated in his last decade has been thought symptomatic of his retreat from public life.[22] In other words, the song cycle retained its reputation as a means to express individual subjectivity. Such singularity, however, was now considered less a symbol of modernity than an old-fashioned indulgence. The final cycles of Shostakovich and Britten were not experimental or radical; twelve-tone methods were outdated by the 1960s. They were late works in part because the branch of the genre to which they belonged seemed to have reached its own late period.

The alliance between song cycle and late style has continued.[23] One of the last works by Polish composer Witold Lutosławski was the song cycle *Chantefleurs et chantefables* (*Song-flowers and Song-stories*, 1990), charming illustrative settings of whimsical, childlike poems by French surrealist poet Robert Desnos. By contrast the Desnos text chosen by nonagenarian Henri Dutilleux as the final song of his cycle *Le Temps l'horloge* (*Time, Clock* 2007) speaks in valedictory tones. The poet died of typhus in the Nazi concentration camps; what is known as 'Le dernier poème' ('The last poem') is supposed to have been found on his body.[24] 'I have loved your shadow so much', the persona explains, 'nothing more is left to me of you / All that remains to me is to be the shadow among shadows . . . To be the shadow that will come and come again into your sunny life'.[25] While it can be read as a statement of love, and would thus belong to the confessional mode of late style, it also captures something of the way a sense of history has inflected composers' approaches to the song cycle in recent decades.

Chapter 11

Rebirth

Pop song cycles

Song cycles and concept albums have been compared several times in this book, with examples from Serge Gainsbourg, The Streets, The Who, Joni Mitchell and The Magnetic Fields. The prospect of discussing popular and art songs side by side is daunting, and no doubt will raise some critical eyebrows if not hackles. However, there are a number of reasons for doing so. In many ways the history of the concept album replays, in compressed form, previous developments in the song cycle. They share an impulse towards gathering songs, according to ever grander and more complex themes. They also nurture particular performance and listening habits. It is not simply that the popular version mimics the classical, though. Too often we consider popular and classical music as existing in separate spheres, rather than acknowledging the ways in which they influence each other and, as importantly, influence our ideas about, in this instance, cycles and why they matter.

Musical genres can be classified in numerous ways: formal and technical features, perceptions of musical meaning, audiences, types of listening spaces, the value systems of particular communities, and how the music is distributed and consumed.[1] Variation in a single category can decide between genres. For example, here is one attempt to define the concept album, by musicologist Travis A. Jackson:

> a concept album is paradigmatically an original recorded project that through its thematic, harmonic, timbral and/or sonic materials as well as its lyrical forms (when applicable) can be read as coalescing around a limited set of ideas. Whatever concept seems to permeate the recording, it is...dependent on the recording medium.[2]

Almost all of this could be transferred to a definition of the song cycle. Jackson's description of the creative process raises some controversial topics in popular-music studies. For a start, implicit emphasis is placed on the importance of original composition: unlike standard pop albums, which typically focus on hit singles that have already been released, concept albums are usually structured around a predetermined musical or lyrical (or sometimes iconographic) idea. The question of who decides that structure raises a number of issues about authorship, occasionally resulting in situations closer to the classical model of solo creator than the collaborative practices typical of popular genres. Where concept albums differ from song cycles most clearly is that their composition takes place through recording. As media theorist Marshall McLuhan famously argued, 'the medium is the message'; the concept album's dissemination primarily through recordings marks it as belonging to the realm of popular, not classical music (which even when it depends on recorded sounds still privileges live performance).[3] However, the emphasis placed by musicians and listeners on the compositional integrity of concept albums reveals a similar set of values to those that frame the composition and interpretation of song cycles.

Initially, as in classical music, 'albums' were boxes in which individual shellac records (78rpm), which played for about four-and-a-half minutes, could be collected. The advent of long-playing vinyl records ($33\frac{1}{3}$ rpm) in 1948 transformed the listening experience of classical, jazz and folk audiences, but it was some time before pop musicians took full advantage of the extended format. Record companies were primarily interested in the new 7-inch 45rpm single, brought out the following year by RCA Victor.[4] Mass produced and cheap, the single was affordable by pop's main market of teenage girls; remember that at this stage 'pop' was used as a catch-all term for music that ranged from Broadway show-tunes to the first stirrings of rock 'n' roll, and that crooner Pat Boone had almost as many hits through the 1950s as Elvis Presley.[5] Once manufacturers began to produce more versatile record players that could play all speeds, however, LP sales of pop music took off, fundamentally changing the perception and ambition of pop music.

The standard American pop album consisted of five or six songs on each of its two sides (the British version included seven per side) with the all-important singles – often already released – prominently positioned. The order of tracks was usually determined in the post-production stage by A&R (artists and repertoire) personnel and producers, not the musicians. Typically, the tracks were a mix of original numbers and cover versions. What happened next echoes the way in which publishers – and, gradually, composers – began to produce collections and then cycles in the early nineteenth century (see Chapter 1). The eight *Songbook* albums released between 1956 and 1964 by jazz singer Ella Fitzgerald, each dedicated to a particular songwriter, perhaps came closest to the single-composer model of classical music (think of the *Six mélodies chantées par Jenny Lind* published in Paris, 1855).[6] Then there were 'topical' albums: barbershop quartet The Four Freshmen released a series of albums based around particular instruments (*The Four Freshmen and Five Trombones* (1955), ... *and Five Trumpets* (1957)), ethnic identities (*Voices in Latin*, 1958); or time-honoured themes (*Voices in Love*, 1958; *Love Lost*, 1959). Occasionally they included vocal interludes that enabled smooth modulations between songs. There also began to be albums structured around external narratives, in the form of original cast albums of Broadway shows such as *South Pacific* (the best-selling album in America in 1949–51), which extracted lyric highpoints from the narrative for home consumption, in a similar manner to Schumann's Lieder drawn from Goethe's novel *Wilhelm Meister* (op. 98a). Finally, there were albums that pursued an 'internal plot'. In *The Letter* (1959), devised by composer–arranger Gordon Jenkins, songs sung by Judy Garland were interwoven with a letter read aloud over string accompaniment by movie star John Ireland (and also pasted on the album's cover), which began: 'My dearest dear, I write this letter because I have no other choice. Life without you is intolerable... New York has changed so much since it was ours... As I write to you, and then think back through the years, I hear music. Our life together seems almost like a concert, with music accenting each scene.' The narrative set-up of *The Letter* implies that it is to be listened to in one sitting, as if it were a stage show or radio drama (or, to take a nineteenth-century example, one of the *Liederspiel* versions of Müller's *Die schöne Müllerin*). However, *The Letter* was still geared towards promoting particular numbers as singles, suggesting that the concept of an album was not yet fully formed.

Probably more significant in terms of changing popular perception was an album such as Frank Sinatra's *In the Wee Small Hours* (Capitol, 1955), deliberately crafted to create a particular atmosphere. The newly written title track introduced a sequence of sixteen ballads: some jazz standards, some original. The songs were presented in lush arrangements by Nelson Riddle which created a characteristic, even coherent, sound world for the album: an important step towards the more production-orientated albums of the 1960s. Their lyrical topic was familiar: lost love. Sung by Sinatra, though, they accrued extra glamour: the ex was a film star (Ava Gardner), the friends Hollywood actors and jazz musicians known as the Rat Pack, the dark side alleged links with organised crime. Sinatra had reinvented himself for the mature market, rather than the teenagers he had wooed with light-hearted numbers in the 1940s.[7] All of this made *In the Wee Small Hours* attractive to older audiences who listened to albums in the comfort of their homes instead of dancing to singles. Records may well have been chosen as mood music, but also repaid attentive listening; so too did improvements in sound quality such as high fidelity and stereo. Advertising was geared towards a new market of (mostly male) audiophiles, attracted by technological developments as much as musical ones.[8]

By the end of the 1950s, sales of LPs outnumbered singles in the United States, and pop musicians wanted their share. The relative length of albums nurtured creative ambition, as did developments in recording methods. The conventional view of recording as a document of live performance began to be queried: instead, new sound worlds that could only be created in a studio began to be explored (hence the distinction between studio and live or compilation albums). Producers began to assume more creative responsibilities.[9] One of the most innovative was

Phil Spector, who used unusual combinations of instruments and over-dubbing to create distinctive, expansive textures, which he called a 'wall of sound'.[10] For most listeners, a song such as The Ronettes' 'Be My Baby' (1963) was just a girl-group hit.[11] But Spector's production techniques, his 'little symphonies for the kids', would be a strong influence on what are often counted among the most famous concept albums, although their categorisation as such is in some ways problematic: The Beach Boys' *Pet Sounds* (1966) and The Beatles' *Sgt Pepper's Lonely Hearts Club Band* (1967).[12]

Both bands had formed in the early 1960s. On the surface they were very different. The Beach Boys grew up in California, and brought together doo-wop, *a cappella* vocal singing in the style of The Four Freshmen and rock 'n' roll in songs that celebrated those quintessential West Coast activities of surfing and driving.[13] The Beatles earned their rock 'n' roll stripes playing clubs in their hometown of Liverpool and in Hamburg. However, the courses of both bands' careers reveal the influence the LP format and recording technology had on changing concepts of the scope of popular music albums. Not least significant was a gradual investment in original authorship. For example, The Beach Boys' first album, *Surfin' Safari* (1961) included three covers out of twelve tracks; all the rest were credited to members of the band: Brian Wilson, Mike Love and their collaborator Gary Usher. By their third album, *Surfer Girl* (1963), all tracks except two traditional instrumentals were by the band (and Wilson was credited as sole producer, a role he would continue until he left The Beach Boys in 1967). The Beatles' first album, *Please Please Me* (1963), was essentially a recording of their live set; it is interesting in comparison to The Beach Boys that six out of fourteen songs were covers. On their next album, *With The Beatles* (also released in 1963) the ratio was fifty–fifty. From their third album *A Hard Day's Night* (1964), though, all the songs were written by members of the band: most often by John Lennon and Paul McCartney.

Collaborative creation was typical of popular music: it represented the joint effort of songwriters, arrangers, performers, engineers and producers.[14] The sharing of song-writing duties and so on is often cited as one of the fundamental differences between pop and classical music; the latter has long leaned on a lone creator model. Another distinguishing feature of pop song versus art song is The Beatles' and The Beach Boys' practice of dividing vocal performance between members of a band, thus preventing a single identity or persona from taking precedence: in theory any of them could sing about or understand a particular experience, which served to broaden audience sympathy (see, we all feel this way). A collaborative model for creation seems counterintuitive to constructing an album around a concept, as illustrated by the Beatles' sixth album, *Rubber Soul* (1965). The Beatles forsook straightforward romantic pop songs in favour of numbers more akin to wry short stories, such as 'Norwegian Wood', 'Drive my Car' and the autobiographical 'In my Life' (one catalyst for this shift, particularly for Lennon, was Bob Dylan).[15] In keeping with imagining new protagonists for their songs, the band explored a range of musical genres and instruments unfamiliar to most Western listeners, such as the Indian sitar, as well as distorted conventional instrumental sounds and special effects. This emphasis on narrative and experimentation was one reason why *Rubber Soul* was described as an album to which to listen, rather than dance: a crucial aesthetic turn, as was *Rubber Soul* being seen to mark the band's transition from pop to rock music.[16] What seems more surprising is producer George Martin's claim that the album was 'an entity of its own' rather than 'a collection of singles'.[17] How could such a stylistically diverse, and multiply authored group of songs be considered – in Brian Wilson's words – 'to all belong together'? One reason, perhaps, was that *Rubber Soul* was the first record The Beatles worked on uninterrupted by going on tour. Gradually, pre-recording and studio creation were merging. In the process, a more prominent role was assigned to producers who, much as arrangers had done earlier, could create a distinctive sound world for an entire album. Martin was often referred to as the fifth Beatle, which at least made him part of the group. In the case of The Beach Boys' *Pet Sounds*, though, one band member took over production, which shifted the power balance more towards the lone creator model.

Brian Wilson had found touring overwhelming and from 1964 left the rest of the Beach Boys to play live while he spent his time writing material in the studio (as yet touring and recording were not financially dependent on one another). The album he created in response to *Rubber Soul* in many ways could not have been made outside a studio: indeed, Wilson later said of *Pet Sounds* 'It wasn't really a *song* concept album, or *lyrically* a concept album: it was really a *production* concept album'.[18] A possible reason for Wilson's privileging of production was his lack of interest in the lyrics: he told others his ideas (in this case Tony Asher) and asked for them to be put more poetically. That said, while members of the band came in to record their signature close harmonies and vocal solos, Wilson was lead vocalist on all but one number (indeed, he used multi-tracking on 'God Only Knows' so that all the counterpoint was created by his voice). In other words, the collective persona previously characteristic of The Beach Boys was beginning to be eroded. Most importantly, the musical world of *Pet Sounds* belonged to Wilson; taking his cue from Spector, he and his engineers recorded found sounds (bicycle bells, dog whistles, trains), and combined the usual band set-up of guitars, keyboards and drums with session musicians on harpsichord, strings, woodwind, brass, percussion and theremin. The backing tracks were recorded live onto a four-track, then transferred to one track of an eight-track recording for the rest of the session, making ample use of echo and reverb effects.

The order in which *Pet Sounds* was put together emphasises Wilson's preoccupation with production over songs or lyrics. There was no predetermined narrative.

Three of the tracks were already laid down in some way: a version of the West Indian folk song 'Sloop John B' had been recorded in 1965 but put aside to record the album *Beach Boys' Party!*; the instrumental 'Pet Sounds' was originally 'Run James Run', perhaps because it was intended for a Bond movie; and 'Don't Talk (Put Your Head on My Shoulder)' started out as a wordless chorale. Only after the whole album was recorded did Wilson begin to put the songs into an order, taking into account the two-side format of the LP, which created a natural break. The thirteen tracks of *Pet Sounds* follow a well-worn song-cycle route from young love to its loss. The first side looks forward to marriage (the upbeat 'Wouldn't It Be Nice'), reassures the object of his affections that he's not like other guys ('I'm waiting for the day . . . when you can love again'), and tries to persuade her to go away with him (the instrumental 'Let's Go Away for a While'). The second side begins with 'God Only Knows' – still professing love, though now with qualifications ('If you should ever leave me . . . '). It becomes bitterer as he advises the woman's next lover 'You've got to keep in mind love is here today / and it's gone tomorrow'. The final song finds her attractions fading with time: 'could we ever bring them back once they have gone? Caroline, no'. The instrumental postlude fades out to the sounds of a clanging railway signal and barking dogs. It is an odd encroachment of the real world – a nod towards early recordings' fascination with documenting everyday sounds, perhaps, or to the *musique concrète* of French composer Pierre Schaeffer.[19] But it could also simply signal that life goes on, whatever our disappointments; perhaps it then serves a similar function to the postludes of Schumann's *Dichterliebe* and *Frauenliebe und -leben.*

The rest of The Beach Boys were unsure about Wilson's departure from their established sound and Californian themes. Doubtless, they also recognised that the album was above all his creation. *Pet Sounds* made clear the potential for studio composition – or using the studio as instrument, as it is sometimes explained – to transform notions of authorship. When someone like Wilson could write songs, perform and produce them, the input of other band members began to seem inconsequential. It was also clear from the way *Pet Sounds* was put together that Wilson had distinct aesthetic ambitions for the album: he described it as 'a collection of art pieces, each designed to stand alone, yet which belong together'.[20] We are close to song-cycle territory here. The progression from writing single songs to putting them in collections and finally to arranging them according to a concept, replays the progression from Lied to song cycle during the nineteenth century. And, just as those song cycles became ever grander in scale and design, shifting from piano to orchestral accompaniment, and even becoming symphonies, Wilson – and many of those who followed – was entranced by the prestige of big works. His invocation of 'art' thus has less to do with crossing whatever divides exist between high and low genres than with the expansion of his creative universe.

Ultimately Wilson was disappointed that *Pet Sounds* was not as great a commercial success in the USA as other albums by The Beach Boys. It was, though, popular in other countries, and recognised as setting new standards by other musicians – McCartney in particular declared it a major inspiration. By the mid-1960s, The Beatles were disenchanted with playing live: the extensive travelling was exhausting, the fans screamed so loudly nothing could be heard anyway, and the band were prone to getting into trouble with local authorities – from Imelda Marcos to the American Bible Belt. More to the point, the kind of music they were now creating in the studio, on albums such as *Rubber Soul* and, subsequently, *Revolver* (1966) could not be reproduced on stage, even if they could afford it.

The Beatles gave their last commercial concert in San Francisco on 29 August 1966; in December of that year they began recording material for their new album at London's Abbey Road Studios. It took over four months to complete *Sgt Pepper's Lonely Hearts Club Band*, released in June 1967.[21] Spending so long in the studio would have been unthinkable when they were starting out (their first album was recorded in twelve hours). Now, of course, they had record company EMI's backing to do so, but the extra time taken was also caused by increased technological and musical experimentation.[22]

The stylistic diversity and collaborative creative processes that had characterised *Rubber Soul*, and which I suggested undercut claims about the album's coherence, were also a feature of *Sgt Pepper*: indeed, the album's variety is one reason why we might query it being labelled a concept album. While individual members usually claimed 'ownership' of a particular track, accounts of how *Sgt Pepper* was put together make clear the extent of teamwork involved in its creation. The idea of adopting an alter ego seems to have been McCartney's, who explained that 'it would be nice to lose our identities, to submerge ourselves in the persona of a fake group'. 'Sergeant Pepper's Lonely Hearts Club Band', the first track, fuses Edwardiana with the heavy rock guitar of contemporary groups such as The Jimi Hendrix Experience and Cream. The introduction of the character Billy Shears, in the final order of the album, implies he is drummer Ringo Starr, who sings 'With a Little Help from My Friends'. From then on, though, there is no obvious narrative to the album until the end; at long-time friend and factotum Neil Aspinall's suggestion, the penultimate track reprises the title song. While this lack of consistency has been taken by some to indicate that *Sgt Pepper* lost its 'concept' in production, it seems from the story of the album's creation that it was never taken very seriously by the band. Rather, 'losing their identity' as The Beatles encouraged them further along the path of story-telling songs ('She's Leaving Home') and songs in or about characters ('Lovely Rita', 'Being for the Benefit of Mr Kite').[23] The Indian *dilruba* (a bowed lute) on 'Within Without You', the psychedelia of 'Lucy in the Sky with Diamonds', and even the barnyard noises of 'Good Morning Good Morning' (responding to an irritating cornflakes commercial) testify to the wide scope of musical styles and lyrical material available to The Beatles by this stage in their career.

If *Sgt Pepper* is a concept album it is, as Wilson described *Pet Sounds*, a *production* concept album. While none of The Beatles had Brian Wilson's studio skills, their long-time producer Martin enabled them to explore a broad spectrum of musical styles and instruments; sounds could also be manipulated by a range of devices such as multi-tracking, overdubbing, fade-ins, reversed playback, varispeed (enabling different takes to be stitched together, and as a means to change pitch and timbre), echo and Doppler effects, and so on.[24] Such editing techniques allowed for not only more complex timbres but also structures to be assembled. The length of tracks increased accordingly. This affected not only the scope of particular songs, but also the way in which albums were organised. The hit singles and fillers model was no longer in play (no singles were released from *Sgt Pepper*, although, as we'll come to later, tracks from the album were played on the radio) and in its place came an approach to the album's overall trajectory similar to some of the song cycles discussed in previous chapters. Tracks of relatively extended duration were carefully placed, functioning as highpoints, interludes or postludes. For instance, the reprise of 'Sergeant Pepper' was followed by the first track to be recorded, 'A Day in the Life'. At five and a half minutes, it was two minutes longer than anything The Beatles had previously recorded. It was also the most ambitiously structured number on the album; it incorporated sections written separately by Lennon ('I read the news today') and McCartney ('Grab your coat') and culminated in a multi-tracked glissando for orchestra (for which Martin turned to aleatoric techniques of avant-garde composers such as Karlheinz Stockhausen and Luciano Berio). The glissando eventually resolves onto a major triad, but the record was still not quite finished, for its run-out groove was filled with gobbledygook; a postlude to the postlude, if you will. Touches like these encourage the view that *Sgt Pepper* was intended to have a clearer shape, and a stronger sense of structural integrity, than found on their previous albums.

Recent scholars have been determined to prove the musical coherence of *Sgt Pepper*, with talk of tonal schemes and motivic cross-references.[25] Such an approach probably tells us more about their listening strategies and analytical methodologies than the creative principles of The Beatles. Unity was felt to be important among listeners at the time of the album's release, but on rather different terms: for many it appeared to capture the psychedelic feel of 1967, the so-called 'summer of love'.[26] *Sgt Pepper*'s immediate influence on other musicians seems to have been threefold: it encouraged elaborate record cover designs, studio experimentation and an approach to album formatting that, if not always clear in concept, nonetheless exhibited a hitherto unknown degree of care over overall shape.

The visual impact of albums took on special significance when recordings became the medium through which new music was first encountered. It was no coincidence that *Sgt Pepper*, which marked The Beatles' retirement from public performance, had the most elaborate cover of all their albums. Designed by pop artist Peter Blake, it showed The Beatles in costume as the titular band, posed between a flower arrangement that spelt out the group's name and a collage of the great and the good. Album cover design might seem irrelevant to musical concerns, but elaborate packaging could encourage purchasers to treat the LP as a precious object; they could pore over the design and wonder why Karl Marx was included alongside Marilyn Monroe and Stockhausen. Another innovation was the appearance of the song lyrics on the inner gatefold, a practice reminiscent of providing audiences at Lieder recitals with the texts to be sung. The cover of *Sgt Pepper* was sufficiently iconic to spawn parodies, one of them Frank Zappa and the Mothers of Invention's *We're Only in It for the Money* (1968), on which the group were shown in drag, between 'Mothers' spelt out in vegetables and a collage of famous and infamous faces.[27] But it was taken as a serious model by many, including The Rolling Stones, who featured a three-dimensional portrait of the band and an impossible maze on the gatefold of *Their Satanic Majesties Request* (1967); and by The Small Faces, the cover of whose *Ogdens' Nut Gone Flake* (1968) carefully mimicked the distinctive label of a Liverpudlian brand of tobacco.

Their Satanic Majesties Request demonstrated the perils of over-indulging in the studio. It was the Stones' first and only attempt at producing themselves, and its experimentation is a one-off in their output. The band added to their usual set-up a full orchestra and a variety of exotic percussion and keyboard instruments (electric dulcimer, mellotron, harpsichord, Indian tablas), as well as a smorgasbord of special effects. The A-side closes by revisiting the first track, 'Sing This All Together': eight minutes of the band and session musicians jamming, replete with vocal drones, speech and shrieks; a minute from the end the original song hazily re-emerges, then disappears again into electronic noise.[28]

The Stones had envisioned *Their Satanic Majesties Request* as a continuous work with no spaces between tracks and interlocking themes throughout, as Zappa achieved with *Lumpy Gravy* in 1968.[29] If we follow the habitual song-cycle hierarchy of privileging musical coherence over poetic links, we might take these examples as among the first rank of concept albums. However, most LPs given that label in the late 1960s earned it because they boasted guiding narratives.[30] For example, the concept of *Ogdens' Nut Gone Flake* had nothing to do with its first side – a fairly conventional selection of different styles – but with the second, which consisted of songs to accompany a fey fairytale devised by comic writer Stanley Unwin. The Pretty Things, a London group, recorded what is usually referred to as one of the first rock concept albums, *S.F. Sorrow* (1968), at Abbey Road while The Beatles were working on *Sgt Pepper*; it included in the sleeve notes, along with the songs' lyrics, chapters of a story by singer-guitarist Phil May charting the life of fictional character Sebastian F. Sorrow.[31]

There are other ways in which the categorisation of some of these albums as 'concept' is ambiguous. One is their relationship to live performance. *Pet Sounds* and *Sgt Pepper* had both been studio creations and, while they have since been heard in concert, they were not while the bands were still together.[32] The Pretty Things, by contrast, performed *S.F. Sorrow* live, with May's story read aloud. While there is a precedent for this in both the song cycle and the concept album – in the *Liederspiel* origins of Schubert's *Die schöne Müllerin*, or in Judy Garland's *The Letter* – the standard reference is to another, even grander, genre: the album has been classified as one of the first rock operas, a precedent for The Who's *Tommy* (1969). The distinction between genres here is especially blurred: rock opera is generally thought to rely on verbal rather than musical narrative; concept albums, on the other hand, can rely on one or the other, or both. In a way, the crossover between them is simply another instance of musicians being attracted to the cultural prestige of big forms – and, no less importantly, of them playing for a wider market. Yet this particular shift between genres was probably not what *The Times* critic (and author of books on Richard Strauss and others) William Mann had meant when he predicted that, in the wake of *Sgt Pepper* '[s]ooner or later some group will take the next logical step and produce an LP which is a popsong-cycle, a Tin Pan Alley *Dichterliebe*.[33] Or what American singer Judy Collins envisioned when she foresaw, with true 1960s spirit, that 'we will have pop song cycles like classical Lieder, but we will create our own words, music, and orchestrations, because we are a generation of whole people.[34]

The album of the late 1960s that best suited their brief was, in fact, called *Song Cycle* (1968).[35] It was by American Van Dyke Parks, who had worked as lyricist on The Beach Boys' abandoned post-*Pet Sounds* project, *Smile*.[36] Parks did not quite create all the words and music (two tracks were covers of songs by Randy Newman and Donovan), but he did produce an idiosyncratic sound world, making full use of the studio (doubtless to the record company's chagrin: *Song Cycle* has the reputation of being one of the most expensive albums ever made, and while critically lauded it was not a commercial success). The twelve songs are loosely connected by Californian locale: they wander from Vine Street to Palm Desert, Laurel Canyon Boulevard and back, along the way making character sketches of widows, migrant farm workers and parents waiting for their soldier son to come home. Utopianism – the dream of life in California – and disillusionment (particularly in response to the Vietnam War), are broader concerns.[37] Most striking is the range of musical styles. *Song Cycle* begins with whirring guitars, as if it has suddenly tuned into a bluegrass station; they are replaced by schmaltzy crooning to orchestral accompaniment (Parks commenting 'That's a take, but I'm sad to say it never made the grade'), then honky-tonk piano ('I sold the guitar today'), then a passage for chamber orchestra with some jazz-inflected repeated rhythms before, finally, beginning the Newman cover, with orchestra – and a passing allusion to Beethoven's 'Ode to Joy'. The self-consciousness with which Parks comments on the album's making, along with a complicated musical patchwork that perpetually breaks down the structure of individual songs, demonstrates not only his historical awareness of American popular music but also an artistic ambition betrayed by adopting the bland but, in this context, aesthetically loaded title.

'Rock music is finally becoming composed music', began a review of *Song Cycle* in the newly founded magazine *Rolling Stone*.[38] It was an important transition. Many musicians – and critics, such as those who wrote for *Rolling Stone* – were keen to view rock as a 'legitimate art form' rather than mere entertainment.[39] Attempts to compare classical and popular music on equal terms were prone to accusations of pretentiousness, as critics who hailed The Beatles as their generation's Schubert swiftly discovered. Yet it is obvious from the examples discussed above that many of the technical features and aesthetic qualities that characterised what set itself up as serious rock music were related to those that defined what was considered serious classical music (technical innovation, narrative invention, connections between the constituent parts). The common ground between rock and classical genres here is indicated by the use of song cycle and concept album as interchangeable terms.[40] The most significant distinction between them had to do with the connections they make between work and recording. While putting song cycles onto disc changed the way in which they were listened to, as discussed in Chapter 9, there continued to be multiple takes on a work such as *Winterreise*. A concept album, on the other hand, was designed for the recording medium, and need only exist in that form (subsequent live renditions of some of these albums will be discussed in a moment).

Recording of any kind facilitates repeat listening. It is worth drawing attention again to the fact that listeners determine an album's concept as much as its creators. An example of this process is described by musicologist Lloyd Whitesell, who remembers his college roommate 'lying on the living room couch in the dark, listening to *Blue* for the umpteenth time. This time, though, he told me he had had a revelation: Joni [Mitchell] intended the album to be a song cycle'. The anecdote neatly demonstrates how such definitions can be, as Whitesell puts it, 'decided at the point of consumption', and can transform perceptions of the original.[41]

Joni Mitchell was neither a rock nor a studio-based musician: she belonged to the singer-songwriter tradition of the folk scene. That, and her gender, suffices to distinguish her from the majority of examples in this chapter.[42] Although other Joni Mitchell albums make more deliberate musical connections, there are still a number of reasons to hear *Blue* as a cycle. The ten songs were written during a break from live performance and so, unlike other albums, first became known to audiences in recorded form: fewer singles were released from *Blue* than the preceding *Ladies in the Canyon* (1970).[43] Whitesell refers to the 'melancholy and bittersweet tones' of *Blue*, along with its multiple references to the colour of the title, as the main way in which the album is unified.[44] A consistent sound world is also created through instrumentation: a bass makes an appearance on one track, pedal steel on two, and percussion on three, but mostly emphasis is placed on Mitchell's voice, accompanied by piano, dulcimer and guitar.

Mitchell admitted she wrote the songs on *Blue* in the aftermath of a painful break-up. Her emotionally direct lyrics, and the album's relatively stripped-down instrumentation, were very different from the fantasy narratives used by The Small Faces or The Pretty Things and convey a greater sense of ownership over their material. In truth she was no less dependent on collaborative creation during recording than members of a band – other musicians, engineers and producers still had important parts to play. Another album from 1971, Marvin Gaye's *What's Going On*, is sometimes credited with destroying the myth of single authorship in popular music, and with being the first soul concept album. Motown had never prioritised albums, never mind concept albums, preferring to concentrate on the (then) more profitable singles market. Still more significantly, for the first time on a Motown record, all the people involved – all thirty-nine of them – were credited. The name of arranger David van DePitte was even on the front cover (albeit in tiny print).

Collaboration had been part of the creative process from the start. The title track was originally by Renaldo 'Obie' Benson, a member of American vocal quartet Four Tops. He had written it after witnessing a skirmish between protestors and police at the People's Park in Berkeley, California, in 1969. His own group were not interested, nor was protest singer Joan Baez, but eventually Gaye was persuaded to make it his own; he worked it over with songwriter Al Cleveland – in Benson's words making it 'more ghetto, more natural . . . more like a story than a song' – and the single was released on 20 January 1971.[45] Two months later Gaye returned to the studio to record the album, which was released in May. The sense of political and personal unease felt in 'What's going on?' had chimed with the experiences Gaye's brother Frankie reported on returning home after serving three years in Vietnam, and the singer's grief over the recent death of fellow musician Tammi Terrell. Gaye asked the question 'What's happening?' of the world around him, and his answers were songs about poverty, racism, police brutality, heroin addiction, environmental destruction and, finally, the redemptive power of love.

The album opens as if overhearing African-American voices welcoming someone home – perhaps back from war. The voices are joined by alto saxophone, drums and bass, which set up the groove before Gaye and the backing singers enter. Famously, the sax line was recorded while the musician was warming up and the overall impression is of improvisation; spoken voices are heard throughout the track, suggesting a fluid boundary between the studio and the outside world. In all this, *What's Going On* contrasted with the glossy production, regular metrical structures, rhythm and syncopation of the standard Motown repertoire from which Gaye had emerged (think The Temptations' 'My Girl'). What is more, there is scant sense of separate tracks. All the songs are interwoven; once the lyrics of one have ended, the instrumental backdrop melts into the next with no sound breaks or fadeouts (this had been achieved by splicing the tracks together and then applying overdubs to the whole album, rather than individual songs).[46] There are also recurring harmonic sequences and themes, the most striking of which is the arching line for voices and upper strings heard in 'What's Going On' at the bridge at the end of the first chorus and at the beginning of the second song, 'What's Happening, Brother'.[47] There is no grand climax; Gaye ends the album by singing its opening vocal line, this time over scattershot piano improvisation; the final track's conga rhythms return, gradually to disappear from earshot.

According to one of its engineers, Laurence Miles, *What's Going On* 'was to be an intimate listening experience. We were mixing it for people sitting in their living rooms, listening to the album straight through' – in other words, trying to nurture the kind of listening our earlier anecdote accorded Joni Mitchell.[48] This was a departure for soul records, which usually focused on dance, and earned it critical recognition: 'ambitious, personal albums may be a glut on the market elsewhere' a *Rolling Stone* review began, 'but at Motown they're something new', before going on to describe how 'gradually the concept of the album takes shape and its wholeness became very affecting'.[49] Gaye's own record company was less convinced of its commercial potential. The crosscurrents between musical aesthetics and racial politics of the early 1970s are too complicated to go into here, but it is apparent that while *What's Going On* proved highly influential in musical terms – not least by encouraging other 'ambitious, personal' records by African-American artists (including Janet Jackson's *Rhythm Nation 1814* (1989), similarly intended to protest against social injustice)[50] – so far as critics were concerned, the genre remained firmly white male territory.

Audience demographics were deliberately taken into account in the USA by a new format of radio broadcasting, album-orientated rock (AOR).[51] New 'freeform' or 'progressive' radio stations from the late 1960s had developed a non-singles chart approach to programming; DJs would play tracks from within albums, and even portions of complete albums. Although initially the mix of styles was eclectic, increasingly they were 'demographically determined', which meant that they turned almost exclusively to rock. It was through this radio association that the term 'progressive rock' was coined. The self-consciously elaborate lyrics and music of British groups such as Emerson, Lake and Palmer, or Yes, seemed ideally suited to the concept album format: whimsical narratives were particularly favoured. Some seemed to take themselves very seriously: see both ELP's concept album *Tarkus* and their virtuosic, tight-trousered live rendition of Musorgsky's *Pictures at an Exhibition*, both from 1971, and Yes's *Tales from Topographic Oceans* (1973).[52] Others tried to introduce an element of parody. Ian Anderson of Jethro Tull, for instance, claimed that the motivation behind *Thick as a Brick* (1972) was to answer critics who labelled them progressive rock, and who had described their previous record, *Aqualung* (1971), as a concept album.[53] They decided to produce something excessively bombastic, he said, and so they did: *Thick as a Brick* consisted of one 45-minute track, a coming-of-age tale relayed in the words of a boy called Gerald Bostock, or 'Little Milton'. The music incorporated a number of recurring themes, fluctuations in tempo and metre and a prominent role for solo flute. The sixteen-page cover was a mock-up of a local newspaper, its articles including the album's lyrics alongside spoof news reports and quizzes.

The absurd aspects of Jethro Tull's quasi-theatrical approach to *Thick as a Brick* were not found on what is often thought the quintessential concept album of the 1970s, Pink Floyd's *The Dark Side of the Moon* (1973). Pink Floyd had concentrated on making albums since their original singer, Syd Barrett, left in 1967 and, in contrast to many of the rock groups of the time, nurtured something of an 'anti-image'. Instead of focusing attention on the performers, they turned the spotlight on the imagery of their albums.[54] The front cover of *The Dark Side of the Moon* shows a prism refracting white light; the back illustrates the reverse. Across the inner gatefold runs a graphic realisation of a heartbeat – the sound that begins and ends the album.

Pink Floyd had developed the material for the album during their British tour of 1972 – it was introduced to the audience as 'The Dark Side of the Moon: A Piece for Assorted Lunatics'. When they arrived in the studio they were then able to lay down the basic structure for the whole album.[55] Much as in *What's Going On*, segues between tracks allowed the music to run continuously.[56] The return of particular musical figures serves to create cohesion, but the more recognisable features of the album's acoustic universe are the recurring sounds that both characterise individual tracks and connect parts to the whole: there are speech fragments, ticking clocks ('Time'), the sounds of a cash register ('Money'), wordless female vocals ('The Great Gig in the Sky'), a saxophone, giggles and, of course, the beating heart.[57] What perhaps distinguishes the 'concept' of this album from many of the other rock offerings from the 1970s is that it did not rely on a narrative.[58] While it is less explicit than the social commentary of Gaye's album, according to one critic the lyrics for *The Dark Side of the Moon* 'analyse the social and psychological pitfalls of the dream of youth culture'; isolation, greed, madness and death are their prime preoccupations.[59]

The success of *The Dark Side of the Moon* and of Pink Floyd's subsequent albums, as well as the popularity of their live shows, meant that by the end of the decade they were playing to stadium-sized audiences from whom they felt increasingly distanced. In need of another hit to sustain them financially, songwriter Roger Waters offered the band two concepts: they chose *The Wall*, which was released as a double album in 1979. It follows the life story of Pink. Each trauma he suffers is another 'brick in the wall' between him and the rest of the world: in childhood his father dies, his mother is overprotective, he is bullied at school; then he becomes a rock star and suffers the usual woes caused by too much sex, drugs and fame. Pink completes the wall around himself and then, in his isolation, imagines he has become a fascist dictator, his concerts resembling Nazi rallies. Eventually he places himself on trial, realises his mistake in removing himself from the world, and begins to tear the wall down. The last song ends 'isn't this where?', linking back to the first, which began, to the same melody, 'we came in?'.

The Wall was lavishly produced with backing by full orchestra, the New York City Opera chorus, a choir of schoolchildren (heard on the hit single 'We Don't Need No Education'), as well as a panoply of recorded sounds (phone calls, street noise, television broadcasts). On its release it was played in its entirety on BBC Radio 1. It also became an extravagant live show, which toured in 1980–1. During the performance a 40-foot wall was constructed between band and audience; animations illustrating the story were projected on it (giant inflatable figures also represented some of the characters) and at the end it collapsed. The show was recognised as a milestone in production values, and an adaptation of it was distributed as a film.

As is doubtless apparent, *The Wall* was more in the vein of a rock opera than a concept album; however, the fact that it was also referred to by the latter term gives a sense of the grand scale the genre attempted by the end of the 1970s.[60] Progressive rock and the concept albums it spawned were, however, falling out of fashion. The growing practice of bands using tours to promote their albums became, in some ways, the concept album's legacy.[61] Albums were increasingly presented as distinct entities: even if they had no explicit concept they might be listened to as if they did. Indeed, most albums (in most but not all genres) were expected to possess a degree of 'conceptness', whether simply by maintaining a particular mood or sound world, or by the overall trajectory of the sequence of songs. New concept albums did appear over the next two decades, but they were few in number and often idiosyncratic: they ranged from Chicago band Styx's *Paradise Theatre* (1981) and Pink Floyd's final offering, the relatively modest *The Final Cut* (1983), to Prince and The Revolution's *Purple Rain* (1984), which fell somewhere between film soundtrack and 'external narrative' song cycle, hardcore punk band Hüsker Dü's *Zen Arcade* (1984), Marilyn Mansun's parody *Antichrist Superstar* (1996) and The Magnetic Fields' *69 Love Songs* (1999; see Chapter 4). New formats (cassette tapes in the 1980s, CDs in the 1990s), prompted reissues of albums from earlier decades, but it was not until the relatively recent trend for bands from the 1960s and 1970s to re-form, or for tribute bands to reproduce complete albums live, that nostalgia for the concept album format began to accumulate.[62]

A rekindled interest in creating concept albums was detected by critics in British band Radiohead's *OK Computer* (1997), which circles around themes of modern malaise and, perhaps tellingly, nods towards a number of artists we have discussed – Phil Spector, The Beach Boys, The Beatles, Marvin Gaye and Pink Floyd among others – through both its production values and structural features such as the 6.5-minute multi-sectional track 'Paranoid Android'.[63] While Radiohead denied that *OK Computer* was a concept album, they admitted that they had tried to create a feeling of continuity. If we can agree that listeners, rather than musicians, often decide an album's concept, then tussling over how this particular example should be categorised is fruitless. What is important is that *OK Computer* was released shortly before a new recording technology that was to change perceptions of albums altogether: with hindsight, it may even stand as the format's last hurrah.[64]

The effect of digital recording technology on listening practices has already been mentioned in Chapter 9; it is worth considering again here because it has, to date, been adopted mostly by popular music markets. An MP3, as it is commonly known, is a digital file that compresses audio data. Some sound quality is lost in the process of compression (one reason why the format is not as popular among classical music listeners, although to many the difference is negligible); however, the advantage of MP3 files is that they can easily be transmitted via the Internet.[65] Music can thus be shared or sold quickly and to wider audiences than ever before. The trend has fundamentally altered the status of record companies and copyright legislation. It also has the potential to change the way we listen to concept albums, because it is now possible to download single songs instead of always investing in the complete package.

It is said that record companies are loath to lose the album as a format. However, it is becoming apparent that some musicians are no less beholden to it as a medium.[66] For example, after parting company with EMI in 2007, Radiohead decided to release their next album independently: what is more, *In Rainbows* was initially made available only as a digital download (in the UK between 10 October and 10 December 2007; it became available in standard CD format at the end of the year). Consumers were asked to make whatever financial contribution they liked, a suggestion considered a radical challenge to record-company procedure. They could only download all ten tracks, though, implying that the album possessed integrity. As if to prove the point, enthusiasts could also purchase a limited edition 'disc box': packaged as a hardcover book, it housed not only a digital file of the album, but also two CD versions (with additional tracks), plus two 12-inch 45rpm vinyl records, lyric booklet, digital photos and printed artwork. The disc box for *In Rainbows* is reminiscent both of the post-war albums, intended as collectibles, and – in volume, if not in style – the extravagant covers of psychedelic-era concept albums. The latter also come to mind with other recent albums that concoct complex narratives such as Ry Cooder's California trilogy (*Chávez Ravine* (2005), *My Name is Buddy* (2007), *I, Flathead* (2008)) or Portland band The Decemberists' *The Hazards of Love* (2009), or grand musical schemes such as Muse's *The Resistance* (2009), the first album the band have produced themselves, which ends with a 13-minute three-part symphony, 'Exogenesis: Overture; Cross-Pollination; Redemption'. The concept of the album will not fade away, it seems.

If we seem to have strayed a long way from the connection between song cycles and concept albums, the quick way home is this: the examples given here make plain that the impulse to create coherent groups of songs or tracks, whether for the pleasures of story-telling or for the sake of technical and formal experimentation, is still with us in both popular and classical forms of music-making. Although the means of delivery are constantly changing, the cyclic or conceptual aspects of the projects remain in many ways the same: they are age-old, in the best and worst sense. The previous chapter ended by suggesting that newly composed song cycles are haunted by history. Along similar lines, the tendency among bands to deny that theirs are concept albums suggests the format is deeply uncool, if curiously alluring.

This is not to say that song cycle and concept album have always remained firmly in separate camps, with no correspondence between them beyond quibbles over terminology. As a postlude to this chapter – and to this book – we might consider a few examples of musicians borrowing across genres. For some composers, popular music seems to be a source for modern texts. For example, American composer John Corigliano's *Mr Tambourine Man: Seven Poems by Bob Dylan* (2008) takes Dylan's lyrics as the basis for a seven-song orchestral song cycle: Corigliano explained that he had no knowledge of Dylan's songs; he wanted to respond to the poetry on his own terms. He did not shirk from setting some famous texts, from 'Mr Tambourine Man' to 'Blowin' in the Wind' to 'All Along the Watchtower', and the effect of hearing the familiar words in an entirely contrasting setting can be unsettling. More successful – quite possibly because I am less well versed in East German rock band Rammstein – is *Mein Herz brennt* (2004), a song cycle by Torsten Rasch. The orchestral and vocal writing is firmly in the tradition of Mahler and Strauss: a good match for the angst of the lyrics. Very different in tone – but similarly attuned to the affinities between the emotions expressed in nineteenth-century Lieder and how we might reconfigure them today – is Gabriel Kahane's *Craigslistlieder* (2008), an eight-song, pastiche Max Reger cycle that sets personal ads from the Internet site Craigslist.

Not all creators of song cycles these days are classically trained, and some of those best known for their concept albums have strayed from the studio – one such is Brian Wilson, who premiered *That Lucky Old Sun (A Narrative)* in concert in 2007 (a recording was issued the following year). 'Nowadays, the wistful godfather of pop music chooses to express himself in song cycles, rather than three-minute doses of sunshine', commented one reviewer.[67] Wilson had not done it alone though; he had reunited with Scott Bennett from The Beach Boys and Van Dyke Parks, who provided interludes of spoken narrative. Their theme? What else but Southern California. The album is in five rounds of songs, divided at irregular intervals by Parks's interjections, and featuring four reprises of the opening title song. The final track begins in nostalgic mood, with Wilson singing to piano accompaniment: 'I had this dream singing with my brothers in harmony.' As the sun sets over the sea he drives away: 'love songs, pretty girls, didn't want it to end . . .' It is uncharacteristically upbeat, perhaps, but makes for a classic song-cycle ending.

Notes

1 Concepts

1 The song cycles of Schubert and Schumann, Rosen points out, have never needed apology or resuscitation, unlike their efforts in other genres, such as opera or chamber music. Charles Rosen, *The Romantic Generation* (Cambridge, MA: Harvard University Press, 1995), p. 125.

2 David Ferris, *Schumann's Eichendorff 'Liederkreis': The Genre of the Romantic Cycle* (Oxford University Press, 2000), p. 24; and John Daverio, 'The Song Cycle: Journeys through a Romantic Landscape', in Rufus Hallmark (ed.), *German Lieder in the Nineteenth Century* (New York: Schirmer, 1996), p. 282.

3 See M.H. Abrams, *The Mirror and the Lamp: Romantic Theory and the Critical Tradition* (Oxford University Press, 1953), p. 93.

4 Ruth Bingham, 'The Early Nineteenth-Century Song Cycle', in James Parsons (ed.), *The Cambridge Companion to the Lied* (Cambridge University Press, 2004), pp. 104–6.

5 See Schumann's 1836 review of Loewe's *Esther*, in *Gesammelte Schriften über Musik und Musiker*, ed. Martin Kreisig (Leipzig: Breitkopf und Härtel, 1914), vol. 1, pp. 269–70, and Oswald Lorenz's review of Loewe's *Gregor auf dem Stein*, *Neue Zeitschrift für Musik* 4 (1837), p. 141.

6 There is, of course, the multi-authored *Word and Music Studies: Essays on the Song Cycle and on Defining the Field*, ed. Walter Bernhart and Werner Wolf (Amsterdam and Atlanta, GA: Rodopi, 2001); and there are chapters on the song cycle in Parsons (ed.), *The Cambridge Companion to the Lied* and Hallmark (ed.), *German Lieder in the Nineteenth Century*.

7 *Musikalisches Lexicon auf Grundlage des Lexicon's von H.Ch. Koch*, ed. Arrey von Dommer, 2nd edition of *H.Ch. Koch's musikalisches Lexikon* (Heidelberg: J.C.B. Mohr, 1964), pp. 513–14. Translation from Ferris, *Schumann's Eichendorff 'Liederkreis'*, p. 9. Inge van Rij refers to a slightly earlier publication, Dommer's *Elemente der Musik* (Leipzig: Weigel, 1862), p. 234, which also gives *An die ferne Geliebte* as the model for the song cycle. See *Brahms's Song Collections* (Cambridge University Press, 2006), p. 5.

8 Undated letter from 1816; see Richard Stokes, *The Book of Lieder: The Original Texts of Over 1000 Songs* (London: Faber and Faber, 2005), p. 3.

9 Schumann, *Gesammelte Schriften*, vol. 2, p. 147.

10 Schlegel's *Abendröte* was first published in *Musenalmanach für das Jahr 1802*. Schubert probably used a later edition, as he writes 'Abendröthe. Erster Theil' at the head of the manuscript, a division Schlegel only added in 1809.

11 Richard Kramer, *Distant Cycles: Schubert and the Conceiving of Song* (University of Chicago Press, 1994), p. 215.

12 For more on the individual songs, see Kramer, *Distant Cycles*, p. 199; Kristina Muxfeldt, 'Schubert's Songs: The Transformation of a Genre', in Christopher H. Gibbs (ed.), *The Cambridge Companion to Schubert* (Cambridge University Press, 1997), p. 126; and Susan Youens, *Schubert's Late Lieder: Beyond the Song Cycles* (Cambridge University Press, 2002), p. 290.

13 See Richard Kramer, 'Posthumous Schubert', *19th-Century Music* 14 (1990), p. 197.

14 See Kramer, *Distant Cycles*, p. 145; and Harry Goldschmidt, 'Welches war die ursprüngliche Reihenfolge in Schuberts Heine-Liedern?', *Deutsches Jahrbuch der Musikwissenschaft für 1972* (1974), pp. 52–62. Martin Chusid points out that Maurice J.E. Brown had already reordered the songs according to the sequence in Heine's *Heimkehr*; see Martin Chusid (ed.), *A Companion to Schubert's 'Schwanengesang': History, Poets, Analysis, Performance* (New Haven, CT: Yale University Press, 2000), p. 160.

15 See Edward T. Cone, 'Repetition and Correspondence in *Schwanengesang*', in Chusid (ed.), *A Companion to Schubert's 'Schwanengesang'*, pp. 53–89.

16 For an extended discussion of the Heine settings see Susan Youens, *Heinrich Heine and the Lied* (Cambridge University Press, 2007), pp. 1–88.

17 According to Daverio's Schumann-inspired criteria for song cycles, nine sets of songs from the 1840 *Liederjahr* qualify: the Heine *Liederkreis* op. 24, *Myrthen* op. 25, the Eichendorff *Liederkreis* op. 39, *Dichterliebe* op. 48, the Reinick *Gedichte* op. 36, the Kerner *Liederreihe* op. 35, and the Rückert *Gedichte* op. 37. *Robert Schumann: Herald of 'A New Poetic Age'* (Oxford University Press, 1997), p. 213.

18 Beate Perrey has recently argued that we should return to Schumann's original version of twenty songs, though she claims that to do so is in keeping with *Dichterliebe*'s fragmentary character. *Schumann's 'Dichterliebe' and Early Romantic Poetics: The Fragmentation of Desire* (Cambridge University Press, 2002), p. 121. Berthold Hoeckner gives an alternative perspective, saying that the elimination of the four songs 'streamlined the tonal path and tightened the narrative progression'; see 'Paths through *Dichterliebe*', *19th-Century Music* 30 (2006), pp. 65–80; here p. 76.

19 Schumann could have written the ending of the final song in C♯ instead of D♭; maybe he thought the latter would be easier to read or, Berthold Hoeckner suggests, he deliberately chose D♭ to make the relationship less obvious. See Rufus Hallmark, *The Genesis of 'Dichterliebe': A Source Study* (Ann Arbor, MI: UMI Research Press, 1979), p. 110.

20 Translation from Stokes, *The Book of Lieder*, pp. 468–9.

21 Keith W. Daniel, *Francis Poulenc: His Artistic Development and Musical Style* (Ann Arbor, MI: UMI Research Press, 1982), p. 243.

22 Francis Poulenc, *Diary of My Songs*, trans. Winifred Radford (London: Victor Gollancz, 1985), pp. 33 and 35.

23 André Schaffner, 1946 review in *Contrepoints*; and Roland Manuel, quoted in Henri Hell, *Francis Poulenc: musicien français* (Paris: Fayard, 1978), p. 137.

24 Poulenc, *Diary of My Songs*, p. 35.

25 See Sidney Buckland, 'The Coherence of Opposites: Éluard, Poulenc and the Poems of *Tel jour, telle nuit*', in Sidney Buckland and Myriam Chimènes (eds.), *Francis Poulenc: Music, Art and Literature* (Aldershot: Ashgate, 1999), pp. 145–77; and Jean Burgos, 'Éluard ou les rituels de régéneration', *Pour une poétique de l'imaginaire* (Paris: Seuil, 1982), p. 331.

26 Poulenc, *Diary of My Songs*, p. 35.

27 Poulenc, *Diary of My Songs*, p. 35.

28 Poulenc, *Diary of My Songs*, p. 36.

29 According to Birkin, *Histoire de Melody Nelson* was a tribute to her; see Sylvie Simmons, *Serge Gainsbourg: A Fistful of Gitanes* (London: Helter Skelter, 2002), pp. 92–3.

30 *Only Connect* festival, 21 October 2006; they were accompanied by musicians Dargie Wright, Big Jim Sullivan, Herbie Flowers, Vic Flick, the Children's String Quartet, Crouch End Festival Chorus and the BBC Concert Orchestra.

31 *A Grand* is his second album; 'Skinner likes to establish a concept and a set of rules for each album so that each represents a distinct period'. 'I'm the Pablo Picasso of geezer garage, aren't I?': Interview with Dorian Lynskey, 29 August 2008, *The Guardian*, Film and Music, p. 3.

2 Wanderers and balladeers

1 Andrew Cusack, *The Wanderer in 19th-Century German Literature: Intellectual History and Cultural Criticism* (Rochester, NY: Camden House, 2008).

2 Susan Youens's books on *Die schöne Müllerin* and *Winterreise* have provided much of the background material found here and should be referred to for more in-depth discussion of both cycles. See *Retracing a Winter's Journey: Schubert's 'Winterreise'* (Ithaca, NY: Cornell University Press, 1992); *Schubert: 'Die schöne Müllerin'* (Cambridge University Press, 1992); and *Schubert, Müller, and 'Die schöne Müllerin'* (Cambridge University Press, 1997).

3 Youens, *Schubert, Müller, and 'Die schöne Müllerin'*, p. xiii; and Lawrence Kramer, *Franz Schubert: Sexuality, Subjectivity, Song* (Cambridge University Press, 1998), p. 132.

4 See Youens, *Schubert, Müller, and 'Die schöne Müllerin'*, p. 3.

5 For more on Berger's settings, see Youens, *Schubert: 'Die schöne Müllerin'*, pp. 8–9.

6 See Jürgen Thym, 'Crosscurrents in Song: Five Distinctive Voices', in Rufus Hallmark (ed.), *German Lieder in the Nineteenth Century* (New York: Schirmer, 1996), p. 159; and Ludwig Finscher, 'Balladen – und Lied-Opera, Balladen – und Liedzyklus: Über Ordnungsprinzipien im Liedschaffen Carl Loewes', *Carl Loewe, 1796–1869* (Kassel: Bärenreiter, 1997), pp. 356–71.

7 See, for example, John Daverio's *Robert Schumann: Herald of 'A New Poetic Age'* (Oxford University Press, 1997), p. 213.

8 Tieck's tale initially appeared in *Volksmärchen herausgegeben von Peter Lebrecht* in 1797; Brahms probably used the later *Phantasus, eine Sammlung von Märchen, Erzählungen, Schauspielen, und Novellen* (1812–16).

9 See his March 1870 letter to Adolf Schubring, *Briefwechsel* (Tutzing: Hans Schneider, 1974), vol. 14, p. 219.

10 See letter to Rieter-Biedermann, 14 September 1875, *Briefwechsel*, vol. 14, p. 250.

11 Max Kalbeck, *Johannes Brahms* (Berlin: Deutsche Brahms Gesellschaft, 1908), vol. 1, p. 429.

12 Carolyn Abbate makes this argument from the opposite direction – considering instances of ballads in opera – in *Unsung Voices: Opera and Musical Narrative in the Nineteenth Century* (Princeton University Press, 1991), pp. 69–96.

13 'Tenor sets off on musical journey' (19 January 2004), http://news.bbc.co.uk/1/hi/england/3409903.stm (accessed on 3 July 2010). I am grateful to David Pisaro for sharing the film of his project with me.

14 For more on this see Reinhold Brinkmann, 'Schubert's Political Landscape', in David Wellbery, Judith Ryan and Hans Ulrich Gumbrecht (eds.), *A New History of German Literature* (Cambridge, MA: Harvard University Press, 2004), p. 542.

15 Luise Eitel Peake, 'Kreutzer's *Wanderlieder*: The Other *Winterreise*', *Musical Quarterly* 65 (1979), pp. 83–102.

16 *Allgemeine musikalische Zeitung mit besonderer Rücksicht auf den österreichischen Kaiserstadt, Wien* 2 (1818), p. 478; quoted in Barbara Turchin, 'The Nineteenth-century *Wanderlieder* Cycle', *The Journal of Musicology* 5 (1987), pp. 498–525; here p. 501.

17 The continuation appeared in a journal the following year; the complete set was then published in a revised and reordered version in the already mentioned *Gedichte aus den hinterlassenen Papieren eines reisenden Waldhornisten*.

18 Wilhelm Müller, 'Ueber die neueste lyrische Poesie der Deutscher: Ludwig Uhland und Justinus Kerner', *Hermes, oder kritisches Jahrbuch der Literatur* 28 (1827), p. 105; cited in Turchin, 'The Nineteenth-century *Wanderlieder* Cycle', p. 509, which discusses derivatives of Kreutzer's *Wanderlieder* at greater length than there is space for here.

19 See Otto Erich Deutsch, *Schubert: Memoirs by his Friends*, trans. Rosamond Ley and John Nowell (New York: Macmillan, 1958), p. 27.

20 See Youens, *Schubert, Müller and 'Die schöne Müllerin'*, p. 140.

21 Letter to Dr Friedrich Löhr, 1 January 1885, *Selected Letters of Gustav Mahler*, ed. Knud Martner, trans. Eithne Wilkins, Ernst Kaiser and Bill Hopkins (New York: Farrar, Straus and Giroux, 1979), p. 31.

22 For a detailed discussion of the relationship between imagery in the two cycles see Youens, 'Schubert, Mahler and the Weight of the Past: *Lieder eines fahrenden Gesellen* and *Winterreise*', *Music and Letters* 67 (1986), pp. 48–61.

23 See Donald Mitchell, *Gustav Mahler*, vol. 2, *The Wunderhorn Years* (London: Faber, 1975), p. 94.

24 For more on the relationship between the *Gesellen* songs and the First Symphony see Raymond Knapp, *Symphonic Metamorphoses: Subjectivity and Alienation in Mahler's Re-cycled Songs* (Middletown, CT: Wesleyan University Press, 2003), pp. 151–93; and

Julian Johnson, *Mahler's Voices: Expression and Irony in the Songs and Symphonies* (Oxford University Press, 2009), pp. 19–21.

25 John Daverio, 'The Song Cycle: Journeys through a Romantic Landscape', in Rufus Hallmark (ed.), *German Lieder in the Nineteenth Century* (New York: Schirmer, 1996), p. 302; see also Marjorie W. Hirsch, *Romantic Lieder and the Search for Lost Paradise* (Cambridge University Press, 2008), pp. 214–45.

3 Performance

1 On the spread of the piano in the United Kingdom see Derek B. Scott, *The Singing Bourgeois: Songs of the Victorian Drawing Room and Parlour* (Milton Keynes: Open University Press, 1989), pp. 45–59.

2 See Scott Messing, *Schubert in the European Imagination*, vol. 1, *The Romantic and Victorian Eras* (Rochester University Press, 2006), pp. 166–7.

3 Matthias Hausmann, '"Sag an, wer lehrt dich Lieder...?" Probleme der Auf-führungspraxis in Schuberts Liedern aus Sängersicht', *Schubert durch die Brille: Internationales Franz Schubert-Mitteilungen* 21 (1998), pp. 9–18.

4 For more on musical albums see James Davies, 'Julia's Gift: The Social Life of Scores, c. 1830', *Journal of the Royal Musical Association* 131 (2006), pp. 287–309.

5 Anton Ottenwald, quoted in Michael Hall, *Schubert's Song Sets* (Aldershot: Ashgate, 2003), p. 131.

6 See Youens, *Schubert: 'Die schöne Müllerin'*, pp. 18–22.

7 Quoted in Youens, *Schubert: 'Die schöne Müllerin'*, p. 14. For more on Vogl's and Sonnleithner's delivery see Martha Elliott, *Singing in Style: A Guide to Vocal Performance Practice* (New Haven, CT: Yale University Press, 2006), pp. 167, 172.

8 Youens, *Schubert: 'Die schöne Müllerin'*, p. 15.

9 Quoted in Jon W. Finson, *Robert Schumann: The Book of Songs* (Cambridge, MA: Harvard University Press), p. 181.

10 *Letters of Clara Schumann and Johannes Brahms, 1853–1896*, ed. Berthold Litzmann (New York: Vienna House, 1973), vol. 1, p. 73.

11 On Clara's performance of *Frauenliebe*, see Edward F. Kravitt, *The Lied: Mirror of Late Romanticism* (New Haven, CT: Yale University Press, 1996), pp. 18–19.

12 Youens, *Schubert, Müller and 'Die schöne Müllerin'*, p. 164.

13 Although Brahms later complained about singers making selections from his *Boukets*, as discussed in Chapter 2 he did not expect, or endorse, complete performances of the *Magelone* cycle he dedicated to Stockhausen. For more see Renate and Kurt Hofmann, *Johannes Brahms als Pianist und Dirigent: Chronologie seines Wirkens als Interpret* (Tutzing: Hans Schneider, 2006).

14 Quoted in Kravitt, *The Lied*, p. 55.

15 Singers' awareness of the need to calibrate their performances for different spaces is evident in various treatises, from that by Viennese Conservatoire teacher Mathilde Marchesi to Lilli Lehmann's *How to Sing* (1924), trans. Richard Aldrich (New York: Dover, 1993).

16 George Grove, quoted in John Warrack, 'Raimund von zur Mühlen', *Grove Music Online*, accessed 26 February 2010.

17 August Reißmann, *Das deutsche Lied in seiner historischen Entwicklung* (Kassel: Oswald Bertram, 1861).

18 Carl E. Schorske, *Fin-de-siècle Vienna: Politics and Culture* (New York: Vintage, 1981), pp. 24–115.

19 See Kravitt, *The Lied*, p. 20.

20 Scott Messing, 'Gustav Klimt's Schubert', *Schubert in the European Imagination*, vol. 2, *Fin-de-siècle Vienna* (University of Rochester Press, 2007), pp. 70–94.

21 H. Arnold Smith, 'Baron Raimund von Zur-Mühlen: The Passing of a Great Artist', *The Musical Times* 73 (1932), p. 317.

22 Letter 18 October 1899, *Edward Elgar: Letters of a Lifetime*, ed. Jerrold Northrop Moore (Oxford: Clarendon Press, 1990), p. 80.

23 Quoted in Lorraine Gorrell, *Discordant Melody: Alexander Zemlinsky, His Songs, and the Second Viennese School* (Westport, CT: Greenwood Press, 2002), p. 191.

24 See David P. Schroeder, 'Alban Berg and Peter Altenberg: Intimate Art and the Aesthetics of Life', *Journal of the American Musicological Society* 46 (1993), pp. 261–94; and René Leibowitz, 'Alban Berg's Five Orchestral Songs after Postcard Texts by Peter Altenberg, op. 4', *Musical Quarterly* 75 (1991), pp. 487–511.

4 Gendered voices

1 See Marcia J. Citron, 'Women and the Lied, 1775–1850', in Jane Bowers and Judith Tick (eds.), *Women Making Music: The Western Art Tradition, 1150–1950* (Urbana and Chicago, IL: University of Illinois Press, 1986), pp. 224–49, here pp. 225–7; and David Gramit, *Cultivating Music: The Aspirations, Interests, and Limits of German Musical Culture, 1770–1848* (Berkeley, CA: University of California Press, 2002), pp. 113–14.

2 For more on the imagery in Chamisso and the Schumanns' letters see Kristina Muxfeldt, '*Frauenliebe und Leben* Now and Then', *19th-Century Music* 25 (2001), pp. 27–48.

3 The figure seems to have become something of a symbol for married life, recurring in later cycles to indicate connubial bliss, as in the first song 'Sei Mein!' ('Be mine!') from Peter Cornelius's *An Bertha* (*To Bertha*, 1862–5), and Jules Massenet's *Poème du souvenir* (*Poem of remembrance*, 1868). For more on *Poème du souvenir* see Paul Yates, *The Song Cycle in Nineteenth-Century France and Debussy's 'Recueil Vasnier'* (PhD, Cambridge, 2002), p. 85.

4 Ruth A. Solie, 'Whose Life? The Gendered Self in Schumann's *Frauenliebe* Songs', in Steven Paul Scher (ed.), *Music and Text: Critical Inquiries* (Cambridge University Press, 1992), pp. 219–40.

5 Muxfeldt, '*Frauenliebe und Leben* Now and Then'.

6 The family of Vienna Conservatory teacher Mathilde Marchesi, for example, would not allow her to appear in theatres, even though she included Italian arias in her concert

repertoire; see her autobiography, *Marchesi and Music: Passages from the Life of a Famous Singing Teacher* (London and New York: Harper, 1897).

7 According to Janet Schmalfeldt, 'Coming Home', *Music Theory Online* 10 (2004) [28].

8 Cited by Jürgen Thym, 'Crosscurrents in Song: Five Distinctive Voices', in Hallmark (ed.), *German Lieder in the Nineteenth Century*, pp. 153–85; here p. 176.

9 Coenraad Bos, as told by Ashley Pettis, *The Well-Tempered Accompanist* (Bryn Mawr, PA: Theodore Presser, 1949), p. 132.

10 Bos, *The Well-Tempered Accompanist*, p. 134.

11 See Hans Joachim Köhler's edition of *Frauenliebe und -leben* (Leipzig: Peters, 1987); Rufus Hallmark's new edition is forthcoming. To Bos's amusement, no critic at the time ever seemed to notice the change; he recorded his version with the American Helen Traubel for Victor, and apparently also convinced Julia Culp of its merits, though her 1909 recording – the cycle's first – keeps to Schumann's published score.

12 Bos, *The Well-Tempered Accompanist*, p. 132.

13 Review of Schumann-Heink recital in New York's Carnegie Hall, *New York Times*, 6 February 1904.

14 Gerhardt, for one, continued to use gestures, as noted by J.B. Steane in *The Grand Tradition: 70 Years of Singing on Record* (London: Duckworth, 1974), p. 226.

15 Lehmann recorded *Winterreise* and *Frauenliebe und -leben* in the 1940s: see Michael H. Kater, *Never Sang for Hitler: The Life and Times of Lotte Lehmann, 1888–1976* (Cambridge University Press, 2008), p. 223.

16 Poulenc explained that he needed 'to believe in the words' he heard sung: 'I admit that when a lady begins: "J'aime tes yeux, j'aime ta bouche, O ma rebelle, o ma farouche" (I love your eyes, I love your mouth, oh my rebellious one, oh my shy one), in spite of Fauré's music I am not convinced, for fear of being too convinced.' Pierre Bernac, *Francis Poulenc: The Man and His Songs*, trans. Winifred Radford (London: Victor Gollancz, 1977), p. 129.

17 See Kater, *Never Sang for Hitler*, p. 145: Kater points out that by this stage in her career Lehmann was increasingly careful about using higher registers. Gerhardt explained that 'the tessitura of some of the songs [from *Winterreise*] was a little uncomfortable for me, but [given] that Schubert had published two versions, one for tenor and one for baritone, and, being a mezzo-soprano myself, I did not think it sacrilege to sing some of them in a lower key'. Elena Gerhardt, *Recital* (London: Methuen, 1953), p. 110.

18 Terry Castle, 'In Praise of Brigitte Fassbaender (A Musical Emanation)', in *The Apparitional Lesbian: Female Homosexuality and Modern Culture* (New York: Columbia University Press, 1993), pp. 200–38; here p. 229.

19 Hardly any baritones have braved *Frauenliebe und -leben* since the 1920s, with the exception of Matthias Goerne (2006), who reported that his teacher Dietrich Fischer-Dieskau thought the idea 'stupid, ridiculous and wrong'. See interview with Ivan Hewett, 'I understand how to be a woman', *Daily Telegraph*, 13 April 2006.

20 Aaron Copland and Vivian Perlis, *Copland: Since 1943* (New York: St Martin's Press, 1989), p. 158; for an extended discussion of the cycle see Larry Starr and Michael J.

Budds, *The Dickinson Songs of Aaron Copland*, Parts 1 and 2 (Hillside, NY: Pendragon Press, 2002).

21 Elaine Showalter, 'Feminist Criticism in the Wilderness', in *The New Feminist Criticism: Essays on Women's Literature and Theory* (London: Virago, 1986); Cixous's essay 'The Laugh of the Medusa' is reproduced in Robyn R. Warhol and Diana Price Herndl (eds.), *An Anthology of Literary Theory and Criticism* (New Brunswick, NJ: Rutgers University Press, 1991).

22 See the Charlie Rose interview (20 March 2000) with Norman, Morrison, Pinkola Estés and Weir at www.charlierose.com/view/interview/3795 (accessed on 3 July 2010).

23 An analysis of 'Both Sides Now' is provided in Lloyd Whitesell's *The Music of Joni Mitchell* (Oxford University Press, 2008), pp. 143–7.

24 Liner notes to *Both Sides Now* (Reprise, 2000).

25 For more see Caroline O'Meara, 'The Raincoats: Breaking Down Rock's Masculinities', *Popular Music* 22 (2003), pp. 299–313.

26 Quoted in Simon Reynolds, *Rip It Up and Start Again: Postpunk 1978–1984* (London: Faber and Faber, 2005), p. 214.

27 For more on the original album see John Dougan, *The Who Sell Out* (New York: Continuum, 2006).

5 Between opera and symphony

1 For an overview of the genre, see Günter Buhles, 'Das Orchesterlied: Facetten einer faszinierenden Gattung', *Das Orchester* 54 (2006), pp. 33–6; Edward Kravitt, 'The Orchestral Lied: An Inquiry into its Style and Unexpected Flowering around 1900', *The Musical Review* 37 (1976), pp. 209–26; and Hermann Danuser, 'Der Orchestergesang des fin-de-siècle: Eine historische und ästhetische Skizze', *Musikforschung* 30 (1977), pp. 425–52.

2 For example, Adolphe Nourrit sang 'Die junge Nonne' (as 'La Religieuse') with instrumental accompaniment at François Habeneck's Société des Concerts du Conservatoire in 1835; see Annegret Fauser, *Der Orchestergesang in Frankreich zwischen 1870 und 1920* (Laaber Verlag, 1994), pp. 6–12.

3 Richard Strauss revised Berlioz's *Treatise on Instrumentation*, while the conductor and composer Felix Weingartner was one of the editors of the Berlioz Complete Edition for Breitkopf und Härtel. Felix Mottl also conducted Berlioz often.

4 For more on the cycle's compositional and publication history, see Peter Bloom, 'In the Shadows of *Les Nuits d'été*', in Peter Bloom (ed.), *Berlioz Studies* (Cambridge University Press, 1992), pp. 80–111: for further discussion of the musical and poetic unity of the cycle see Julian Rushton, '*Les Nuits d'été*: Cycle or Collection', in Bloom (ed.), *Berlioz Studies*, pp. 112–35.

5 At the same time Berlioz reissued the version with piano, bringing it into line with the revisions. Incidentally, these days the cycle is most often performed in its orchestral version, entirely by one singer (usually a mezzo-soprano).

6 Mottl conducted the premiere of *Tristan und Isolde* at the Bayreuth Festival in 1886, and was renowned as a conductor of Wagner and Berlioz; he died in 1911, after collapsing during his 100th performance of *Tristan*! Hans Werner Henze devised an alternative version for chamber orchestra in 1976.

7 John Deathridge, *Wagner: Beyond Good and Evil* (Berkeley, CA: University of California Press, 2008), pp. 123–4.

8 Donald Mitchell has suggested that some of the cycle's music may have been orchestrated for the first time in the First Symphony; see John Williamson, 'The Earliest Completed Works: A Voyage towards the First Symphony', in Donald Mitchell and Andrew Nicholson (eds.), *The Mahler Companion* (Oxford University Press, 2002), pp. 52–3.

9 For an overview of French Wagnerism see Stephen Huebner, *French Opera at the fin-de-siècle: Wagnerism, Nationalism and Style* (Oxford University Press, 1999), pp. 11–21.

10 It was premiered in its piano version and without its interlude, though, because of a crisis in confidence on the part of the composer; the orchestral version was given at the Société Nationale two months later, in April 1893. The last segment of the second poem was published separately with piano accompaniment as 'Le Temps des Lilas'.

11 For more in-depth discussion of these symphonies see Raymond Knapp, *Symphonic Metamorphoses: Subjectivity and Alienation in Mahler's Re-Cycled Songs* (Middletown, CT: Wesleyan University Press, 2003); and Julian Johnson, *Mahler's Voices: Expression and Irony in the Songs and Symphonies* (Oxford University Press, 2009).

12 See Donald Mitchell, 'Mahler's Fourth Symphony', in Mitchell and Nicholson (eds.), *The Mahler Companion*, p. 213, nn. 38 and 39; and William Kinderman, '"Ich bin der Welt abhanden gekommen": Mahler's Rückert Setting and the Aesthetics of Integration in the Fifth Symphony', *Musical Quarterly* 88 (2006), pp. 232–73.

13 Peter Revers, '"... the heart-wrenching sound of farewell": Mahler, Rückert, and the *Kindertotenlieder*', trans. Irene Zedlacher, in Karen Painter (ed.), *Mahler and His World* (Princeton University Press, 2002), pp. 173–83; here pp. 174–5.

14 See Stephen Hefling, 'The Rückert Lieder', in Mitchell and Nicholson (eds.), *The Mahler Companion*, pp. 338–65.

15 See discussion in the previous chapter and Edward Kravitt, 'The Lied in 19th-Century Concert Life', *Journal of the American Musicological Society* 18 (1965), pp. 207–18; here pp. 215–17.

16 See Donald Mitchell, 'Mahler and the Chamber Orchestra', in Mitchell and Nicholson (eds.), *The Mahler Companion*, pp. 226–31.

17 *Die chinesische Flöte* was also the source for Karol Szymanowski's *Love Songs of Hafiz* opp. 24 (1911) and 26 (1914), Anton Webern's *Vier Lieder* op. 13 (1914–18) and Richard Strauss's *Gesänge des Orients* op. 77 (1928).

18 See Fusako Hamao, 'The Sources of the Texts in Mahler's *Das Lied von der Erde*', *19th-Century Music* 19 (1995), pp. 83–95; Stephen E. Hefling compares the original Li-Po poem that became Mahler's 'Der Trunkene im Frühling' with its various translations

and paraphrases in *Mahler: 'Das Lied von der Erde'* (Cambridge University Press, 2000), pp. 38–42.

19 For more on these allusions see Hefling, *Mahler: 'Das Lied'*, pp. 109–10 and 114–15.

20 For more on Mahler's use of pentatonicism, see Hefling, *Mahler: 'Das Lied'*, pp. 86 and 99; for more on the whole-tone scale see Chapter 6.

21 Or, rather, Mahler made the earlier song predict this moment, as he added the line 'und aufblüh'n im Lenz' ('and bloom forth in spring') to forecast the later 'Die liebe Erde allüberall blüht auf im Lenz' ('The beloved earth all over everywhere blooms forth in spring'). See Hefling, *Mahler: 'Das Lied'*, pp. 90–1.

22 See Hefling, *Mahler: 'Das Lied'*, p. 116.

6 Travels abroad

1 Translation from Simon Perry, 'A Voice Unknown: Undercurrents in Mussorgsky's *Sunless*', *19th-Century Music* 28 (2004), pp. 15–49; here p. 31.

2 Alexandra Orlova (comp. and ed.), *Musorgsky Remembered*, trans. Véronique Zaytzeff and Frederick Morrison (Indianapolis, IN: Indiana University Press, 1991), p. 10.

3 Singing student Aleksandra Demidova, in Orlova (comp. and ed.), *Musorgsky Remembered*, p. 128.

4 See Richard Taruskin, *Defining Russia Musically: Historical and Hermeneutical Essays* (Princeton University Press, 1997), p. 55.

5 For more on these songs, and for an overview of nineteenth-century Russian art song, see Gerald Abraham, 'Russia', in Denis Stevens (ed.), *A History of Song* (London: Hutchinson, 1960), pp. 338–75.

6 See Mary S. Woodside, 'Leitmotiv in Russia: Glinka's Use of the Whole-Tone Scale', *19th-Century Music* 14 (1990), pp. 67–74.

7 Richard Taruskin, *Stravinsky and the Russian Traditions: A Biography of the Works through Mavra* (Oxford University Press, 1996), p. 1,357.

8 See Richard Taruskin, 'Realism as Preached and Practiced: The Russian Opera Dialogue', *Musical Quarterly* 56 (1970), pp. 431–54; here p. 443.

9 On the influence of folk song on Musorgsky, see Petra Weber-Bockholdt, *Die Lieder Mussorgskijs: Herkunft und Erscheinungsform* (Munich: Wilhelm Fink, 1982).

10 This point is made by Caryl Emerson, *The Life of Musorgsky* (Cambridge University Press, 1999), pp. 73–5. The first song was composed in 1868, joined by four more in 1870 and two in 1872.

11 For a close reading of the fourth song see Michael Russ, 'Be Bored: Reading a Mussorgsky Song', *19th-Century Music* 20 (1996), pp. 27–45.

12 For more detailed discussion see Perry, 'A Voice Unknown'.

13 The view is the much more recent Taruskin's: see his *Musorgsky: Eight Essays and an Epilogue* (Princeton University Press, 1993), pp. 384–5.

14 Emerson, *The Life of Musorgsky*, p. 129.

15 Letter to Golenischschev-Kutuzov, August 1877; cited in Emerson, *The Life of Musorgsky*, p. 125.

16 Glazunov and Rimsky-Korsakov orchestrated alternate songs for a version published in 1882; Dmitri Shostakovich orchestrated all of them in 1962.

17 On Tchaikovsky's sadness see Nicholas Slonimsky, *Writings on Music: Russian and Soviet Music and Composers* (New York: Routledge, 2004), p. 29; and Richard D. Sylvester, *Tchaikovsky's Complete Songs: A Companion with Texts and Translations* (Bloomington, IN: Indiana University Press, 2004), p. 270.

18 See Timothy L. Jackson, *Tchaikovsky: Symphony no. 6 (Pathétique)* (Cambridge University Press, 1999); and David Brown, *Tchaikovsky: A Biographical and Critical Study*, vol. 3, *The Years of Fame and Fortune, 1878–1893* (London: Victor Gollancz, 1992), p. 432.

19 Taruskin, *Defining Russia Musically*, pp. xi–xii.

20 Alphonse Daudet, *Le Nabab: moeurs parisiennes* (Paris and Geneva: Éditions Slatkin, 1997), p. 487.

21 Frits Noske, *French Song from Berlioz to Duparc*, trans. Rita Benton (New York: Dover, 1970).

22 J.G. Prod'homme, 'Schubert's Works in France', *Musical Quarterly* 14 (1928), pp. 495–514; here p. 497.

23 Anon, 'Les Mélodies de François Schubert', *La France musicale* 1 (18 March 1838), pp. 3–4.

24 *Revue gazette et musicale*, 6 December 1840; quoted in David Tunley, *Salons, Singers and Songs: A Background to Romantic French Song* (Aldershot: Ashgate, 2002), p. 98.

25 Ernst Legouvé, *Soixante ans de souvenirs* (Paris: Hetzel, 1888), vol. 3, p. 176. Translation from Prod'homme, 'Schubert's Works in France', p. 497. Liszt and Wagner could also be listed, as they composed some *mélodies* while in Paris, suggesting a sense of a distinct French tradition.

26 On 7 December 1898 at the Théâtre d'Application; it was presented as *La Belle Meunière*, and audience members were given a two-page summary of the story; the translator, Maurice Chassang's wife, Madame Marthe, read the preface beforehand.

27 Paul J.D. Yates, *The Song Cycle in 19th-Century France and Debussy's 'Recueil Vasnier'* (PhD, University of Cambridge, 2002), p. 71.

28 This tendency was encouraged by the publication between 1875 and 1914 of Massenet's songs in eight volumes, dismembering the original cycles; as these are now the only editions in print, we have to reassemble the cycles today, perhaps explaining their relative unfamiliarity.

29 The *Cinq Mélodies* include 'Mandoline', 'En sourdine' and 'À Clymène' from *Fêtes galantes* and 'Green' and 'Spleen' from *Romances sans paroles*.

30 'Lydia' is referred to in songs two, four and five, and is found in the piano part in song three; see Carlo Caballero, *Fauré and French Musical Aesthetics* (Cambridge University Press, 2001), pp. 238–9.

31 Debussy had originally sold what became *Fêtes galantes (I)* to Hartmann but unfortunately the publisher had just gone bankrupt; his successor, Fromont, released them following the success of the opera *Pelléas et Mélisande*. 'I' consists of 'En sourdine',

'Clair de lune' and 'Fantoches'; they were all revisions of settings composed ten years earlier; 'II' of 'Les Ingénus', 'Le Faune' and 'Colloque sentimental'.

32 See Jann Pasler, '*Pelléas* and Power: Forces behind the Reception of Debussy's Opera', *19th-Century Music* 10 (1987), pp. 243–64.

33 For more on Debussy's opera see Robert Orledge, *Debussy and the Theatre* (Cambridge University Press, 1982); and Carolyn Abbate, '*Tristan* in the Composition of *Pelléas*', *19th-Century Music* 5 (1981), pp. 117–41.

34 The phrase is Adorno's: see *The Philosophy of New Music*, trans. Robert Hullot-Kentor (Minneapolis, MN: University of Minnesota Press, 2006), p. 156.

35 At least as it was published in its final version: the two poems appeared side-by-side in the journal *L'Artiste* on 1 July 1868, along with 'Les Ingénus' and three other poems as 'Nouvelles Fêtes galantes'. 'Clair de lune' and 'Mandoline' were the first poems to be published, in *La Gazette rimée*, 20 February 1867. Paul Verlaine, *Oeuvres poétiques complètes*, ed. Y.G. le Dantec, revised by Jacques Borel (Paris: Gallimard, 1962), pp. 101–2.

36 For more see Stephen Rumph, 'Debussy's *Trois Chansons de Bilitis*: Song, Opera, and the Death of the Subject', *The Journal of Musicology* 12 (1994), pp. 464–90; here p. 488; see also Susan Youens, 'Debussy's Setting of Verlaine's "Colloque sentimental": From the Past to the Present', *Studies in Music* 15 (1981), pp. 93–105.

37 On *Haugtussa* see Daniel M. Grimley, *Grieg: Music, Landscape and Norwegian Identity* (Woodbridge: The Boydell Press, 2006), pp. 109–46; and Susan McClary, 'Playing the Identity Card: Of Grieg, Indians and Women', *19th-Century Music* 31 (2008), pp. 217–27. On *The Diary* see John Tyrrell, *Janáček: Years of a Life*, Vol. 2, *(1914–1928) Tsar of the Forests* (London: Faber and Faber, 2007), *passim*.

38 See Jann Pasler, 'Race, Orientalism and Distinction in the Wake of the "Yellow Peril"', in Georgina Born and David Hesmondhalgh (eds.), *Western Music and its Others* (Berkeley, CA: University of California Press, 2000), pp. 86–118.

39 For further discussion, primarily with regard to literature, see Edward W. Said, *Culture and Imperialism* (London: Vintage, 1993).

40 See Annegret Fauser, *Musical Encounters at the 1889 Paris World Fair* (University of Rochester Press, 2005).

41 For more see Susan Youens, *Hugo Wolf: The Vocal Music* (Cambridge University Press, 1992), pp. 200–3.

42 For more see Robert Orledge, 'Evocations of exoticism', in Deborah Mawer (ed.), *The Cambridge Companion to Ravel* (Cambridge University Press, 2000), pp. 27–46.

43 For more see Peter Kaminsky, 'Vocal Music and the Lures of Exoticism and Irony', in Mawer (ed.), *The Cambridge Companion to Ravel*, pp. 162–87; here pp. 178–84.

44 Arthur Hoérée, 'L'Oeuvre vocal', *R&M* December 1938, p. 104; cited in Rollo H. Myers, *Ravel* (London: Dent, 1977), p. 128. Bathori had worked closely with Debussy and Satie: see the biographical overview in her *On the Interpretation of the Mélodies of Claude Debussy*, trans. Linda Laurent (Stuyvesant, NY: Pendragon, 1998), pp. 1–19.

45 Op. 24 was composed for voice and piano; three years later, Szymanowski returned to the Hafiz poems to create a new eight-song cycle for voice and orchestra, only using

three of the numbers from the first set: the first and fifth, 'Wünsche' and 'Der Verliebte Ostwind', and the fourth, 'Tanz'.

46 Alistair Wightman, *Karol Szymanowski: His Life and Work* (Aldershot: Ashgate, 1999), p. 138; Wightman compares melodic aspects of two songs from op. 26 to a characteristic arabic melodic unit, or *ajnā*; see p. 139.

47 For extended discussion of the cycle see Stephen Downes, *Szymanowski: Eroticism and the Voices of Mythology* (Aldershot: Ashgate, RMA Monographs, 2003), pp. 38–53.

48 Quoted in Jim Samson, *The Music of Szymanowski* (London: Kahn and Averill, 1980), p. 153.

49 Quoted in Wightman, *Karol Szymanowski*, p. 251.

50 See his letter to Zofia Kochańska, 20 June 1921, cited in Wightman, *Karol Szymanowski*, p. 252.

51 For more on this see Jim Samson, *Music in Transition: A Study of Tonal Expansion and Atonality (1900–1920)* (Oxford University Press, 1995), pp. 200–4; and 'Szymanowski and Polish Nationalism', *The Musical Times* 131 (1990), pp. 135–7.

52 Karol Szymanowski, 'Thoughts on Polish Criticism in Music Today' (from *The Warsaw New Literary Review* July 1920), in *Karol Szymanowski and Jan Smeterlin: Correspondence and Essays*, trans. Bugusław Maciejewski and Felix Aprahamian (London: Allegro Press, 1970), pp. 85–92; here 91.

7 Modern subjects

1 Webern will not be dealt with in detail here: his Trakl cycle, op. 14, is discussed at length in Anne C. Shreffler, *Webern and the Lyric Impulse: Songs and Fragments on Poems of Georg Trakl* (Oxford: Clarendon Press, 1994). Hindemith, Schoeck and Britten are discussed in Chapter 8. For more on the NMC Songbook see www.nmcrec.co.uk.

2 Letter to Emil Hertzska quoted in H.H. Stuckenschmidt, *Arnold Schoenberg: His Life, World and Work*, trans. Humphrey Searle (New York: Schirmer, 1978), p. 135.

3 On the chronology of *Gurrelieder* see Walter Frisch, *The Early Works of Arnold Schoenberg, 1893–1908* (Berkeley, CA: University of California Press, 1993), pp. 140–57.

4 See Alexander Zemlinsky, 'Jugenderinnerungen', in *Arnold Schoenberg zum 60. Geburtstag* (Vienna: Universal, 1934), pp. 33–5.

5 Jacobsen's *Gurresange* were written in 1868–9 and published posthumously in 1886. The version of Robert Franz Arnold's German translation that Schoenberg used appeared in 1897.

6 Alban Berg, *Arnold Schönberg. Gurrelieder Führer* (Leipzig and Vienna: Universal, 1913), p. 45; see also Frisch, *The Early Works of Arnold Schoenberg*, pp. 153–6.

7 For more on the harmonic language of *Gurrelieder* see Ethan Haimo, *Schoenberg's Transformation of Musical Language* (Cambridge University Press, 2006), pp. 58–65; and Frisch, *The Early Works of Arnold Schoenberg*, pp. 140–57.

8 The revised version requires six soloists and four choirs (three four-part male choirs and one eight-part mixed choir). The orchestra is also huge, asking for 80 strings, 25 winds, 25 brass, 4 harps, celeste and percussion (including heavy chains).

9 The concert took place on 14 January 1910, at the Wiener Verein für Kunst und Kultur. See Julie Brown, 'Schoenberg's Early Wagnerisms: Atonality and the Redemption of Ahaseurus', *Cambridge Opera Journal* 6 (1994), pp. 51–80, esp. p. 53.

10 1910 programme note, excerpted in Brown, 'Schoenberg's Early Wagnerisms', p. 53, from Willi Reich, *Schoenberg: A Critical Biography*, trans. Leo Black (New York: Praeger, 1971), pp. 48–9.

11 The other two works were the two op. 14 songs and the Three Piano Pieces op. 11.

12 Stéphane Mallarmé, 'Réponse à une Enquête' (1891), quoted in Guy Michaud, *La Doctrine symboliste: Documents* (Paris: Nizet, 1955), p. 74.

13 For a similar argument about Alban Berg's *Altenberg Lieder* op. 4, see David P. Schroeder, 'Alban Berg and Peter Altenberg: Intimate Art and the Aesthetics of Life', *Journal of the American Musicological Society* 46 (1993), pp. 261–94.

14 See Albrecht Dümling, 'Public Loneliness: Atonality and the Crisis of Subjectivity in Schönberg's Opus 15', in Konrad Boehmer (ed.), *Schönberg and Kandinsky: An Historic Encounter* (Amsterdam: Harwood, 1997), pp. 101–97.

15 For an extended reading of the first song see Julie Brown, 'Schoenberg's Musical Prose as Allegory', *Music Analysis* 14 (1995), pp. 161–91.

16 The quote is Otto Julius Bierbaum's characterisation of cabarets in his novel *Stilpe* (1897), which was a further inspiration for Ernst von Wolzogen's establishment of the *Überbrettl*.

17 M. Green and J. Swan, *The Triumph of Pierrot: The Commedia dell'Arte and the Modern Imagination* (New York: Macmillan, 1986), p. 26; on Schoenberg, see pp. 195–232.

18 Susan Youens, 'The Texts of *Pierrot lunaire*', *Journal of the Arnold Schoenberg Institute* 8 (1987), pp. 94–115; and Glenn Watkins, *Pyramids at the Louvre: Music, Culture, and Collage from Stravinsky to the Postmodernists* (Cambridge, MA: Harvard University Press, 1994), p. 283.

19 For more on this see Jonathan Dunsby's detailed account of the work in *Schoenberg: 'Pierrot lunaire'* (Cambridge University Press, 1992), pp. 28–72.

20 Alan Lessem, *Music and Text in the Works of Arnold Schoenberg: The Critical Years 1908–1922* (Ann Arbor, MI: UMI Research Press, 1979), p. 126.

21 Quoted in Dunsby, *Schoenberg: 'Pierrot lunaire'*, p. 45.

22 For a historical overview see Jacqueline Waeber, *En musique dans le texte: Le Mélodrame, de Rousseau à Schoenberg* (Paris: Van Dieren Editeur, 2006).

23 Edward F. Kravitt, 'The Influence of Theatrical Declamation upon Composers of the Late Romantic Era', *Acta Musicologica* 34 (1962), pp. 18–28.

24 Pierre Boulez, 'Trajectories: Ravel, Stravinsky, Schoenberg', *Notes of an Apprenticeship*, trans. Paul Thévenin (New York: Knopf, 1968), pp. 242–67. On the relationship between Stravinsky's *Trois Poésies* and *Pierrot*, see Stephen Walsh, *The Music of Stravinsky* (Oxford: Clarendon Press, 1993); on Ravel's songs see Robert Gronquist, 'Ravel's *Trois Poèmes de Stéphane Mallarmé*', *Musical Quarterly* 64 (1978), pp. 507–23.

25 See Andrew Meyer, 'Schoenberg's *Pierrot* in Paris: Rezeption, Projektion und Einfluss', in Mark Delaere and Jan Herman (eds.), *Pierrot lunaire: Albert Giraud – Otto*

Erich Hartleben – Arnold Schoenberg: A Collection of Musicological and Literary Studies (Louvain and Paris: Éditions Peeters, 2004), pp. 173–92; and David Metzer, 'The New York Reception of *Pierrot lunaire*: The 1923 Premiere and its Aftermath', *Musical Quarterly* 78 (1994), pp. 669–99.

26 See Lorraine Gorrell, *Discordant Melody: Alexander Zemlinsky, His Songs, and the Second Viennese School* (Westport, CT: Greenwood Press, 2002), p. 253 n. 76, quoting Darius Milhaud, 'Of Arnold Schoenberg on His Seventieth Birthday: Personal Recollections', *Musical Quarterly* 30 (1944), pp. 379–84, esp. 383.

27 According to a letter to Zemlinsky of 2 October 1912, Schoenberg had arranged at least 25 rehearsals before the work's premiere. Quoted in Dunsby, *Schoenberg: 'Pierrot lunaire'*, p. 25. See Gorrell, *Discordant Melody*, pp. 8–88. David Metzer points out that a further reason for the objection was that Schoenberg had planned to present *Pierrot* alongside *Gurrelieder* on an American tour in 1923. The International Composers' Guild was eventually granted permission to perform *Pierrot* by the score's publishers. Schoenberg conducted the work in New York on 17 November 1940. Metzer, 'The New York Reception of *Pierrot lunaire*', p. 670.

28 Stephen Lloyd, 'Poetry through a Megaphone', in *William Walton: Muse of Fire* (Woodbridge: Boydell Press, 2001), pp. 28–58.

29 See Roger Marsh, 'A Multicoloured Approach: Rediscovering Albert Giraud's *Pierrot lunaire*', *Twentieth-Century Music* 4 (2007), pp. 97–121.

30 In 1970, following Birtwistle's departure, the group was renamed The Fires of London, and continued until 1987. Other ensembles have also taken *Pierrot*'s configuration as their guide: for example, the Da Capo Chamber Players, eighth blackbird and Finnish group Uusinta Lunaire. Jonathan Cross briefly discusses further *Pierrot*-inspired pieces by Davies, Birtwistle and Henze in *The Stravinsky Legacy* (Cambridge University Press, 1998), p. 145.

31 See Cross, *The Stravinsky Legacy*, p. 145.

32 For some commentators, though, Maxwell Davies's evocation of the sound world of *Pierrot lunaire* in *Eight Songs for a Mad King* just reveals the extent of his dependence on the past; see David Metzer, *Quotation and Cultural Meaning in Twentieth-Century Music* (Cambridge University Press, 2003), p. 104.

8 The death of the song cycle

1 Mary Lawton, *Schumann-Heink: The Last of the Titans* (New York, 1928; reprint 1977), p. 331. Richard Strauss and Elisabeth Schumann also toured the East Coast immediately after the end of the war, with the intention of promoting German music.

2 Alfred Einstein, *Observer* review of 200th South-place Sunday concert 4 November 1934, included in Catherine Dower, *Alfred Einstein on Music: Selected Music Criticisms* (New York: Greenwood Press, 1991), p. 178.

3 Quoted in Anton Haefeli and Reinhard Oehlschlägel, 'International Society for Contemporary Music', *Grove Music Online*, accessed 26 February 2010.

4 The literature on music in the Nazi regime is extensive: for an introduction see Pamela M. Potter, 'Music in the Third Reich: The Complex Task of "Germanization"', in Jonathan Huener and Francis R. Nicosia (eds.), *The Arts in Nazi Germany: Continuity, Conformity, Change* (New York and Oxford: Berghahn, 2006), pp. 85–104.

5 See Gerhardt's account in *Recital* (London: Methuen, 1953), pp. 114–19. The broadcasters were arrested because they were not members of the Nazi party; Kohl was the only one to be released.

6 Arnold Toynbee, 'Whither Mankind?' (26 March 1931), quoted in Richard Overy, *The Morbid Age: Britain Between the Wars* (London: Penguin, 2009), p. 37.

7 See Arnold Whittall, *Serialism* (Cambridge University Press, 2008).

8 For an introduction see Stephen Hinton, 'Weill: *Neue Sachlichkeit*, Surrealism and *Gebrauchsmusik*', in Kim H. Kowalke (ed.), *A New Orpheus: Essays on Kurt Weill* (New Haven, CT: Yale University Press, 1986), pp. 61–82; and 'Aspects of Hindemith's *Neue Sachlichkeit*', *Hindemith-Jahrbuch* 14 (1987), pp. 22–107.

9 Berg's first serial piece was a song; see also Anne Shreffler, '"Mein Weg geht jetzt vorüber": The Vocal Origins of Webern's Twelve-Tone Compositions', *Journal of the American Musicological Society* 47 (1994), pp. 275–339.

10 For more on the significance of Krenek's opera see Claire Taylor-Jay, *The Artist Operas of Pfitzner, Krenek and Hindemith* (Aldershot: Ashgate, 2004).

11 On Zemlinsky's op. 29 see Malcolm S. Cole, 'Afrika singt: Austro-German Echoes of the Harlem Renaissance', *Journal of the American Musicological Society* 30 (1977), pp. 72–95; and Anthony Beaumont, *Zemlinsky* (London: Faber and Faber, 2000), p. 360. Krenek experimented with tonality in the cycles *Fiedellieder* op. 64 (1930) and *Durch die Nacht* op. 67 (1930–1), and with twelve-note clusters in *Gesänge des späten Jahres* op. 71 (1931).

12 See his talk to the Schubert Congress in 1928, cited in John L. Stewart, *Ernst Krenek: The Man and His Music* (Berkeley, CA: University of California Press, 1991), p. 99.

13 Marie Rolf and Elizabeth West Marvin argue that op. 27 is structurally unified and should be considered as a coherent cycle, in 'Analytical Issues and Interpretive Decisions in Two Songs by Richard Strauss', *Intégral* 4 (1990), pp. 67–103.

14 Self-quotation was not unknown to earlier works: 'Traum durch die Dämmerung' op. 29, no. 1 ('The Dream in Twilight') and 'Befreit' op. 39 ('Released'), composed in 1895, are quoted in the tone poem *Ein Heldenleben* (1898).

15 For more on the *Krämerspiegel* see Norman del Mar, *Richard Strauss: A Critical Commentary on his Life and Works* (London: Barrie and Jenkins, 1972), vol. 3, pp. 358–65.

16 For more see Siglind Bruhn, *Musical Ekphrasis in Rilke's 'Marien-Leben'* (Amsterdam: Rodolpi, 2000), p. 72.

17 Geoffrey Skelton, *Paul Hindemith: The Man Behind the Music* (London: Victor Gollancz, 1977), pp. 76–7.

18 Hindemith initially revised the cycle in 1936–9, then again in 1941 and in 1947–8. Four songs were orchestrated in 1939, followed by two more in 1959.

19 For further discussion see Michael Kater, *Composers of the Nazi Era: Eight Portraits* (New York: Cambridge University Press, 2000), pp. 144–82.

20 Christa Jost, 'Hans Pfitzner und das romantische Lied', *Mitteilungen der Hans-Pfitzner-Gesellschaft* 57 (1997), pp. 5–33.

21 Hans Pfitzner, note to *Alte Weisen: Acht Gedichte von Gottfried Keller für eine Singstimme mit Klavier* op. 33 (London: Boosey and Hawkes, 1943).

22 Fischer-Dieskau remembers Schoeck filling notebooks with 'a unified theme'; see his *Echoes of a Lifetime*, trans. Ruth Hein (London: Macmillan, 1989), p. 278.

23 Quoted in Werner Vogel, *Othmar Schoeck im Gespräch* (Zurich: Atlantis, 1965), p. 129; quoted in Derrick Puffett, *The Song Cycles of Othmar Schoeck* (Bern and Stuttgart: Haupt, 1982), p. 177.

24 Vogel, *Othmar Schoeck im Gespräch*, p. 113, quoted in Puffett, *The Song Cycles of Othmar Schoeck*, p. 178.

25 The spare orchestration has been said to refer to Weill and to Stravinsky's *L'Histoire du soldat* (1918); see Chris Walton, *Othmar Schoeck: Life and Works* (University of Rochester Press, 2009), p. 123.

26 For extended discussion of *Gaselen* see Puffett, *The Song Cycles of Othmar Schoeck*, pp. 177–200; on Beethoven's influence especially see pp. 182 and 191.

27 On Schoeck's Hesse cycle op. 44 (1929) see James Parsons, 'The Lied in the Modern Age: To Mid Century', in James Parsons (ed.), *The Cambridge Companion to the Lied* (Cambridge University Press, 2004), pp. 291–4.

28 For further discussion see Stephen Banfield, *Sensibility and English Song: Critical Studies of the Early 20th Century* (Cambridge University Press, 1985), vol. 1, especially pp. 233–47.

29 Wilfrid Mellers, 'Blue Remembered Hills', *Between Old Worlds and New: Occasional Writings on Music* (London: Cygnus Arts, 1997), p. 99.

30 For a brief biographical overview and discussion of Housman's homosexuality see Richard Perceval Graves, *A.E. Housman: The Scholar-Poet* (Oxford University Press, 1981), pp. 103–4.

31 Edwin Evans, 'English Song and *On Wenlock Edge*', *The Musical Times* 59 (June 1918), pp. 247–9; Ernest Newman, 'Concerning *A Shropshire Lad* and Other Matters', *The Musical Times* (September 1918), pp. 393–8.

32 Michael Barlow, *Whom the Gods Love: The Life and Music of George Butterworth* (London: Toccata Press, 1997), p. 63.

33 *A Shropshire Lad* XXVII, in *The Works of A.E. Housman* (Ware: Wordsworth Editions, 1994), p. 43.

34 Newman, 'Concerning *A Shropshire Lad*', p. 397.

35 Newman, 'Concerning *A Shropshire Lad*', p. 397.

36 Constant Lambert, *Music Ho! A Study of Music in Decline* (London: Faber and Faber, 1934), pp. 175 and 172. For a more complex take on Vaughan Williams's approach to folk song see Alain Frogley 'Constructing Englishness in Music: National Character and the Reception of Ralph Vaughan Williams', in Alain Frogley (ed.), *Vaughan Williams Studies* (Cambridge University Press, 1996), pp. 1–22.

37 Lambert, *Music Ho!*, p. 284.

38 Philip Brett, 'Benjamin Britten: Return to England, 1942–50', *Grove Music Online*, accessed 26 February 2010.

39 For more see Arnold Whittall, *The Music of Britten and Tippett: Studies in Themes and Techniques* (Cambridge University Press, 1982), pp. 80–3.

40 For a more detailed account see David Neumeyer, *The Music of Paul Hindemith* (New Haven, CT: Yale University Press, 1986), pp. 137–58.

41 According to his preface, songs 9 and 14 represent the dynamic highpoint and song 11 the expressive crux.

42 *Das Marienleben II* has been taken as an exemplar of the theories Hindemith expounded in *The Craft of Musical Composition*, trans. Otto Ortmann and Arthur Mendel (London: Schott, 1939).

43 Oliver Kemble, 'Good night, Vienna', *The Manchester Guardian* (20 August 1947), p. 3.

44 See Bryan Gilliam, *The Life of Richard Strauss* (Cambridge University Press, 1999), p. 179. Around the same time that he composed the Eichendorff and Hesse settings, Strauss orchestrated 'Ruhe, meine Seele!', a Karl Henckell poem he had included in his op. 27 set.

45 They were recognised at the time as a 'deliberately valedictory offering'; see, for example, Arthur Hutchings's review of 'Strauss's Four Last Songs' arranged for piano, *The Musical Times* 91 (1950), pp. 465–8.

46 The main reason for his visit, though, was to unfreeze some business royalties; as had happened to him during the previous war, he had been unable to access funds from his British publishers.

47 Orchestral works and suites derived from his operas were performed by the Royal Philharmonic Orchestra, conducted by Sir Thomas Beecham and Norman del Mar. Neville Cardus, 'Richard Strauss in London', *The Manchester Guardian* (7 October 1947), p. 3.

48 'Profile: Richard Strauss', *The Observer* (12 October 1947), p. 6.

9 Performance

1 Initially cylinders rather than discs had been used. For an introduction to the history of recording technology see Timothy Day, *A Century of Recorded Music: Listening to Musical History* (New Haven, CT: Yale University Press, 2000).

2 Desmond Shawe-Taylor, 'Elena Gerhardt and the Gramophone', in Elena Gerhardt, *Recital* (London: Methuen, 1953), p. 170. The eight songs were 'Gute Nacht', 'Der Lindenbaum', 'Wasserflut', 'Frühlingstraum', 'Die Post', 'Der Krähe', 'Der Wegweiser' and 'Der Leiermann'.

3 On the background of the Wolf Society see Day, *A Century of Recorded Music*, pp. 69–70.

4 For an account of the relationship between recording and music education in the USA see Mark Katz, *Capturing Sound: How Technology has Changed Music* (Berkeley, CA: University of California Press, 2004), pp. 48–71.

5 Compton Mackenzie, *The Gramophone* 9: 102 (1931), p. 203; quoted in Day, *A Century of Recorded Music*, p. 70.

6 For more on the importance of records' tangibility see Katz, *Capturing Sound*, pp. 9–12.

7 Gerhardt soon returned to the stage as a participant in Dame Myra Hess's National Gallery midday concerts, the success of which spawned lunchtime recitals around the country. In her memoirs she remembers performing Schubert's complete *Winterreise* in Reading. See *Recital*, pp. 125–30. The BBC soon began broadcasting Lieder again.

8 Fischer-Dieskau was not the first to record *Winterreise*; the first complete recording was made by baritone Hans Duhan, accompanied by Ferdinand Foll and Lena Orthmann in 1928 for HMV: it ran to twenty-four sides. Soprano Lotte Lehmann, tenors Max Meili and Peter Anders, and baritones Marko Rothmuller, Karl Schmitt-Walter and Hans Hotter all recorded the cycle during the 1940s: Anders and Hotter even made more than one version.

9 Dietrich Fischer-Dieskau, *Echoes of a Lifetime*, trans. Ruth Hein (London: Macmillan, 1989), p. 11.

10 Fischer-Dieskau, *Echoes of a Lifetime*, pp. 43 and 312. Later in life he would host gramophone evenings at his home; see Hans A. Neunzig, *Dietrich Fischer-Dieskau: A Biography*, trans. Kenneth S. Whitton (London: Duckworth, 1998), p. 79.

11 J.B. Steane, *The Grand Tradition: 70 Years of Singing on Record* (London: Duckworth, 1974), p. 223.

12 Fortunately, the technology was available by this point for them to do something about it. Although Fischer-Dieskau was notorious for not requiring multiple takes or edits, at least he could repeat things in the studio if necessary.

13 Letter from Lehmann to Fischer-Dieskau, 16 November 1960; quoted in Neunzig, *Dietrich Fischer-Dieskau*, p. 102.

14 Fischer-Dieskau, *Echoes of a Lifetime*, p. 183.

15 For a sample Schubert programme see Neunzig, *Dietrich Fischer-Dieskau*, pp. 74–7.

16 Fischer-Dieskau's re-recordings tended to 'preserve and develop earlier insights', but also reduced emphasis and increased smoothness and beauty of singing. Steane, *The Grand Tradition*, p. 493.

17 Arthur Komar (ed.), *'Dichterliebe' by Robert Schumann: An Authoritative Score, Historical Background, Essays in Analysis, Views and Comments* (London: Chappell, 1971), p. 63.

18 Lotte Lehmann, *Eighteen Song Cycles: Studies in their Interpretation*, with an introduction by Neville Cardus (London: Cassell, 1945; reprinted 1971).

19 Karla Höcker on Fischer-Dieskau, quoted in Neunzig, *Dietrich Fischer-Dieskau*, p. 46.

20 Lehmann, *Eighteen Song Cycles*, p. 9.

21 Pierre Bernac, *Francis Poulenc: The Man and His Songs*, trans. Winifred Radford, with a foreword by Lennox Berkeley (London: Victor Gollancz, 1977), esp. pp. 103–5, on *Les Yeux fertiles*.

22 For example see Roland Barthes's view of him in his essay 'The Grain of the Voice', the starting point for Jonathan Dunsby's 'Roland Barthes and the Grain of Panzéra's Voice', *Journal of the Royal Musical Association* 134 (2009), pp. 113–32.

23 Steane, *The Grand Tradition*, p. 495.

24 Beyond *Winterreise*, there are examples of adaptations such as Ragnar Kjartansson's performance/video of *SCHUMANN machine* (2008), in which the tuxedo-clad artist

sips prosecco and smokes cigars while performing, repeatedly, 'Hör ich das Liedchen klingen' from *Dichterliebe*.

25 David Blayney Brown, catalogue for Mariele Neudecker exhibition 'Over and Over, Again and Again' (St Ives: Tate, 2004).

26 Review by Anna Picard, 'Winterreise, Wigmore Hall', *The Independent* (31 March 2002).

27 The new versions included releases by Mark Padmore and Paul Lewis (Harmonia Mundi), Steve Davislin and Anthony Romaniuk (Melba) and Jules Bastin and Ursula Kneihs (Pavane).

10 Afterlife

1 Alan Bennett, *The Habit of Art* (London: Faber and Faber, 2009), p. 50.

2 See Orin Moe, 'William Grant Still: *Songs of Separation*', *Black Music Research Journal* 1 (1980), pp. 18–36; Larry Starr, *The Dickinson Songs of Aaron Copland* (Hillsdale, NY: Pendragon Press, 2002); and Barbara B. Heyman, *Samuel Barber: The Composer and His Music* (Oxford University Press, 1995).

3 For more on Hölderlin see Laura Tunbridge, *Schumann's Late Style* (Cambridge University Press, 2007), pp. 175–6.

4 Philip Brett, 'Benjamin Britten: Transition and Triumph, 1955–1962', *Grove Music Online*, accessed 26 February 2010.

5 Hugh Wood, 'Britten's Hölderlin Songs', *The Musical Times* 104 (1963), pp. 781–3.

6 There have been cycles and collections by Aribert Reimann (*Hölderlin-Fragmente*, 1963), Wolfgang Rihm (*Hölderlin-Fragmente*, 1977) and Wilhelm Killmayer (*Hölderlin-Lieder*, 1989), among others.

7 See Bjorn Heile, *The Music of Mauricio Kagel* (Aldershot: Ashgate, 2006), pp. 128–33.

8 See Pousseur's essay, *Schumann, le poète (vingt-cinq moments d'une lecture de 'Dichterliebe')* (Paris: Méridiens-Klincksieck, 1993).

9 For more see David Metzer, 'The Paths from and to Abstraction in Stockhausen's *Gesang der Jünglinge*', *Modernism/Modernity* 11 (2004), pp. 695–721; and his *Musical Modernism at the Turn of the Twenty-First Century* (Cambridge University Press, 2009); and P. Decroupet and E. Ungeheuer, 'Through the Sensory Looking Glass: The Aesthetic and Social Functions of *Gesang der Jünglinge*', *Perspectives of New Music* 36 (1998–9), pp. 97–142.

10 According to David Osmond-Smith, Berberian's performance styles in *Aria* incorporated jazz, lyric contralto, *Sprechstimme*, dramatic, Marlene Dietrich, coloratura, folk, oriental, baby and nasal. See 'The Tenth Oscillator: The Work of Cathy Berberian 1958–1966', *Tempo* 58 (2004), pp. 2–13.

11 For more detailed discussion see David Osmond-Smith, *Berio* (Oxford University Press, 1991), p. 68.

12 www.georgecrumb.net/comp/ancien-p.html (accessed 8 January 2010).

13 Quoted in Julian Anderson, 'Gérard Grisey', *Grove Music Online*, accessed 26 February 2010.

14 Steve Reich, 'Early Works', in *Writings on Music 1965–2000*, ed. Paul Hillier (Oxford University Press, 2002), p. 21.

15 Brian Ferneyhough, *Collected Writings*, ed. James Boros and Richard Toop (Amsterdam: Harwood Academic Press, 1995), p. 292.

16 Brian Ferneyhough, *Collected Writings*, pp. 296–7.

17 Richard Toop, 'Brian Ferneyhough's *Etudes Transcendentales*: A Composer's Diary (Part I)', *Eonta* 1 (1991), pp. 55–89.

18 Another recent example is Michael Finnissy's *Whitman* (1980; revised 2004–5), which relates the biography of nineteenth-century American poet Walt Whitman, taking musical cues from his poems and diaries. Or Ned Rorem's *Evidence of Things Not Seen*, made up of three sets of thirty-six poems, divided into 'Beginnings', 'Middles' and 'Ends'.

19 'Moscow Christmas: A Diary (December 1966)', *Peter Pears: Travel Diaries 1936–1978*, ed. Philip Reed (Woodbridge: Boydell Press, 1995), p. 150.

20 'Armenian Holiday: A Diary (August 1965)', *Peter Pears: Travel Diaries*, pp. 132–3.

21 See Francis Maes, 'Between Reality and Transcendence: Shostakovich's Songs', in Pauline Fairclough and David Fanning (eds.), *The Shostakovich Companion* (Cambridge University Press, 2008), pp. 231–58.

22 Maes, 'Between Reality and Transcendence'.

23 Elliott Carter seems to be enjoying an extended late period, during which he has produced *Of Challenge and of Love* (1994) and *In the Distances of Sleep* (2006).

24 In fact it was a journalist's reworking of a poem from 1926; see Katharine Conley, 'The Myth of the "Dernier poème": Robert Desnos and French Cultural Memory', in Mieke Bal, Jonathan V. Crewe and Leo Spitzer (eds.), *Acts of Memory: Cultural Recall in the Present* (Hanover, NH: University Press of New England, 1999), pp. 134–46. Poulenc set the Poème as a *mélodie* in 1956.

25 Robert Desnos, *Domaine publique*, ed. René Bertelé (Paris: Gallimard, 1953), p. 408; translated in Conley, 'The Myth of the "Dernier poème"', p. 136.

11 Rebirth

1 Franco Fabbri, 'A Theory of Musical Genres: Two Applications', in David Horn and Philip Tagg (eds.), *Popular Music Perspectives* (Göteborg: International Association for the Study of Popular Music, 1981), pp. 52–81.

2 Unpublished paper by Travis A. Jackson, '*What's Going On*: Authorship, Accidents and the Concept Album' (2004). Quoted with the author's permission.

3 McLuhan first used the phrase in *Understanding Media: The Extensions of Man* (1964; reprinted London: Routledge, 2001).

4 Michael Chanan, *Repeated Takes: A Short History of Recording and its Effects on Music* (London: Verso, 1995), p. 112.

5 For an excellent account of the impact of recording see Elijah Wald, *How the Beatles Destroyed Rock 'n' Roll: An Alternative History of American Popular Music* (Oxford

University Press, 2009); Wald usefully points out the gender bias of popular music criticism, and reminds us of the importance of female markets.

6 There were songbooks of Cole Porter, and Rodgers and Hart (both in arrangements by Buddy Bregman, released 1956); Duke Ellington (arr. Ellington and Billy Strayhorn, 1957); Irving Berlin (arr. Paul Weston, 1958); George and Ira Gershwin (arr. Nelson Riddle, 1959); Harold Arlen (arr. Billy May, 1961); Jerome Kern (arr. Riddle, 1963); and Johnny Mercer (arr. Riddle, 1964).

7 See Susan Nanes, 'Maturity and Masculinity: Frank Sinatra in the 1950s', in Kristi S. Long and Matthew Nadelhaft (eds.), *America Under Construction: Boundaries and Identities in Popular Culture* (New York: Garland, 1997), pp. 19–36; especially 33–4.

8 See Wald, *How the Beatles Destroyed Rock 'n' Roll*, pp. 184–98.

9 Virgil Moorefield compares the producer to the film auteur; see *The Producer as Composer: Shaping the Sound of Popular Music* (Cambridge, MA: The MIT Press, 2005).

10 Ronnie Spector, 'Phil Spector and the Wall of Sound', in Theo Canteforis (ed.), *The Rock History Reader* (New York: Routledge, 2007), pp. 45–51.

11 Wald, *How the Beatles Destroyed Rock 'n' Roll*, p. 236.

12 See Daniel Harrison, 'After Sundown: The Beach Boys' Experimental Music', in John Covach and Graeme M. Boone (eds.), *Understanding Rock: Essays in Musical Analysis* (Oxford University Press, 1997), pp. 33–58.

13 David Leaf, *The Beach Boys and the California Myth* (New York: Grosset and Dunlap, 1978).

14 For more on the collaborative nature of recording see Albin J. Zak III, *The Poetics of Rock: Cutting Tracks, Making Records* (Berkeley, CA: University of California Press, 2001), pp. 163–4.

15 For extended discussion of Dylan's songwriting skills in the mid-1960s see Greil Marcus, *Like a Rolling Stone: Bob Dylan at the Crossroads* (London: Faber and Faber, 2005).

16 Walter Everett, *The Beatles as Musicians: The Quarrymen through 'Rubber Soul'* (Oxford University Press, 2001), p. 312. On the transition from pop to rock see Theodor Gracyk, *Rhythm and Noise: An Aesthetics of Rock* (Durham, NC: Duke University Press, 1996).

17 Keith Badman, *The Beatles off the Record* (London: Omnibus Press, 2000), p. 188.

18 Quoted in Charles L. Granata, *I Just Wasn't Made For These Times: Brian Wilson and The Making of 'Pet Sounds'* (London: Unanimous, 2003), p. 235.

19 Wald points out that the first stereo LP (1957) had the Dukes of Dixieland on one side and a selection of train sounds on the other; *How The Beatles Destroyed Rock 'n' Roll*, p. 188.

20 Philip Lambert, 'Brian Wilson's *Pet Sounds*', *Twentieth-Century Music* 5 (2008), pp. 109–33.

21 'Strawberry Fields' and 'Penny Lane' came from the same recording sessions but did not make it onto the album. Instead they were released as a double A-side single. UK chart protocol prevented anything issued as a single from being included on an LP in the same year.

22 Ian MacDonald's *Revolution in the Head: Beatles Records and the Sixties* (London: Pimlico, 1995) usefully documents tracks in chronological order.

23 As Sheila Whiteley points out, there is never any doubt that this is The Beatles. *The Space Between the Notes: Rock and the Counter-Culture* (London: Routledge, 1992), pp. 40–1.

24 See Mark Lewisohn, *The Beatles: Recording Sessions* (New York: Harmonium Books, 1988); George Martin, *All You Need is Ears* (New York: St Martin's Press, 1979); and George Martin and William Pearson, *Summer of Love: The Making of Sgt Pepper* (London: Macmillan, 1994).

25 Allan F. Moore, *The Beatles: Sgt Pepper's Lonely Hearts Club Band* (Cambridge University Press, 1997).

26 In *The Times*, critic Kenneth Tynan declared the release of *Sgt Pepper* 'a decisive moment in the history of Western civilisation'. Controversy surrounded the band with claims that certain songs endorsed drug use. MacDonald probably rightly describes responses to the album as more of a 'cultural "contact high"'; both 'the most authentic aural simulation of the psychedelic experience ever created' and 'a distillation of the spirit of 1967 as it was felt by vast numbers across the Western world who had never taken drugs in their lives'. *Revolution in the Head*, p. 199.

27 The bright colours of *Sgt Pepper*'s inside cover were also lampooned, as were The Beatles' music and lyrics: see James Borders, 'Form and the Concept Album: Aspects of Modernism in Frank Zappa's Early Releases', *Perspectives of New Music* 39 (2001), pp. 118–60.

28 British cultural theorist Paul Willis explained that hippies' claims that they preferred LPs to singles because they were 'clearly for listening to' really meant that they were suitable to take drugs to; see *Profane Culture* (London: Routledge Falmer, 1978).

29 The two sides of Zappa's album, labelled Lumpy Gravy Part I and II, were the first to play continuously, without gaps between tracks; see Borders, 'Form and the Concept Album', p. 125.

30 Indeed, Wilfrid Mellers argued that the concept album should be considered primarily a literary, rather than a musical, form: see *The Twilight of the Gods: The Music of The Beatles* (New York: Viking Press, 1974), pp. 89–93.

31 While the austerity of Bob Dylan's *John Wesley Harding* (1968) is generally considered to fly in the face of the era's psychedelic inclinations, he included a fantastical story in the liner notes – something to do with three kings and three buddies – which referenced the album's songs.

32 Wilson performed his album live in 2000 (and recorded it in 2002); American pop group Cheap Trick gave and recorded a live performance of *Sgt Pepper* to mark the album's fortieth anniversary.

33 William Mann, 'The Beatles Revive Hopes of Progress in Pop Music', *The Times*, 29 May 1967 (Issue 56,953, col. E).

34 Quoted in J. Marks, *Rock and Other Four Letter Words* (New York: Bantam Books, 1968), p. 15.

35 There are other contenders from 1968, from Van Morrison's *Astral Weeks* to Joan Baez's collaboration with Peter Schickele (P.D.Q. Bach), *Baptism: A Journey through Our Time*.

36 *Smile* relayed American history through the eyes of a time-travelling bicyclist on a journey from Plymouth Rock to Hawaii. Brian Wilson and Parks returned to complete the project in 2002. For more, see Domenic Priore, *Smile: the Story of Brian Wilson's Lost Masterpiece* (London: Sanctuary, 2005).

37 For more on the album see Carter Dale, 'What's Still Left of My Memory: Recovery and Reorientation in the Songs of Van Dyke Park', *Popular Music and Society* 27 (2004), pp. 387–405.

38 Review by Jim Miller, 24 February 1968; see www.rollingstone.com (accessed 30 December 2009).

39 Bernard Gendron, *Between Montmartre and the Mudd Club: Popular Music and the Avant-Garde* (University of Chicago Press, 2002), p. 61; quoted in Lloyd Whitesell, *The Music of Joni Mitchell* (Oxford University Press, 2008), p. 4.

40 See, for instance, Carys Wyn Jones, *The Rock Canon: Canonical Values in the Reception of Rock Albums* (Aldershot: Ashgate, 2008), p. 43.

41 Whitesell, *The Music of Joni Mitchell*, pp. 194–5.

42 On the gender politics of Mitchell's early career see Stuart Henderson, 'All Pink and Clean and Full of Wonder? Gendering "Joni Mitchell", 1966–1974', *Left History* 10 (2005), pp. 83–109.

43 Mitchell had considered including some earlier material but decided against it at a late stage in the recording process.

44 Whitesell, *The Music of Joni Mitchell*, p. 196; his chapter 'Collections and Cycles' discusses *Song to a Seagull* (1968), *For the Roses* (1972), *Hejira* (1976), and *Don Juan's Reckless Daughter* (1977), pp. 195–226.

45 Ben Edmonds, *Marvin Gaye: 'What's Going On' and the Last Days of Motown* (London: MOJO books, 2001), pp. 97–8. The single's B-side was 'God is Love', which in altered form would become the fifth track on the album.

46 Suzanne E. Smith, *Dancing in the Street: Motown and the Cultural Politics of Detroit* (Cambridge, MA: Harvard University Press, 1999), p. 238.

47 A table of tonal, metrical and structural features of the album is provided by Kevin J. Holm-Hudson, 'Worked Out within the Grooves: The Sound and Structure of *The Dark Side of the Moon*', in Russell Reising (ed.), *'Speak to Me': The Legacy of Pink Floyd's 'The Dark Side of the Moon'* (Aldershot: Ashgate, 2005), pp. 78–80.

48 Quoted in Edmonds, *Marvin Gaye*, p. 196.

49 Vince Aletti, review 5 August 1971, *Rolling Stone*.

50 Another black female artist who created what are often referred to as disco concept albums was Donna Summer; see her *Four Seasons of Love* (1976), which consists of four extended tracks: Side 1, 'Spring Affair' and 'Summer Fever'; Side 2, 'Autumn Changes' and 'Winter Melody'.

51 For more see R. Serge Denisoff and William K. Schurk, *Tarnished Gold: The Record Industry Revisited* (London: Transaction, 1986), pp. 253–5.

52 It was not insignificant that ELP were something of a super group: trained classical musicians, who had previously played with The Nice, King Crimson and Atomic
Rooster. For more on the phenomenon of art rock see Jim Curtis, *Rock Eras: Interpretations of Music and Society, 1954–1984* (Bowling Green University Press, 2003),
pp. 278–85; and on the rock elite see Jason Toynbee, *Making Popular Music: Musicians,
Creativity and Institutions* (London: Bloomsbury, 2000), p. 93.

53 For serious consideration of their music see Allan F. Moore, *Aqualung* (London: Continuum, 2004); and 'Jethro Tull and the Case for Modernism in Mass Culture', in Allan F.
Moore (ed.), *Analysing Popular Music* (Cambridge University Press, 2003), pp. 158–72.

54 Cliff Jones, *Echoes: The Stories Behind Every Pink Floyd Song* (London: Carlton, 1996),
p. 6.

55 John Harris, *The Dark Side of the Moon: The Making of the Pink Floyd Masterpiece*
(London: HarperPerennial, 2006).

56 Holm-Hudson also points out the influence of electronic pioneers Paul Beaver and
Bernard Krause, who had recently released three albums: *In a Wild Sanctuary* (1970),
Gandharva (1971) and *All Good Men* (1972). 'Worked Out within the Grooves',
pp. 71–3.

57 On unifying aspects of the album's musical design see Shaugn O'Donnell, '"On the
Path": Tracing Tonal Coherence in *The Dark Side of the Moon*', in Reising (ed.), *'Speak
to Me'*, pp. 87–103; and Phil Rose, *Which One's Pink? An Analysis of the Concept Albums
of Roger Waters and Pink Floyd* (London: Collector's Guide Publishing, 1998).

58 Even if some listeners have found one for it in *The Wizard of Oz*; see Lee Baron and Ian
Inglis, '"We're Not in Kansas Anymore": Music, Myth and Narrative Structure in *The
Dark Side of the Moon*', in Reising (ed.), *'Speak to Me'*, pp. 56–66.

59 Ger Tillekens, 'The Keys to Quiet Desperation: Modulating Between Misery and Madness', in Reising (ed.), *'Speak to Me'*, pp. 104–22; here p. 105; and Sheila Whiteley, *The
Space Between the Notes*, pp. 103–10.

60 The divide between concept album and rock musical is often blurred during the creative
process; David Bowie had initially intended *The Rise and Fall of Ziggy Stardust and the
Spiders from Mars* (1972) to be a television or stage show and, more recently, Fatboy
Slim's and David Byrne's *Here Lies Love*, conceived as a musical about Imelda Marcos,
has been repackaged as a concept album.

61 According to Allan F. Moore: 'The concept album, far from vanishing, has grown to the
extent that all rock tours have acquired particular identities, existing largely to promote
a particular album.' See his *Rock: The Primary Text – Developing a Musicology of Rock*
(Aldershot: Ashgate, 2001), p. 92.

62 Interestingly, those live performances are often recorded. For example, Heart performed
their 1976 debut album *Dreamboat Annie* live in 2007 and released a recording the
following year, while at least two Genesis tribute bands have reproduced the 1974
album *The Lamb Lies Down on Broadway* in concert (ReGenesis, 2001; The Musical
Box, 2004–5).

63 Dai Griffiths, *Radiohead's 'OK Computer'* (New York: Continuum International Publishing Group, 2004).

64 Tim Footman, *Welcome to the Machine: OK Computer and the Death of the Classic Album* (New Malden: Chrome Dreams, 2008).

65 See Katz, *Capturing Sound*, pp. 160–3.

66 In March 2010 Pink Floyd won a court ruling preventing EMI selling individual tracks from their albums without the band's permission.

67 Kitty Empire, 'The Boy is Back in Town', review of Brian Wilson at the Royal Festival Hall, 16 September 2007, *The Observer* 'Review', p. 19.

Guide to further reading

General

Bernhart, W. and W. Wolf, eds., *Word and Music Studies: Essays on the Song Cycle and on Defining the Field* (Amsterdam: Rodopi, 2001).

Hallmark, R., ed., *German Lieder in the 19th Century* (New York: Schirmer, 1996).

Kramer, L., *Music and Poetry: The Nineteenth Century and After* (Berkeley, CA: University of California Press, 1994).

Kravitt, E.F., *The Lied: Mirror of Late Romanticism* (New Haven, CT: Yale University Press, 1996).

Parsons, J., ed., *The Cambridge Companion to the Lied* (Cambridge University Press, 2004).

Rosen, C., *The Romantic Generation* (Cambridge, MA: Harvard University Press, 1995).

Stokes, R., *The Book of Lieder: The Original Texts of Over 1000 Songs* (London: Faber and Faber, 2005).

Early cycles

Peake, L.E., 'The Antecedents of Beethoven's Liederkreis', *Music and Letters* 153 (1982), 242–60.

   'Kreutzer's *Wanderlieder*: The Other *Winterreise*', *Musical Quarterly* 65 (1979), 83–102.

Turchin, B. 'The 19th-century *Wanderlieder* Cycle', *Journal of Musicology* 5 (1987), 498–525.

Schubert

Chusid, M., ed., *A Companion to Schubert's 'Schwanengesang': History, Poets, Analysis, Performance* (New Haven, CT: Yale University Press, 2000).

Gibbs, C., ed., *The Cambridge Companion to Schubert* (Cambridge University Press, 1997).

Kramer, L., *Franz Schubert: Sexuality, Subjectivity, Song* (Cambridge University Press, 1998).

Kramer, R., *Distant Cycles: Schubert and the Conceiving of Song* (University of Chicago Press, 1994).

Messing, S., *Schubert in the European Imagination*, 2 vols. (University of Rochester Press, 2007).

Youens, S., *Schubert's Late Lieder: Beyond the Song Cycles* (Cambridge University Press, 2002).

Schubert, Müller and 'Die schöne Müllerin' (Cambridge University Press, 1997).

Schubert: 'Die schöne Müllerin' (Cambridge University Press, 1992).

Retracing a Winter's Journey: Schubert's 'Winterreise' (Ithaca, NY: Cornell University Press, 1992).

'Behind the Scenes: *Die schöne Müllerin* before Schubert', *19th-Century Music* 15 (1991–2), 3–22.

Schumann

Daverio, J., *Robert Schumann: Herald of a 'New Poetic Age'* (Oxford University Press, 1997).

Ferris, D., *Schumann's Eichendorff Liederkreis and the Genre of the Romantic Cycle* (Oxford University Press, 2000).

Finson, J.W., *Robert Schumann: The Book of Songs* (Cambridge, MA: Harvard University Press, 2007).

Hoecker, B., 'Paths Through *Dichterliebe*', *19th-Century Music* 30 (2006), 65–80.

Muxfeldt, K., '*Frauenliebe und Leben* Now and Then', *19th-Century Music* 25 (2001), 27–48.

Perrey, B.J., *Schumann's 'Dichterliebe' and Early Romantic Poetics: Fragmentation of Desire* (Cambridge University Press, 2002).

Mahler

Johnson, J., *Mahler's Voices: Expression and Irony in the Songs and Symphonies* (Oxford University Press, 2009).

Knapp, R., *Symphonic Metamorphoses: Subjectivity and Alienation in Mahler's Re-Cycled Songs* (Middletown, CT: Wesleyan University Press, 2003).

Youens, S., 'Schubert, Mahler and the Weight of the Past: *Lieder eines fahrenden Gesellen* and *Winterreise*', *Music and Letters* 67 (1986), 48–61.

French cycles

Bloom, P., ed., *Berlioz Studies* (Cambridge University Press, 1992).

Buckland, S. and M. Chimènes, eds., *Francis Poulenc: Music, Art and Literature* (Aldershot: Ashgate, 1999).

Caballero, C., *Fauré and French Musical Aesthetics* (Cambridge University Press, 2001).

Fauser, A., *Musical Encounters at the 1889 Paris World Fair* (University of Rochester Press, 2005).

Irvine, D., *Massenet: A Chronicle of his Life and Times* (Portland, OR: Amadeus Press, 1994).

Mawer, D., ed., *The Cambridge Companion to Ravel* (Cambridge University Press, 2000).

Noske, F., *French Song from Berlioz to Duparc: The Origin and Development of the Mélodie*, trans. Rita Benton (New York: Dover, 1970).

Russian cycles

Emerson, C., *The Life of Musorgsky* (Cambridge University Press, 1999).

Perry, S., 'A Voice Unknown: Undercurrents in Mussorgsky's *Sunless*', *19th-Century Music* 28 (2004), 15–49.

Sylvester, R.D., *Tchaikovsky's Complete Songs: A Companion with Texts and Translations* (Bloomington, IN: University of Indiana Press, 2004).

Taruskin, *Defining Russia Musically: Historical and Hermeneutical Essays* (Princeton University Press, 1997).

   Musorgsky: Eight Essays and an Epilogue (Princeton University Press, 1993).

Orchestral cycles

Hefling, S., *Mahler: 'Das Lied von der Erde'* (Cambridge University Press, 2000).

Kravitt, E.F., 'The Orchestral Lied: An Inquiry into its Style and Unexpected Flowering around 1900', *The Musical Review* 37 (1976), 209–26.

Mitchell, D. and A. Nicholson, eds., *The Mahler Companion* (Oxford University Press, 2002).

Painter, K., ed., *Mahler and His World* (Princeton University Press, 2002).

Twentieth-century cycles

Banfield, S., *Sensibility and English Song: Critical Studies of the Early 20th Century*, 2 vols. (Cambridge University Press, 1985).

Brown, J.A., 'Schoenberg's Musical Prose as Allegory', *Music Analysis* 14 (1995), 161–91.

   'Schoenberg's Early Wagnerisms: Atonality and the Redemption of Ahaseurus', *Cambridge Opera Journal* 6 (1994), 51–80.

Bruhn, S., *Musical Ekphrasis in Rilke's 'Marien-Leben'* (Amsterdam: Rodopi, 2000).

Dunsby, J., *Schoenberg: 'Pierrot lunaire'* (Cambridge University Press, 1992).

Fairclough, P. and D.J. Fanning, *The Cambridge Companion to Shostakovich* (Cambridge University Press, 2008).

Ferneyhough, B., *Collected Writings*, ed. J. Boros and R. Toop (Amsterdam: Harwood Academic Press, 1995).

Frisch, W., *The Early Works of Arnold Schoenberg, 1893–1908* (Berkeley, CA: University of California Press, 1993).

Gilliam, B., *The Life of Richard Strauss* (Cambridge University Press, 1999).

Haimo, E., *Schoenberg's Transformation of Musical Language* (Cambridge University Press, 2006).

Heile, B., *The Music of Mauricio Kagel* (Aldershot: Ashgate, 2006).

Kater, M., *Composers of the Nazi Era: Eight Portraits* (Oxford University Press, 2000).

Metzer, D., *Musical Modernism at the Turn of the 21st Century* (Cambridge University Press, 2009).

   Quotation and Cultural Meaning in Twentieth-Century Music (Cambridge University Press, 2003).

Neumeyer, D., *The Music of Paul Hindemith* (New Haven, CT: Yale University Press, 1986).

Osmond-Smith, D., *Berio* (Oxford University Press, 1991).

Reich, S., *Writings on Music, 1965–2000*, ed. Paul Hillier (Oxford University Press, 2002).

Samson, J., *Music in Transition: A Study of Tonal Expansion and Atonality (1900–1920)* (Oxford University Press, 1995).

   The Music of Szymanowski (London: Kahn and Averill, 1980).

Schreffler, A., *Webern and the Lyric Impulse: Songs and Fragments on Poems of Georg Trakl* (Oxford: Clarendon Press, 1994).

Starr, L. and M.J. Budds, *The Dickinson Songs of Aaron Copland* (Hillside, NY: Pendragon Press, 2002).

Stewart, E., *Ernst Krenek: The Man and His Music* (Berkeley, CA: University of California Press, 1991).

Walton, C., *Othmar Schoeck: Life and Works* (University of Rochester Press, 2009).

Watkins, G., *Pyramids at the Louvre: Music, Culture, and Collage from Stravinsky to the Postmodernists* (Cambridge, MA: Harvard University Press, 1994).

Whittall, A., *The Music of Britten and Tippett: Studies in Themes and Techniques* (Cambridge University Press, 1982).

Wightman, A., *Karol Szymanowski: His Life and Work* (Aldershot: Ashgate, 1999).

Performance

Chanan, M., *Repeated Takes: A Short History of Recording and its Effects on Music* (London: Verso, 1995).

Cook, N., E. Clarke, D. Leech-Wilkinson and J. Rink, *The Cambridge Companion to Recorded Music* (Cambridge University Press, 2009).

Day, T., *A Century of Recorded Music: Listening to Musical History* (New Haven, CT: Yale University Press, 2000).

Elliott, M., *Singing in Style: A Guide to Vocal Performance Practice* (New Haven, CT: Yale University Press, 2006).

Kater, M.H., *Never Sang for Hitler: The Life and Times of Lotte Lehmann, 1886–1976* (Cambridge University Press, 2008).

Katz, M., *Capturing Sound: How Technology Has Changed Music* (Berkeley, CA: University of California Press, 2004).

Scott, D.B., *The Singing Bourgeois: Songs of the Victorian Drawing Room and Parlour* (Milton Keynes: Open University Press, 1989).

Tunley, D., *Salons, Singers and Songs: A Background to Romantic French Song 1830–70* (Aldershot: Ashgate, 2002).

Concept albums

Canteforis, T., ed., *The Rock History Reader* (New York: Routledge, 2007).

Covach, J. and G.M. Boone, *Understanding Rock: Essays in Musical Analysis* (Oxford University Press, 1997).

Curtis, J., *Rock Eras: Interpretations of Music and Society, 1954–1984* (Bowling Green University Press, 2003).

Edmonds, B., *Inner City Blues: Marvin Gaye and the Last Days of the Motown Sound* (Edinburgh: Canongate, 2003).

Everett, W., *The Beatles as Musicians: The Quarrymen through 'Rubber Soul'* (Oxford University Press, 2001).

   The Beatles as Musicians: 'Revolver' through the 'Anthology' (Oxford University Press, 1999).

Footman, T., *Welcome to the Machine: 'OK Computer' and the Death of the Classic Album* (New York: Chrome Dreams, 2008).

Gracyk, T., *Rhythm and Noise: An Aesthetics of Rock* (Durham, NC: Duke University Press, 1996).

Granata, C.L., *I Just Wasn't Made for these Times: Brian Wilson and the Making of 'Pet Sounds'* (London: Unanimous, 2003).

Griffiths, D., *Radiohead's 'OK Computer'* (New York: Continuum, 2004).

Harris, J., *The 'Dark Side of the Moon': the Making of the Pink Floyd Masterpiece* (London: HarperPerennial, 2006).

Lambert, P., 'Brian Wilson's *Pet Sounds*', *Twentieth-Century Music* 5 (2008), 109–33.

MacDonald, I., *Revolution in the Head: Beatles Records and the Sixties* (London: Pimlico, 1995).

Moore, A.F., *Aqualung* (London: Continuum, 2004).

   Rock: The Primary Text – Developing a Musicology of Rock (Aldershot: Ashgate, 2001).

Moorefield, V., *The Producer as Composer: Shaping the Sound of Popular Music* (Cambridge, MA: The MIT Press, 2005).

Reising, R., ed., *'Speak to Me': The Legacy of Pink Floyd's 'The Dark Side of the Moon'* (Aldershot: Ashgate, 2005).

Smith, S.E., *Dancing in the Streets: Motown and the Cultural Politics of Detroit* (Cambridge, MA: Harvard University Press, 1999).

Wald, E., *How the Beatles Destroyed Rock 'n' Roll: An Alternative History of American Popular Music* (Oxford University Press, 2009).

Whiteley, S., *The Space Between the Notes: Rock and Counter-Culture* (London: Routledge, 1992).

Whitesell, L., *The Music of Joni Mitchell* (Oxford University Press, 2008).

Womack, K., ed., *The Cambridge Companion to the Beatles* (Cambridge University Press, 2009).

Zak, A., *The Poetics of Rock: Cutting Tracks, Making Records* (University of California Press, 2001).

Index

Abbey Road, 147, 175, 178
Ahna, Pauline de, 126
Albani, Emma, 54
   and Schumann, *Frauenliebe und -leben*, 54
Alden, David, 151, 152
Anderson, Ian. *See* Jethro Tull
Anderson, Marian, 55
André, Johann, 43, 44
Andrews, Julie, 60
Angelou, Maya, 56
Arnim, Achim von. *See* Brentano
Asher, Tony, 173
Aspinall, Neil, 175
Auden, W.H., 153
Auric, Georges. *See* Les Six
Austria, 2, 32
   Schubert centenary, 47, 126
   Schubert's reputation in, 38
   Vienna, 41, 44, 45, 46, 77
      Liederabende in, 45–9
      post-war (WWI), 124
      and psychoanalysis, 114
      Skandalkonzert, 48
      Tonkünstlerverein, 112, 113
Authorship, 59, 60, 169
   collaboration, 172, 180

Baez, Joan, 60, 180
Bakst, Léon, 103
Balakirev, Mily, 84. *See also* 'Russian Five'
Ballad. *See* Loewe, Carl
Ballets Russes, 103, 120
Banck, Carl, 35
Barber, Samuel, 154
Bardac, Emma, 99
Barenboim, Daniel, 148, 152

Bathori, Jane, 104
Baudelaire, Charles, 96, 114
BBC (British Broadcasting Corporation), 145, 146
Beach Boys, The, 60, 184, 186
   Pet Sounds, 172, 173–5, 178
   Smile, 178
   Surfer Girl, 172
   Surfin' Safari, 172
Beatles, The, 60, 184
   A Hard Day's Night, 172
   Please Please Me, 172
   Revolver, 175
   Rubber Soul, 172, 173, 175
   and Schubert, 179
   Sgt Pepper's Lonely Hearts Club Band, 172, 175–7, 178
      'A Day in the Life', 176
      and Schumann, *Dichterliebe*, 178
   With The Beatles, 172
Beckett, Samuel, 151, 155
Beethoven, Ludwig van, 47, 64, 80, 118, 144, 149
   allusions to, 126, 179
   An die ferne Geliebte, 4, 6–8
      as model, 8, 21, 130
      performance of, 44, 92
   in Russia, 82
Bennett, Alan, 153
   The Habit of Art, 153
Benson, Renaldo 'Obie'
   Four Tops, 180
Berberian, Cathy, 157
   and Berio, *Circles*, 159
   and Cage, *Aria*, 159
   influence of, 161

Berg, Alban, 124, 125
  *Fünf Orchesterlieder nach
    Ansichtskarten-Texten von Peter
    Altenberg*, 48
Berger, Ludwig, 24
  Die schöne Müllerin, 25
Berio, Luciano, 159, 162, 164
  and The Beatles, *Sgt Pepper*, 176
  Circles, 159, 161
Berlin, Irving, 59
Berlioz, Hector
  Les Nuits d'été, 64, 65–6
Bernac, Pierre, 18, 149
  and Poulenc, 157
Bethge, Hans, 78
Biber, Heinrich, 127
Billing, Klaus, 152
Bingham, Ruth. *See* Song cycle: definitions
Birkin, Jane, 21
Birtwistle, Harrison, 163
  Bogenstrich, 163
  Entr'actes and Sappho Fragments, 163
  The Pierrot Players, 122
  Pulse Shadows, 163
  Semper Dowland, Semper Dolans, 163
Bitonality
  in Mahler, 78
  in Ravel, 104
  in Szymanowski, 108
Bizet, Georges, 92, 93
Blake, Peter, 177
Blake, William, 135, 166
Blok, Alexander, 166
Blues, 58
  in Kagel, *Aus Deutschland*, 156
Boone, Pat, 170
Boosey and Hawkes. *See* Roth, Ernest
Borodin, Alexander. *See* 'Russian Five'
Bos, Coenraad, 54, 145
  Schumann, *Frauenliebe und -leben*, 54
Bostridge, Ian, xv, 151, 152
Bote und Bock, 126
Bouchor, Maurice, 70
Boulez, Pierre, 157, 163
  Le Marteau sans maître, 5, 121, 122, 129, 163
    influence of, 163
  Pli selon pli, 157

Brahms, Johannes, 45, 80, 104, 123, 144,
    149
  on *Die schöne Müllerin*, 44
  as performer, 44
  Romanzen aus Ludwig Tiecks Magelone, 28,
    29–32
  'Treue Liebe dauert lange', 30
  Vier ernste Gesänge, 147
  Zigeunerlieder, 146
Bream, Julian, 155
Brecht, Berthold, 125
Breitkopf und Härtel, 41, 46
Brendel, Alfred, 148, 152
Brentano, Clemens
  Des Knaben Wunderhorn, 24
Brett, Philip, 155
Britten, Benjamin, 32, 80, 112, 124, 149, 153,
    154, 164
  late style, 166
  and Pears, 157
  Peter Grimes, 135
  The Poet's Echo, 166
  Sechs Hölderlin Fragmente, 155, 166
  Serenade, 134
  Songs and Proverbs of William Blake, 166
  twelve-note composition, 167
  Winter Words, 37
Brown, Trisha, 151
Bryars, Gavin
  Jesus' Blood Never Failed Me Yet, 162
Bungert, August, 144
Bussini, Romaine, 45
Bussotti, Sylvano
  Pièces de chair II, 159
Butt, Clara, 48
Butterworth, George, 131
  'Is my team ploughing?' *See* Housman, *A
    Shropshire Lad*

Cage, John, 157
  Aria, 159
  Fontana Mix, 157
Cappi, Pietro. *See* Diabelli
Cardus, Neville, 139
Carreño, Teresa, 144
Carter, Elliott, 154
Carver, Ellen, 151

Castle, Terry, 55
Chabrier, Emmanuel, 104
Chamisso, Adelbert von, 24
    Frauenliebe und -leben, 50, 51
Chaplin, Charlie, 164
Char, René, 121
Chausson, Ernest
    Poème de l'amour et de la mer, 70, 71
    Le Roi Arthus, 71
    Wagnerism, 70
Chopin, Frederyk, 107
Cixous, Hélène, 56
Cleveland, Al, 180
Cline, Patsy, 59
Clooney, Rosemary, 60
Coherence, 1, 2, 4, 5, 6, 7, 9, 16, 31, 143,
        153
    of The Beatles, *Sgt Pepper*, 176
    in concept albums, 175
Collaboration. *See* Authorship
Collins, Judy, 60, 178
Concept album, 20, 60, 61, 169, 183,
        185
    cover art
        The Beatles, *Sgt Pepper*, 177
        Jethro Tull, *Thick as a Brick*, 182
        Pink Floyd, *The Dark Side of the Moon*,
            182
        Radiohead, *In Rainbows*, 185
    definitions, 169, 172
        The Beach Boys, *Pet Sounds*, 173
        The Beatles, *Sgt Pepper*, 175, 176
        'internal plot', 171
        'topical', 170
    Gaye, *What's Going On*, 180
    live performance, 178
    'progressive rock', 182
    and recording, 179
    and rock opera, 178
    and song cycle, 20, 174, 178, 179,
        185
    studio composition, 177, 181
Cooder, Ry, 185
Coolidge, Elizabeth Sprague, 104
Copland, Aaron, 154
    Twelve Poems of Emily Dickinson, 56

Corigliano, John
    Mr Tambourine Man, 185
Cornelius, Peter, 38
Cotton, Charles, 135
Cream, 175
Crumb, George, 162, 164
    Ancient Voices of Children, 161
Cui, César, 82. *See also* 'Russian Five'
Culp, Julia, 46, 144
cummings, e.e., 159

Dalos, Rimma, 56
Dargomïzhsky, Alexander, 82, 86
    The Stone Guest, 85
    'Vostochnïy romans', 84, 85
Daudet, Alphonse, 91
Daverio, John, 39
Davies, Peter Maxwell
    Eight Songs for a Mad King, 122, 161
    The Pierrot Players, 122
Davies, Ray. *See* The Kinks
Debussy, Claude, 93
    Fêtes galantes, 99–101
        'Colloque sentimental', 101
    influence on Vaughan Williams, 132
    influences, 81, 82
    Pelléas et Mélisande, 99
Decemberists, The, 185
DeGaetani, Jan, 161
Demus, Jörg, 148
DePitte, David van, 180
Desnos, Robert, 167
Diabelli, Anton, 41, 44
Diaghilev, Sergei. *See* Ballets Russes
Dillane, Stephen, 152
Dommer, Arrey von, 6, 7
Donovan, 178
Dowland, John, 155, 163
Drake, Julius, xv, 152
Droste-Hülshoff, Annette von, 50
Duparc, Henri, 70
Durey, Louis. *See* Les Six
Dutilleux, Henri
    Le Temps l'horloge, 167
Dvořák, Anton, 150
Dylan, Bob, 60, 172, 185

Eichendorff, Joseph von. *See also* Schumann
    'Im Abendrot', 139. *See also* Strauss, *Vier
        letzte Lieder*
Elgar, Edward
    Sea Pictures, 48
Eliot, T.S., 155
Ellington, Duke, 156
Éluard, Paul, 18
    Poulenc, *Tel jour, telle nuit*, 19
Emerson, Caryl, 88
Emerson, Lake and Palmer
    Tarkus, 181
Eschenbach, Christoph, 149, 152
Evans, Edwin, 132
Exoticism, 81, 84, 108, 109
    in Ravel, 104
    in Szymanowski, 108

Falla, Manuel de, 102
Farrère, Claude, 92
Fassbaender, Brigitte
    Schubert, *Winterreise*, 55
Fauré, Gabriel, 150
    La Bonne Chanson, 96–9
    influence of, 81
    influences on, 96, 97
Feminism. *See* Gender
Ferneyhough, Brian, 164
    Études transcendentales, 163–4
    Carceri d'invenzione, 163
Fink, Bernarda, 150
Fischer, Edwin, 147
Fischer-Dieskau, Dietrich, 144, 149, 150, 152,
        166
    influence of recording, 147
    on Schoeck, 129, 131
    and Schubert, 146, 148
Fitzgerald, Ella, 170
Flagstad, Kirsten, 139
Flaxland, Gustave-Alexandre, 93
Fluctuating tonality
    in Schoenberg, 113, 114
Folk song, 2, 27, 81, 86, 101, 102
    collections, 103
    and exoticism, 83
    Mahler, 38

Joni Mitchell, 179
    parody by Heine, 11
    Szymanowski, 108, 109
    Vaughan Williams, 132
    whole-tone scale, 84
Four Freshmen, The, 170
France
    folk-song collecting, 102
    Les Six, 125
    Paris, 70
        Great Exhibition, 103
        Wagner in, 70
    reception of Schubert in, 92
        romances and *mélodies*, 92
Franz, Robert, 54, 144
Frege, Livia, 43
Freud, Sigmund, 114, 131
Freund, Marya, 120
Friedländer, Max, 47
Furtwängler, Wilhelm, 139

Gainsbourg, Serge
    Histoire de Melody Nelson, 20–1
Galás, Diamanda, 57, 58
    Defixiones, Will and Testament, 57
García Jr, Manuel, 45
Gardner, Ava, 171
Garland, Judy, 171
    The Letter, 178
Gautier, Judith, 78
Gautier, Théophile, 65
Gaye, Marvin, 184
    What's Going On, 180, 181, 182
Geibel, Emmanuel, 104
Gender
    feminism, 56, 61
    performance, 58, 63
    representations of, 51, 60, 61
        écriture feminine, 56, 57
    women singing 'male' cycles, 55, 56, 63
George, Stefan
    Das Buch der hängenden Gärten, 114, 115
Gerhardt, Elena, 55, 124, 144, 146, 147
    Hugo Wolf Society, 145
    Schubert, *Winterreise*, 145
    Schumann, *Frauenliebe und -leben*, 146

Germany, 2
  Berlin
    Überbrettl, 117
    Stockhausen tour, 44
Gerstl, Richard, 115
Giesebrecht, Ludwig Theodor, 28
Gieseking, Walter, 147
Gigli, Beniamino, 147
Giraud, Albert, 120
  Pierrot lunaire, 117
Glanville, Mark
  A Yiddish Winterreise, 151
Glinka, Mikhail, 82, 84
  Ruslan and Lyudmila, 84
Gmeiner, Lulu, 46
Goerne, Matthias, 152
Goethe, Johann Wolfgang von, 2, 3, 25, 32, 156
  'Erlkönig'. *See* Schubert: 'Erlkönig'
  Die Leiden des jungen Werthers
    and *Winterreise*, 151
  Wilhelm Meisters Lehrjahre (Schumann
    setting), 171
Gogol, Nikolai, 85
Golenischschev-Kutuzov, Arkad'evich, 82, 88
Gonson, Claudia. *See* The Magnetic Fields
Grieg, Edvard
  Haugtussa, 102
Grisey, Gérard, 162
  Quatre Chants pour franchir le seuil, 161
Gurney, Ivor
  Ludlow and Teme, *The Western Playland*,
    131
Guthrie, Thomas, 151
Gutmann, Albert, 46

Haden, Petra
  The Who Sell Out, 61
Haefliger, Andreas, 152
Hanslick, Eduard, 44
Harrison, George. *See* The Beatles
Hart, Roy, 122
Hartleben, Otto Erich, 117
  Pierrot lunaire, 118
Hartmann, Georges, 91, 93
Haslinger, Tobias, 9, 10, 42
Hegner, Paula, 145

Heilmann, Hans, 78
Heine, Heinrich
  popularity in Russia, 82
  Schubert, *Schwanengesang*, 9, 10
  Schumann, *Dichterliebe*, 11
  on Spain, 104
Hensel, Luise, 24
Hensel, Wilhelm, 24
Henze, Hans Werner, 149
  Drei Hölderlin Fragmente, 155
  Kammermusik 1958, 155, 163
Herder, Johann Gottfried, 2
Herrmann, Oliver
  Dichterliebe: A Story of Red and Blue, 55, 152
d'Hervey de Saint Denys, Le Marquis, 78
Hesse, Hermann, 130, 139
Heyse, Paul, 104
Hiller, Ferdinand, 92, 104
Hindemith, Paul, 112, 124, 154, 155
  Das Marienleben, 127
  Das Marienleben II, 136–7
Hirayama, Michiko, 161
Hitler, Adolf, 123, 128
HMV, 145, 148
  Winterreise Society, 146
Hölderlin, Friedrich, 155
  Britten, 155
  Henze, 155
Holzmair, Wolfgang, 152
Honegger, Arthur. *See* Les Six
Housman, A.E,
  A Shropshire Lad, 131–4
    'Is my team ploughing?', 132
Hugo, Victor, 92
Humperdinck, Engelbert, 144
  Die Königskinder, 118
Hüsch, Gerhard, 146
Hüsker Dü
  Zen Arcade, 183
Hyperion, 150

International Society for Contemporary Music
    (ISCM), 124, 129

Jackson, Janet
  Rhythm Nation 1814, 181

Jackson, Travis A., 169
Jacobsen, Jens Peter, 113
Janáček, Leoš
    The Diary of One Who Disappeared, 102
Jansen, Gustave, 104
Jazz, 125, 170, 171
    Herbie Hancock, 60
    in Kagel, *Aus Deutschland*, 156
    Neue Sachlichkeit, 125
    recording, 170
    in Zemlinsky, *Symphonische Gesänge*, 125
Jefferson, Blind Lemon, 58
Jeitteles, Alois, 6
Jenkins, Gordon
    The Letter, 171
Jethro Tull
    Aqualung, 182
    Thick as a Brick, 182
Jimi Hendrix Experience, The, 175
Joachim, Amalie, 47

Kagel, Mauricio
    Aus Deutschland, 155
Kahane, Gabriel
    Craigslistlieder, 185
Keats, John, 135
Keenlyside, Simon, 151, 152
Keller, Gottfried, 129, 130
Kerr, Alfred, 126
Kinks, The
    *Lola vs. The Powerman and the
        Money-go-round Part One*, 61
Klingsor, Tristan (Léon Leclère), 103
Knapp, Alexander
    A Yiddish Winterreise, 151
Komar, Arthur, 149
Kramer, Lawrence, 24
Krenek, Ernst, 124
    Jonny spielt auf, 126. *See also Neue
        Sachlichkeit*
    Das Reisebuch aus den österreichischen Alpen,
        125–6, 143
    and Schubert, 153
Kreutzer, Conradin, 33
    influence on Schubert, 34
    Wanderlieder, 33

Kulmann, Elisabeth, 56
Kurtág, György
    Messages of the Late R.V. Troussova, 56, 120
    'A Little Erotic', 56

Lambert, Constant, 134
Lamoureux, Charles, 70
Lang, Josephine, 50
Late style, 154, 167, 168
    Britten, 167
    Schubert, 9
    Shostakovich, 166, 167
    Strauss, 139
Lauer-Kottlar, Beatrice, 127
Leclère, Léon. *See* Klingsor
Legouvé, Ernest, 92
Lehmann, Lotte, 55, 149
    Schumann, 'Ich grolle nicht', 55
Leisner, Emmi, 55, 148
    Brahms, *Vier ernste Gesänge*, 147
Lennon, John, 176. *See also* The Beatles
    influence of Bob Dylan, 172
Leonora, Dar'ia Mikhailovna, 82
Les Six, 125, 129
Lied, Lieder, 2, 3, 4, 25, 29, 64, 69
    performance style, 45
Liederabende. See Performance
Liederspiel, 3, 24, 25
    Müller, *Die schöne Müllerin*, 23, 24, 171
    Schubert, *Die schöne Müllerin*, 178
Lind, Jenny, 93, 170
Liszt, Franz, 43, 92, 118, 144
    transcriptions of Schubert, 41
Loewe, Carl, 4, 27
    Der Bergmann, 28
    Esther, 28, 29
    Gregor auf dem Stein, 28
    influence on Brahms, 29
LP (long-playing record), 42, 143, 147, 148,
        149, 170, 171, 177
    creative impact, 172
    format of *Pet Sounds*, 174
Lübbecke-Job, Emma, 127
Ludwig, Christa, 152
Lutosławski, Witold, 149
    Chantefleurs et chantefables, 167

'lyric I', 2, 154, 161, 164
  in Mahler, 38, 39
  in Schoenberg, 114, 115
  in Schubert, 25

Maeterlinck, Maurice
  Pelléas et Mélisande, 99
Magnetic Fields, The, 62
  69 Love Songs, 62, 183
  Distortion, 62
  I, 62
Mahler, Gustav, 32, 66, 185
  Kindertotenlieder, 72–7
    in *Das Lied von der Erde*, 78
  Des Knaben Wunderhorn, 38, 72
  Das Lied von der Erde, 73, 77–80, 114
    in Crumb, *Ancient Voices of Children*, 161
  Lieder eines fahrenden Gesellen, 37, 38–9, 70,
    72
  Rückert Lieder
    'Ich bin der Welt abhanden gekommen',
    72
  and Schubert, 153
Mallarmé, Stéphane, 114, 115, 157
Mann, William, 178
Mansun, Marilyn
  Antichrist Superstar, 183
Marsh, Roger
  *Albert Giraud's Pierrot lunaire: 50 Rondels
    Bergamasques*, 120
Martin, Frank, 149
Martin, George, 173, 176. *See also* The Beatles
Marx, A.B., 104
Marx, Karl, 177
Massenet, Jules, 92, 118
  Expressions lyriques, 94
  influence of, 81
  Poème d'avril, 91–4
May, Phil. *See* The Pretty Things
McCartney, Paul, 175, 176. *See also* The Beatles
McCormack, John, 147
McLuhan, Marshall, 170
Mélodies, 92
Melodrama. *See* Sprechstimme: precedents for
Mendelssohn, Fanny, 24, 50
Merritt, Stephin, 62. *See also* The Magnetic
  Fields

Messchaert, Johannes, 46, 147
Messiaen, Olivier
  Cinq Rechants, 162
  Harawi, 162
  Tristan, 162
  Turangalîla Symphony, 162
'Mighty Handful'. *See* 'Russian Five'
Miles, Laurence, 181
Milhaud, Darius. *See* Les Six
Mitchell, Joni
  Blue, 179–80
  versions of 'Both Sides Now', 60–1
Mitchell, Katie, 151, 152
Modernism, 5, 153, 155
  concert practices, 47
  fading of, 123
  and popular culture, 116
  and Schoenberg, 112
Monroe, Bill, 59
Monroe, Marilyn, 177
Monteverdi, Claudio, 155
Moore, Gerald, 146, 148, 149
Morrison, Toni, 56
Mothers of Invention, The. *See* Zappa
Motown, 180, 181
Mottl, Felix, 64, 67
MP3. *See* Recording: technology: digital
Mühlen, Raimund von zur, 45, 46, 147
  Die schöne Müllerin, 47
Müller, Hanns Udo, 146
Müller, Wilhelm, 23, 24, 151
  Die schöne Müllerin, 25, 44
  Winterreise, 32, 33, 34, 47
Muse
  The Resistance, 185
musique concrète, 157, 174
Musorgsky, Modest
  comparison to Tchaikovsky, 89
  use of folk song, 86
  influence of, 71, 81, 82, 99
  Khovanshchina, 87, 120
  as Lieder accompanist, 82
  The Nursery, 86, 87
  Songs and Dances of Death, 87–9
    'Serenade', 88
  Sunless, 5, 82, 86–7
Muxfeldt, Kristina, 51

Nationalism, 3, 81
    Britain, 131, 134
    France, 103
    Germany, 124, 128
    interwar, 123
    Poland, 107, 109
    Russia, 82
Nazism, 124, 128, 153, 167
    and Hölderlin, 155
Neudecker, Mariele, 151
Neue Sachlichkeit, 125, 129
Newman, Ernest, 132
Newman, Randy, 178
Nielsen, Carl, 102
Nikisch, Arthur, 144
Norman, Jessye, 56
Nourrit, Adolphe, 92

Opera. *See* Wagner, Richard
    'bleeding chunks', 69, 77
    influence on Brahms, 29
    performance style, 43, 45, 54
Organicism, 2, 14
Orientalism, 84
    in Mahler, 78
    in Ravel, 103
Ottenwald, Anton, 42

Padmore, Mark, 151
Parks, Van Dyke, 186
    Song Cycle, 178, 179
Parny, Evariste-Désiré de, 104
Pears, Peter, 124, 134, 155, 164
    and Britten, 157
Pentatonic scale, 103
    in Mahler, 78, 104
Perahia, Murray, 148
Performance
    amateur, 2, 4, 40, 43, 50, 150
    concert reform, 41, 48
        Mahler, *Kindertotenlieder*, 77
    gender, 53, 58
    gestures, 25, 54
        Gerhardt, 147
        suppression of, 44
    Liederabende, 46
    orchestral song, 64

professional, 4, 43
    Schubertiade. *See* Schubertiade
    transposition, 10
Petrov, Ivan, 82
Pfitzner, Hans
    Alte Weisen, 128, 129
    Herr Oluf, 69
    and Nazism, 128
Pierrot Players, The, 122
Pink Floyd, 184
    The Dark Side of the Moon, 182,
        183
    The Final Cut, 183
    The Wall, 183
Pinkola Estés, Clarissa, 56
Pisaro, David, 32, 151
Plath, Sylvia, 56
Poland
    Skamander movement, 108
Pop Idol, 63
Porter, Cole, 59
Possart, Ernst von
    Strauss, *Enoch Arden*, 118
Poulenc, Francis, 18, 149, 154. *See also* Les Six
    and Bernac, 157
    Litanies à la vierge noire, 19
    Tel jour, telle nuit, 18–20
Pousseur, Henri
    Dichterliebesreigentraum, 156
    Schumann, *Dichterliebe*, 156
Presley, Elvis, 59, 170
Pretty Things, The, 180
    S.F. Sorrow, 177–8
Prey, Hermann, 152
Price, Leontyne
    and Still, 157
Prince and The Revolution
    Purple Rain, 183
Progressive tonality
    in Mahler, 38, 73
    in Tchaikovsky, 90
Publishers
    printing techniques, 40, 93
    role of, 3, 9, 10, 41, 43, 44, 91, 92, 93, 126,
        127, 139
Pushkin, Alexander, 85
    Britten, *The Poet's Echo*, 166

Quasthoff, Thomas, 152

Radio, 49, 59, 60, 144, 145, 146, 171, 176
  AOR (album-oriented radio), 181
Radiohead
  In Rainbows, 184, 185
  OK Computer, 184
Raincoats, The, 61
  'Lola', 61
Rammstein, 185
Rasch, Torsten
  Mein Herz brennt, 185
Rathaus, Daniil, 89, 91
Ravel, Maurice, 103, 120
  Chansons madécasses, 104
    'Aoua!', 104
  Don Quichotte à Dulcinée, 104
  influence on Vaughan Williams, 132
  Shéhérazade, 103, 108
  Trois Poèmes de Stéphane Mallarmé, 120
Realism, 85, 118
Recording, 59, 144
  concept album, 170
  impact on notions of authorship, 59–60
  impact on repertoire, 153
  influence on listening practices, 149, 179
  influence on performance practice, 55, 147
  sold by subscription, 146
  studio composition, 173
  technology, 162, 170, 183
    acoustic, 144
    digital, 150, 184–5
    electric, 145
    high fidelity and stereo, 171
    magnetic tape, 146
    studio composition, 171, 176, 181
    tape loops, 162
    television, 152
    YouTube.com, 150
Reger, Max, 144, 185
Reich, Steve
  It's Gonna Rain, Come Out, 162
Reichardt, Friedrich
  Lieb' und Treue, 25
Rellstab, Ludwig, 9, 24
Rettrich, Pauline, 44

Richault, Charles-Simon, 92, 93
Riddle, Nelson, 171
Rilke, Rainer Maria, 127, 137, 163
Rimbaud, Arthur, 96
Rimsky-Korsakov, Nikolai, 103. *See also*
    'Russian Five'
Rock
  and The Beatles, *Rubber Soul*, 173
  and gender, 60
  Parks, *Song Cycle*, 179
  'progressive rock', 181, 183
Rock opera
  Pink Floyd, *The Wall*, 183
  The Pretty Things, *S.F. Sorrow*, 178
Rodgers and Hammerstein
  Oklahoma!, 59
  South Pacific, 171
Rolling Stone magazine, 179, 181
Rolling Stones, The
  Their Satanic Majesties Request, 177
Romance
  French, 92
  Russian, 83
Romanticism, 2, 4, 155
Ronettes, The, 172
Rorem, Ned, 154
  Ariel, 56
  Women's Voices, 56
Rosen, Charles, 1
Rostropovich, Mstislav, 166
Roth, Ernst, 139
Rubinstein, Anton, 104
Rückert, Friedrich
  Kindertotenlieder, 72
Russia
  and Britten, 166
  Stockhausen tour, 44
'Russian Five', 82, 103

Saint-Saëns, Camille, 99
Samson, Jim, 109
Sand, Georges, 93
Scelsi, Giacinto
  Canti del Capricorno, 161
Schaeffer, Pierre, 174
Schäfer, Christine, 55, 152

Schenker, Heinrich, 129
Schlegel, August Wilhelm, 2
Schlegel, Friedrich
    Abendröte, 8. *See also* Schubert
Schlotke, Otto, 29
Schnabel, Artur, 147
Schober, Franz von, 28
Schoeck, Othmar, 112, 129–31, 149, 154
    Gaselen, 129
Schoenberg, Arnold, 48, 112, 124, 129, 137, 155
    Das Buch der hängenden Gärten, 5, 112,
        114–16, 118
    legacy, 112
    Gurrelieder, 112–14
    influence of, 129
    Pierrot lunaire, 120, 161. *See also* Modernism
    influence of, 120, 122, 156, 163
    'Der kranke Mond', 118
    performance, 120
    Sprechstimme, 56
    Twelve-note composition, 124
    Verein für musikalische Privataufführungen,
        48
Schönstein, Baron Karl von, 43
Schott, 127
Schröder-Devrient, Wilhelmine, 43
    Schumann, *Frauenliebe und -leben*, 53
Schubert, Franz, 4, 8, 40, 118, 144, 146, 149,
    150, 155, 156
    Abendröte, 8–9
    centenary, 126
    'Erlkönig', 28, 41, 92
        publication of, 41
    in France, 65
    influence of, 81
    on Kreutzer's *Wanderlieder*, 33
    The Lady of the Lake, 42
    performance of, 47
    in Russia, 82
    Die schöne Müllerin, 23–7, 32
    'Die böse Farbe', 26, 27
    'Die liebe Farbe', 26, 27
    and Mahler, 38, 39
    performance of, 42, 44, 47, 92, 148
    publication of, 42
    Schwanengesang, 9–10

transcriptions of, 92
Viola, 28
Winterreise, 9, 23, 37, 143, 153, 179
    'Der greise Kopf', 34
    'Gute Nacht', 34, 37
    influence of, 18, 35
    in Kagel, *Aus Deutschland*, 156
    'Der Leiermann', 34, 37
    and Mahler, 37–9
    performance of, 44, 148, 149, 151–2, 164
    Winterreise Society, 146
Schubertiade, 41, 48
    Kagel, *Aus Deutschland*, 156
Schumann, Clara, 11, 44, 45, 50, 51
    on *Frauenliebe und -leben*, 44
Schumann, Elisabeth, 55
Schumann, Robert, 64, 94, 104, 118, 144, 149,
    150, 153, 156, 162
    on Beethoven, 8
    choral ballads, 28, 70
    Dichterliebe, 5, 10–18, 45, 129, 149, 174, 178
    'Am leuchtenden Sommermorgen', 14
    'Ein Jüngling liebt ein Mädchen', 11
    'Im wunderschönen Monat Mai', 14–16
    influence of, 18, 20, 156
    performance of, 44, 148, 149
    publication of, 42
    Eichendorff *Liederkreis* op. 39, 44, 93
    Pfitzner, 128
    in France, 93
    Frauenliebe und -leben, 43, 51–5, 56, 61,
        174
    influence of, 81, 127
    on Loewe's *Esther*, 28
    as model, 115
    in Russia, 82
Schumann-Heink, Ernestine, 123
    Schumann, *Frauenliebe und -leben*, 54
Schwarzkopf, Elisabeth, 46
Seidl, Anton, 9
Shostakovich, Dmitri, 164, 166
    Four Verses by Captain Lebyadkin, 167
    Seven Verses of Alexander Blok, 166
    Suite on Texts by Michelangelo Buonarroti,
        167
Silvestre, Armand, 93, 96

Sims, Shirley. *See* The Magnetic Fields
Sinatra, Frank, 60
  In the Wee Small Hours, 171
Singer-songwriter, 60
  Galás, 58
  Joni Mitchell, 179
Singspiel, 25
Sitwell, Edith, 120
Skinner, Mike (The Streets)
  A Grand Don't Come for Free, 21–2
Small Faces, The, 180
  Ogdens' Nut Gone Flake, 177
Solie, Ruth, 51
Somervell, Arthur, 131
Song cycle
  comparison to concept album, 169
  definitions, 1, 3, 8
    ballad hybrid. *See* Loewe, Carl
    by Bingham, 3–4
    coherence, 14, 20
    by Dommer, 6
    'external-plot cycles', 4
    Frauenliebe und -leben, 51
    'internal plots', 4
    'meta-cycle', 162–4
    titles, 3, 6, 9, 10
    'topical cycles', 3
Sonnleithner, Ignaz, 41
Sorabji, Kaikhosru, 108
Spain, 103
  and Ravel, 104
Spector, Phil, 172, 173, 184
Spengler, Otto, 124
Spina, Carl Anton, 44
Spiri, Anthony, 150
Sprechstimme
  in Boulez, *Le Marteau sans maître*, 121
  in Davies, *Eight Songs for a Mad King*, 122
  in Ferneyhough, *Études transcendentales*, 164
  in Kurtág, *Messages*, 56, 120
  precedents for, 118
  in Schoenberg, *Gurrelieder*, 113
  in Schoenberg, *Pierrot lunaire*, 112, 118, 120
Stägemann, Elisabeth, 24, 25
Starr, Ringo. *See* The Beatles

Stasov, Vladimir, 82, 86
Steiner, Sigmund Anton, 6
Still, William Grant, 154
  and Price, 157
Stockhausen, Julius, 28, 44, 45, 46, 147, 149
  Schumann, *Frauenliebe und -leben*, 53
Stockhausen, Karlheinz, 177
  and The Beatles, *Sgt Pepper*, 176
  Gesang der Jünglinge, 157
Stow, Randolph, 122
Strauss, Richard, 71, 137, 144, 150, 178, 185
  Capriccio, 127
  Enoch Arden, 118
  Krämerspiegel, 126
  Der Rosenkavalier, 126
  Tod und Verklärung, 139
  Vier letzte Lieder, 130, 139–43, 153
Stravinsky, Igor, 120
  Les Noces, 108
  The Rite of Spring, 108
  Trois Poésies de la lyrique japonais, 120
Streets, The. *See* Skinner
Strophic song, 2, 3, 92
  Beethoven, *An die ferne Geliebte*, 6
  Brahms, *Romanzen aus Ludwig Tiecks Magelone*, 29
  Schubert, *Die schöne Müllerin*, 23
  Schubert, *Winterreise*, 34
  vs. through-composed, 4, 9, 113
Styx
  Paradise Theatre, 183
Symbolism, 114
  in Belgium, 117
  in France, 114
  Russian, 71
Symmons Roberts, Michael, 151
Szymanowski, Karol, 107–11
  Słopiewnie, 108, 110
  Songs of the Fairy Princess, 107
  Songs of the Infatuated Muezzin, 108

Tailleferre, Germaine. *See* Les Six
Taruskin, Richard, 91
Taubert, Wilhelm, 104

Tchaikovsky, Pyotr, 89–91, 144
  'Fate' motive, 91
Temptations, The, 181
Tennyson, Alfred, 135
Terrell, Tammi, 180
Thomas, Ambroise, 91
Thomas, Quentin, 32
Tieck, Ludwig, 29, 31
Tippett, Michael, 154
Tuwim, Julian, 108
Twelve-note composition, 129, 137
  Britten, 166, 167
  Schoenberg, 125
  Shostakovich, 167

Uhland, Ludwig, 32, 33
Unwin, Stanley, 177

Vannier, Jean-Claude, 21
  L'Enfant assassin des mouches, 21
Varèse, Edgard, 120
Vasnier, Marie, 99
Vaughan Williams, Ralph, 102, 131, 135
  On Wenlock Edge, 132
    'Is my team ploughing?', 132, 134
  Songs of Travel, 37
Verlaine, Paul
  Fêtes galantes, 96, 99
  La Bonne Chanson, 96
Viñes, Ricardo, 104
Vishnevskaya, Galina, 166
Vogl, Johann Michael, 43
  Schubert, *The Lady of the Lake*, 42
Volkstümlich, 24. *See also* Folk song
Vries, Gerrie de, 151
Vrieslander, Otto, 117

Wadsworth, Matthew, 151
Wagner, Richard, 29
  Bayreuth, 48, 70
  leitmotif, 70, 80
  Lohengrin, 11
  Siegfried, 66
    Mahler, *Das Lied von der Erde*, 80
  Tannhäuser, 70

'Tristan' chord, 70, 100
Tristan und Isolde, 70
  and Debussy, 100
  Schoenberg, *Gurrelieder*, 113
Wesendonck Lieder, 56, 64, 66–9
  'Träume', 66
  and *Tristan und Isolde*, 65, 66, 67
Wagnerism, 38, 70, 117
  Chausson, 70, 71
  Debussy, 99
  Mahler, *Das Lied von der Erde*, 77
  Schoenberg, *Gurrelieder*, 77
Waits, Tom, 162
Walter, Gustav, 46
Walton, William
  Façade, 120
Wanderlieder, 32, 33
  Krenek, *Reisebuch*, 125
  Kreutzer, 33
  Müller, *Winterreise*, 23
  Uhland, 32
Weber, Carl Maria von, 118
  Die Temperamente beim Verluste der Geliebten, 4
Webern, Anton, 112, 124, 125, 155
  arrangement of Schoenberg, *Gurrelieder*, 114
Weigl, Petr
  Winterreise, 55
Weill, Kurt, 124
  Mahagonny 'Songspiel', 125
Weinberg, Mieczysław, 104
Weingartner, Felix
  Wallfahrt nach Kevlaar, 69
Weir, Judith
  woman.life.song, 56
Werner, Erik Nelson, 151
Wesendonck, Mathilde, 66, 69
West, Andrew, 151
Whitesell, Lloyd, 179
Who, The
  The Who Sell Out, 61
  Tommy, 178
Whole-tone scale, 103, 104
  in Dargomïzhsky, 'Vostochnïy romans', 84

Whole-tone scale (*cont.*)
  in Debussy, 99
  in Mahler, 78
  in Musorgsky, *Sunless*, 86
  in Szymanowski, 108
Williams, Alan
  Twelve Storeys High, xv
Wilson, Brian, 173, 176. *See also* The Beach
    Boys
  influence of Spector, 173
  That Lucky Old Sun, 186
Wolf, Hugo, xv, 46, 71, 94, 104, 129, 144, 146,
    149
  Hugo Wolf Society, 145
Women. *See* Gender
  composers, 50
Wüllner, Ludwig, 46, 123

X Factor, 63

Yes
  Tales from Topographic Oceans, 181
Youens, Susan, 24, 44
Ysaÿe, Eugène, 144

Zappa, Frank
  Lumpy Gravy, 177
  We're Only in It for the Money, 177
Zehme, Albertine, 117, 118
Zemlinsky, Alexander, 113, 120, 124
  Symphonische Gesänge op. 3. *See* Jazz
Zender, Hans
  *Schubert's Winterreise: A Composed
    Interpretation*, 156
Zumsteeg, Emilie, 50